THE HISTORICAL MARKERS
of North Georgia

Historical Marker Titles

Georgia Historical Markers – Coastal Counties
ISBN: 0-87797-215-X

The Historical Markers of North Georgia
ISBN: 0-87797-234-6

The Historical Markers of Metro Atlanta
ISBN: 0-87797-216-8
(Not Yet Published)

The Historical Markers of Southwest Georgia
ISBN: 0-87797-241-9
(Not Yet Published)

The Historical Markers of Southeast Georgia
ISBN: 0-87797-242-7
(Not Yet Published)

THE HISTORICAL MARKERS
of North Georgia

The complete text and location of the
various state and non-state historical markers
located throughout forty-four north Georgia counties.

140 Photographs and Illustrations
Almost 200 markers that relate to the Civil War

Kenneth W. Boyd

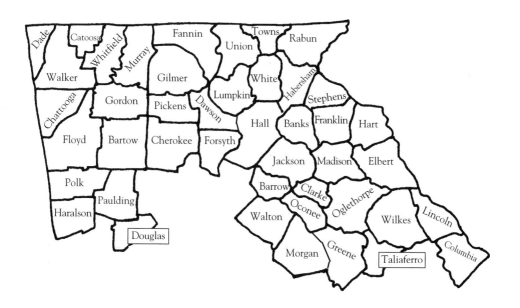

Cherokee Publishing Company
Atlanta, Georgia
1993

Library of Congress Cataloging-in-Publication Data
Boyd, Kenneth W., 1938-
    The historical markers of north Georgia : the complete text and location of
the various state and non-state historical markers located throughout forty-four
north Georgia counties / Kenneth W. Boyd. — 1st edition
        p.   cm.
    Includes index.
    ISBN 0-87797-234-6   (trade paper) : $14.95
    1. Historical markers—Georgia—Guide-books.
    2. Georgia— Description and travel—1981—Guide books.
    3. Georgia—History, Local.   I. Title.
F287.B69   1991
917.5804'43—dc20   91-27463
                                                                   CIP

Copyright © 1993 by Kenneth W. Boyd

This book is printed on acid-free paper which conforms to the American National Standard
Z39.48-1984 Permanence of Paper for Printed Library Materials. Paper that conforms to this
standard's requirements for pH, alkaline reserve and freedom from groundwood is anticipated to
last several hundred years without significant deterioration under normal library use and storage
conditions. ∞

Manufactured in the United States of America

First Edition

ISBN: 0-87797-234-6

    99   98   97   96   95   94   93   10 9 8 7 6 5 4 3 2 1

Front Cover Photo: Joseph E. Johnston, hand-colored mezzotint engraving by A. G. Campbell

Back Cover Photos: Sequoyah, Portrait by Charles Bird King;
Traveler's Rest, courtesy of Georgia Department of Natural Resources;
Ben T. Epps, photo courtesy of Pat Epps

Cover Design: Roger Sawhill, Forte Studios

Index: Pamela H. Naliwajka

Design: Lara C. Boyd and Pamela H. Naliwajka

Cherokee Publishing Company
P O Box 1730, Marietta, Georgia 30061-1730

For

Lara Christine Boyd

and

Pamela Haury Naliwajka

who both worked

very diligently

to make this publication

a reality

CONTENTS

CONTENTS

CONTENTS

SYMBOLS AND ABBREVIATIONS

◆	Marker was missing when surveyed
★	Marker not photographed or compared with printed text
Not Standing	Marker replacement is not likely
BCHS	Barrow County Historical Society
BTC	Bartram Trail Conference
DAR	Daughters of the American Revolution
FFA	Future Farmers of America
GCG	Garden Club of Georgia, Inc.
GHM	Georgia Historical Commission/Department of Natural Resources
GHR	Georgia House Resolution
GPC	Georgia Power Company
GLG	Grand Lodge of Georgia
HCHS	Hall County Historical Society
LGC	Ladies Garden Club
MHS	Methodists Heritage Society
NPS	National Park Service
SCHS	Stephens County Historical Society
TUMC	Tignall United Methodist Charge
UDC	United Daughters of the Confederacy
UMC	United Methodist Church
USN	United States Navy
VFW	Veterans of Foreign Wars
WPA	Works Progress Administration

INTRODUCTION

North Georgia is widely known for its natural and scenic beauty and its marvelous climate. Its history is best remembered by the discovery of gold, the Cherokee Indian Nation and its forced removal (in 1838) over the "Trail of Tears," and General Sherman's relentless march towards Atlanta.

Historical markers commerorate many fascinating incidents in North Georgia's history. These include the erection of a Friendship Monument by Mark Anthony Cooper in honor of his creditors. The famous *Grier's Almanac*, first published in 1807, continues to be published today. Rebecca Felton, in 1922 at the age of 87, became the first woman to serve in the U. S. Senate, having been appointed to finish her deceased husband's term.

The world's only double-barrelled cannon is on display in Athens – a military failure for lack of a means of firing both barrels at the same instant. Dr. Crawford W. Long, in 1842, performed the first surgical operation in which ether was used as an anesthetic. The Appalachian Trail, which stretches more than 2,000 miles to Mount Katahdin, Maine, has its southern starting point on Springer Mountain. And the University of Georgia was the first university in the nation to receive a state charter (1785) for a government-controlled university.

Nancy Hart, a revolutionary heroine who stood six feet tall, captured a band of Tories and considered shooting them too kind – they were hanged. In Kingston, Confederate Memorial Day has been observed continuously since 1865 – the only such record held by any community in the nation. The first garden club in America was founded in Athens in 1891. In the 1850s, Woodland/Barnsley Gardens was developed with elaborate gardens containing over 100 varieties of roses. The gardens are being restored and are now open to the public. Ben Epps built and flew the first airplane in Georgia in 1907.

The gold rush (1832) in Auraria and Dahlonega predated both the Colorado and the California gold rushes. Between 1829 and 1839, about $20 million in gold was mined in the area. The first private mint in the United States was started in Gainesville in 1830.

Fort Yargo, built in 1793 to protect the early settlers, remarkably still stands. The Line Baptist Church traces its history to a time when it was located in Cherokee lands and meetings could not be held at night because all white people had to be off Indian lands by sundown. Sequoyah, in 1821, invented an alphabet for the Cherokee language, which led to the publication of the *Cherokee Phoenix*, a bilingual newspaper for the Indian Nation. The Cherokee capital, New Echota, contained a constitutional government of executive, legislative, and judicial branches. Chief James Vann, once lived in a grand home surrounded by his business ventures and acres of land tilled by his slaves.

An exciting Civil War episode took place in 1862 when a group of northern soldiers in disguise, led by a civilian, seized the locomotive *General* at Big Shanty. Known as the "Andrews Raid," they intended to wreck the state railroad as they fled northward. Most were captured north of Ringgold, and some were eventually hanged.

Conditions were so difficult in Confederate hospitals after the Battle of Chickamauga in 1863 that mule meat was fed to the sick and wounded. In the spring of 1864, General William T. Sherman's forces moved through the valleys and gaps and ridges of North Georgia. With constant flanking movements and battles at Resaca and New Hope Church, Sherman pressed on toward Atlanta. Even after the fall of Atlanta in September, the Fifth Ohio Cavalry burned the once-proud town of Cassville – home to 1,300 persons. So complete was the destruction that only three houses and three churches were left and no rebuilding was ever attempted.

I hope you come to share my captivation with the counties of North Georgia, and with their history as told through the text of historical markers.

ORGANIZATION OF MATERIAL

The marker texts are arranged alphabetically by county and then by city. Within a city, the texts are arranged in a logical geographic sequence. Markers physically standing side by side or close to each other on the street will have their texts next to or close to each other in the book.

METHODS USED TO COMPILE INFORMATION

We have attempted to identify, accurately record the text, and provide the locations, of hundreds of roadside historical markers. Most markers have been located and photographed to ensure that the text in the book accurately records the text on the marker itself. We have not attempted to edit or make corrections to the marker text – in fact, we have diligently attempted to record the text exactly as it appears on the marker. We *have* tucked a number of periods and commas inside quotation marks, and obvious or known inaccuracies in the text have usually been noted. Differences and variations in spellings, capitalizations, or dates have not been tampered with. The errors that remain or those that have been freshly created are solely the responsibility of the compiler.

We have attempted to provide the location of each marker with directions specific enough so that they may be located with relative ease. Distances were usually measured from the local courthouse or post office. If a marker was not present when our survey was made, it is noted by a ♦. If we were unable to photograph a marker, and therefore unable to verify the text, it is noted by a ★. Occasionally we could photograph a marker while it was in the maintenance shop. If a marker is not likely to reappear or be replaced, it is noted by **not standing**. The lack of replacement is usually because the sponsoring organization is not active, although some markers have been intentionally removed or discarded. The organization responsible for erecting the marker and the date of erection, when known, are also noted. Please refer to the list of abbreviations to determine the correct identity of each sponsor.

Since most markers were erected many years ago, lakes have been developed, new roads built, old roads forgotten or blocked off, street names have changed, and many highway route numbers are different. It is likely that there are markers standing that we failed to discover. If you have knowledge of markers (metal markers mounted on a post) not included in this work, please write us at Cherokee Publishing Company, P O Box 1730, Marietta, GA 30061-1730, giving us a description, location, and, if possible, a photo, of the marker text. If you locate a marker with incomplete or inaccurate directions, we would appreciate your forwarding that information to us.

SCOPE AND CRITERIA

This work is a partial, but major revision of the earlier book *Georgia Historical Markers* (1973) by Carroll Proctor Scruggs. The earlier book included only markers erected by the Georgia Historical Commission and the Georgia Department of Natural Resources. This work has been expanded to include the markers erected by the Daughters of the American Revolution, the Garden Club of Georgia, Inc., the Grand Lodge of Georgia, the United Daughters of the Confederacy, the National Park Service, the Methodist Heritage Society, the Works Progress Administration, and a number of independent organizations including a few markers of unknown sponsorship. Plaques, monuments, and statues have been excluded. With few exceptions, only metal historical markers mounted on a post have been included. The photographs that are not credited were taken by the compiler or are from an unidentified source.

DESCRIPTION OF HISTORIC MARKER
PROGRAMS IN GEORGIA

Georgia's Official Historical Marker Program was begun when the Georgia Historical Commission was established in 1951 and continues today under the guidance of the Parks, Recreation and Historic Sites Division of the Department of Natural Resources. The first markers were erected in 1952.

Georgia was the thirteenth and last British colony and one of the thirteen original states. Its history is intimately involved with Indians, colonists, missionaries, traders, goldminers, and the military forces of Great Britain, France, and Spain. Among the purposes of historical marker programs is simple recognition, which serves to identify and encourage the preservation of the wealth of historical resources in Georgia. Markers are an effective way to inform both residents and visitors alike about significant places, events, and people in Georgia's past. Some markers, these "tombstones on posts," will remind us that our liberty is worth fighting and dying for and will remind us of the tremendous sacrifices made by those who passed before. Some places identified by markers contain tangible reminders of the past, such as an old mill, fort, or cemetery. Other markers simply mark the spot where such a structure once stood, or they mark the location of historical events that have unfolded.

There is a heavy concentration of markers relating to the movements of General Sherman through Georgia – after all, many of the structures he passed were burned to the ground. Georgia is probably second in the nation in the number of officially erected markers, with only Texas having more, and Kentucky and Virginia close behind. Fulton County (Atlanta) alone has over 200 markers, which is more than in many states. Chatham County (Savannah) has over 100 markers. Markers can be found on courthouse lawns, mountaintops and front yards, in parks and cemeteries, along major highways, and even on isolated dirt roads.

Generally, the texts for early historical markers were prepared in the office of the Georgia Historical Commission or by the official county historian, without specific judgment criteria. Markers dealing with the Civil War were written and located under contract by two Civil War historians, Wilbur G. Kurtz, Sr., and Colonel Allen P. Julian. Currently, markers may be erected to *persons* who have been dead for at least twenty years and who made a significant impact on Georgia history; *events* that changed the course of Georgia history; *buildings* where the person who made history lived or where the event that changed history occurred; or *places* where Georgia history was made. Today new marker applications are usually initiated by interested citizens, who provide the necessary documentation. A board of reviewers then judges the application against the criteria. Usually only a few applications are approved, because most are judged to be of primarily local significance rather than of statewide or national significance. Such things as balanced and comprehensive coverage of the state, popular appeal, and safety for the marker and reader are also considered. Both new and replacement markers are subject to the same review process.

Many unofficial but historically significant markers have been erected by other organizations. The Atlantic Coastal Highway Commission erected twenty-five markers, of which five remain standing, along the Coastal Highway (U.S. 17/GA. 25) during 1930. The Garden Club of Georgia, Inc., has erected a number of Blue Star Memorial Highway markers and markers that trace the travels of naturalist William Bartram. The Works Progress Administration had a very active marker program during the Depression. The Daughters of the American Colonists, the Daughters of the American Revolution, the United Daughters of the Confederacy, the National Park Service, the Methodist Heritage Society, and the Grand Lodge of Georgia have also erected a number of markers.

MARKER IDENTIFICATION, MAINTENANCE, AND RESTORATION

Historical markers are constant targets of vandals, thieves, motor vehicles, and road equipment. Additional markers are added to the "missing list" each year. It now costs the taxpayer about $1,300 to replace a missing or stolen marker. If you know of stolen, lost or damaged markers, please share your knowledge with someone at the nearest state park or historic site. You may also inform the Parks, Recreation and Historic Sites Division, Georgia Department of Natural Resources, Twin Towers East #1352, 205 Butler Street, SE, Atlanta, GA 30334. Telephone: 404- 656-2770.

The state also maintains a marker repair and restoration shop at Panola Mountain Conservation Park near Atlanta. Ken Carlsrud has become an accomplished artist at bullet-hole patching, reconstruction of letters and arrows, and meticulous gold lettering and painting. Each year the shop can repair or refurbish about 130 markers. Historic Marker Shop, Panola Mountain Conservation Park, 2600 GA Highway 155, Stockbridge, GA. 30281. Telephone: 404-389-7810.

Official Georgia historical markers are easily recognized by their green color with gold lettering and the Georgia State Seal located on top. Each marker has a message space that measures 38 inches by 42 inches. Markers erected by the state usually have a numerical designation in the lower left-hand corner. For example, marker 025-62 indicates Chatham County, the 25th county alphabetically and the 62nd marker erected. The year of erection or replacement is usually found in the lower right-hand corner. Non-state markers may or may not have numerical designations, and we have therefore arbitrarily assigned many numbers in the book as a means of identification.

ACKNOWLEDGMENTS

This compiler is deeply appreciative for the assistance that many, many people gave in the gathering of this material. Among them are: Carolyn Minish, Sharon Hardy, Libby Forehand, Marvin Souder, Jeff Stancil, Mrs. W. Harry Smith, Betty Swords, Pat Epps, Robert Davis, Peggy Callaway, Jeff Dean, Michele Rodgers, Frankie Memborn, Bobby McElwee, Mary Farbrough, Linda Mathews, Kathy Know, Dot Mims, Harold A. Lawrence, and Edward B. Nelson. Sincere thanks to you all.

We would also like to thank Gail Miller of the Georgia Department of Archives and History and Jan Flores of the Georgia Historical Society Library.

David Seibert, a marker "nut" just like the compiler, has graciously compared our text with his own notes and records. As a fortunate result, a number of additional non-state markers have been included and there are fewer errors in this book.

There are several people without whose patience, assistance, interest, cooperation, and encouragement this book simply would never have been published. They are Billy Townsend, Ed Reed, and Kenneth Thomas of the Georgia Parks, Recreation and Historic Sites Division, Kenneth Carlsrud, and the late Al Ewing of the Historical Marker Maintenance Shop section. Thank You!

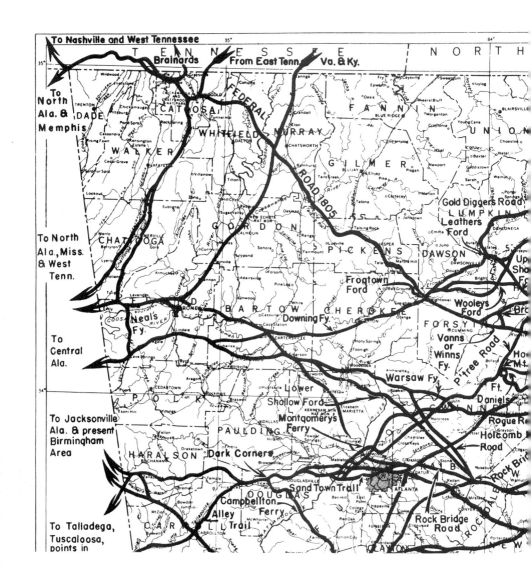

EARLY TRAILS AND ROADS
IN GEORGIA

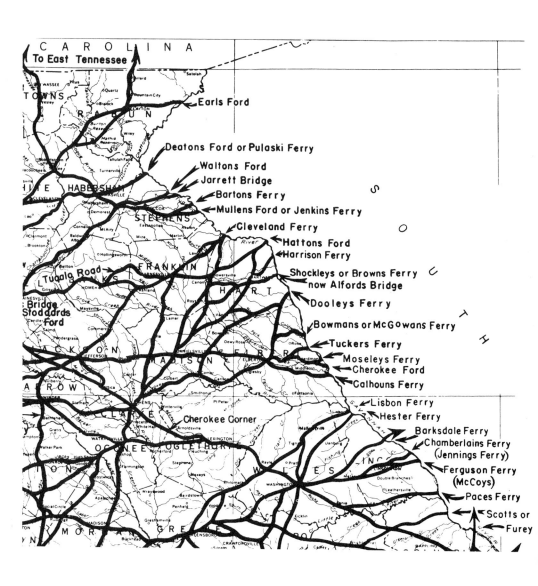

Reproduced from Georgia Early Roads and Trails
circa 1730–1850 by Marion R. Hemperley,
Georgia Department of Archives and History

INDIANS IN GEORGIA

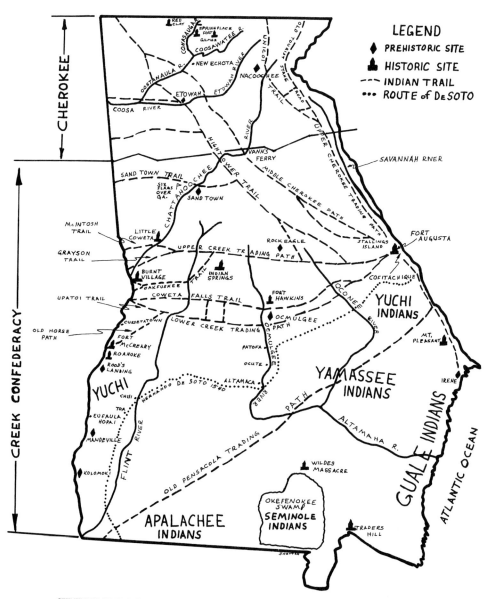

LEGEND
- ◆ PREHISTORIC SITE
- ⛪ HISTORIC SITE
- --- INDIAN TRAIL
- ••• ROUTE of DeSOTO

CHEROKEE

CREEK CONFEDERACY

RED CLAY
SPRINGPLACE FORT GILMER
CONASAUGA R.
COOSAWATEE R.
COOSAWATEE
NEW ECHOTA
NACOOCHEE
COSTANAULA R.
ETOWAH RIVER
UNICOI TURNPIKE
STATE ROAD
ETOWAH
COOSA RIVER
HIGHTOWER TRAIL
VANN'S FERRY
SAVANNAH RIVER
UPPER CHEROKEE TRADING PATH
SAND TOWN TRAIL
CHATTAHOOCHEE RIVER
MIDDLE CHEROKEE PATH
SIX FLAGS OVER GA.
SAND TOWN
McINTOSH TRAIL
LITTLE COWETA
UPPER CREEK TRADING PATH
ROCK EAGLE
STALLINGS ISLAND
FORT AUGUSTA
GRAYSON TRAIL
BURNT VILLAGE
OAKFUSKEE
COWETA FALLS TRAIL
INDIAN SPRINGS
FORT HAWKINS
COFITACHIQUE
UPATOI TRAIL
LOWER CREEK TRADING PATH
OCMULGEE
OCMULGEE PATH
OCONEE RIVER
YUCHI INDIANS
OLD HORSE PATH
CUSSETATOWN
FORT McCREARY
ROANOKE
ROOD'S LANDING
PATOFA
OCUTE
MT. PLEASANT
YUCHI
CHISI
TOA
HERNANDO DE SOTO 1540
ALTAMACA
YAMASSEE INDIANS
IRENE
EUFAULA HOPAI
MANDEVILLE
FLINT RIVER
OCMULGEE RIVER
ALTAMAHA PATH
GUALE INDIANS
ATLANTIC OCEAN
KOLOMOKI
OLD PENSACOLA TRADING
WILDES MASSACRE
ALTAMAHA R.
APALACHEE INDIANS
OKEFENOKEE SWAMP
SEMINOLE INDIANS
TRADERS HILL
J.SOWER

PREPARED BY SIX FLAGS OVER GEORGIA

EARLY INDIAN ROADS AND TRAILS

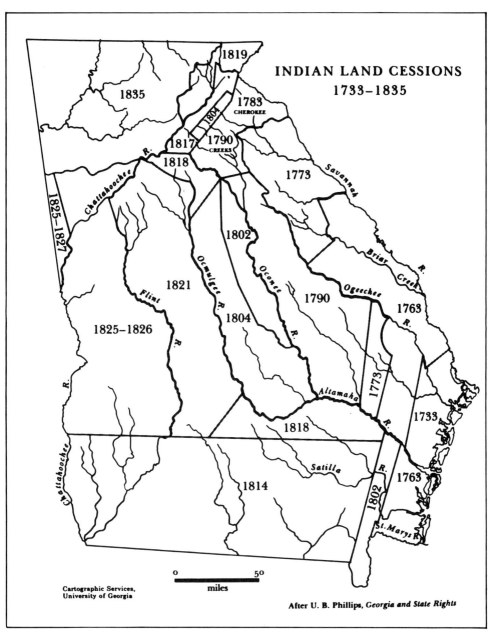

INDIAN LAND CESSIONS
1733–1835

1819

1835

1783
CHEROKEE

1804

1817

1790
CREEKS

1818

1773

1825–1827

Chattahoochee R.

1802

1821

Flint R.

1804

Ocmulgee R.

Oconee R.

1790

Savannah

Briar Creek R.

1763 R.

1825–1826

Altamaha

1773

R.

1733

1818

1763 R.

Chattahoochee R.

Satilla R.

1814

1802

St. Marys R.

0   50
miles

Cartographic Services,
University of Georgia

After U. B. Phillips, *Georgia and State Rights*

ATLANTA   HISTORY

INDIAN LAND CESSIONS
1733–1835

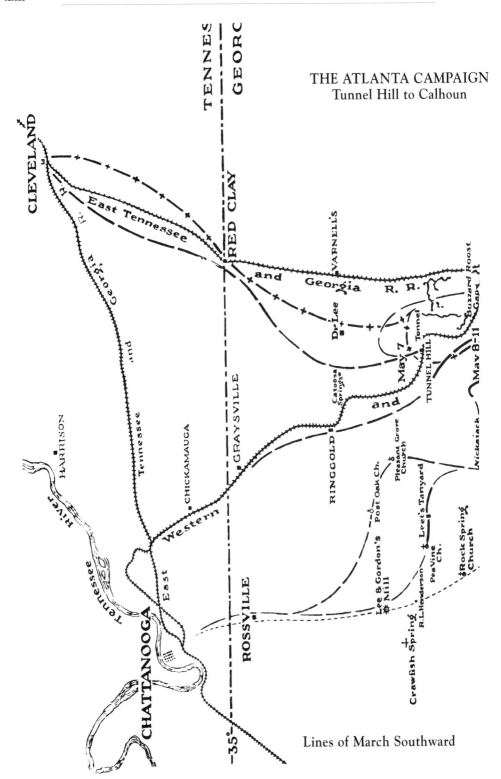

THE ATLANTA CAMPAIGN
Tunnel Hill to Calhoun

Lines of March Southward

MILITARY OPERATIONS

of the
Confederate Army of Tennessee
Commanded By
Gen. Joseph E. Johnston
and
Gen. John B. Hood
and
Federal Forces Consisting of the Army
of the Cumberland
Army of the Tennessee
Army of the Ohio

Commanded By
Maj. Gen. William T. Sherman

IN GEORGIA
May 7 – Sept. 5
1864

THE ATLANTA CAMPAIGN
Calhoun to Cartersville

LINES OF MARCH SOUTHWARD OF THE OPPOSING FORCES
AND THEIR APPROXIMATE ROUTES ARE INDICATED THUS:

CONFEDERATE
Army of the Tennessee · — · — · — · —

FEDERAL
Army of the Cumberland — — — — —
Army of the Tennessee ·····················
Army of the Ohio — + — + — + — +

Compiled from Reports and Atlas of the Official Records and field studies of the area

Drawn by Wilbur G. Kurtz 1957

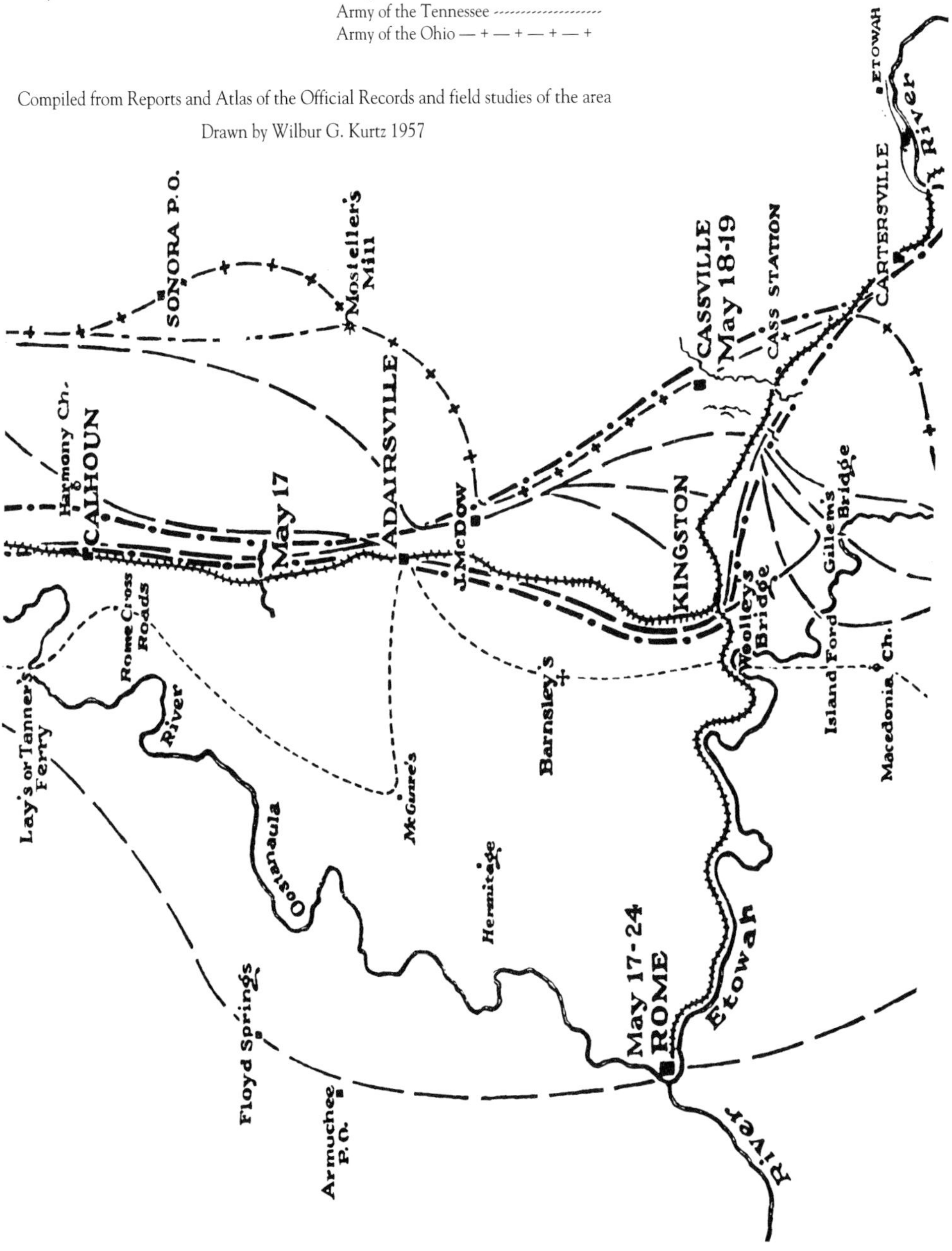

SONORA P.O.

Mosteller's Mill

ETOWAH

River

CARTERSVILLE

CASSVILLE
May 18-19

CASS STATION

Harmony Ch.
CALHOUN

ADAIRSVILLE

May 17

J. McDow

KINGSTON

Gillem's Bridge

Wooley's Bridge

Island Ford

Macedonia Ch.

Rome Cross Roads

Lay's or Tanner's Ferry

Oostanaula River

McGuire's

Barnsley's

Hermitage

Floyd Springs

Armuchee P.O.

May 17-24
ROME

Etowah

River

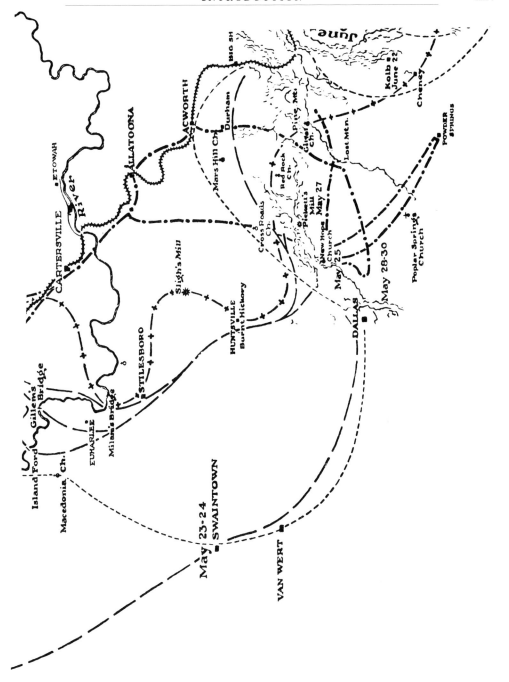

THE ATLANTA CAMPAIGN
Cartersville to New Hope Church

THE ATLANTA CAMPAIGN
Allatoona to Decatur

STONE MTN.
July 18

Browning's Court House
(TUCKER)

Henderson's Mill
July 18

Blake's Mill

OLD CROSS KEYS
Rainy

Durand's Mill

July 22
DECATUR

Georgia R. R.

River

McAfee's Bridge

July 10-17

ROSWELL

July 8
Phillip's Ferry

Power's Ferry
July 12-18

July 18
BUCKHEAD

July 20

July 17
Pace's Ferry

Moore's Mill
Howell's Mill

Paper
Mill

Soap Cr.

MARIETTA

Kennesaw Mtn.

VINING'S

July 4

SMYRNA

July 5-9

Mayson-Turner Ferry

LICK SKILLET

WOODSTOCK

Noonday Ch.

BIG SHANTY

ACWORTH

Durham

Mars Hill Ch.

ALLATOONA

Ross Roads Ch.

Pickett's Mill

Hope May 27

Pine Mtn.

Red Rock Ch.

Gilbert's Ch.

Lost Mtn.

Kolb June 22

Cheney

June 27

POWDER SPRINGS

prings ch.

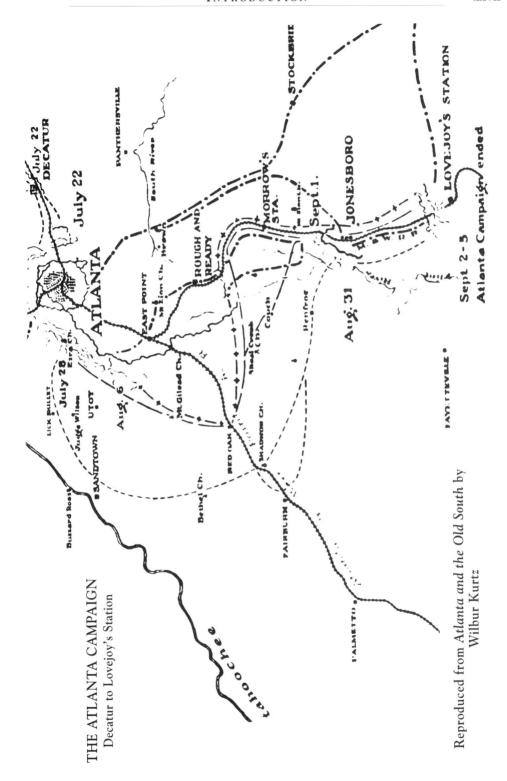

THE ATLANTA CAMPAIGN
Decatur to Lovejoy's Station

Reproduced from *Atlanta and the Old South* by
Wilbur Kurtz

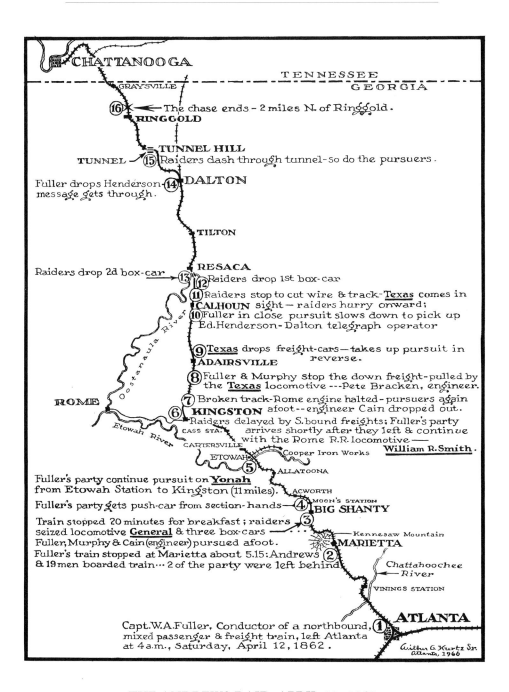

THE ANDREWS RAID–APRIL 12, 1862

Reproduced from
Atlanta and the Old South by Wilbur Kurtz

BANKS COUNTY

Named in honor of noted surgeon
Dr. Richard E. Banks (1784–1850).
County Seat: Homer.

BALDWIN

"HAWKINS LINE"

This line, sometimes called "The Four
Mile Purchase Line," was the boundary
between Georgia and the Cherokee
Nation from 1804 to 1818. It was
established when Georgia bought a
four mile strip from the Indians so as
to take in Wofford's Settlement on
Nancytown Creek. James Blair was
agent for the government, James Vann
and Ketahahee for the Cherokees.

It formed the boundary between Jackson Co. and the Cherokees; later
Franklin Co. and the Cherokees, and
is now the line between Habersham
and Banks Counties.

(Located on US 441/GA 15 on the
south edge of town. GHM 006-2,
1953.)

HOMER

BANKS COUNTY

Banks County was created by Act of
Dec. 11, 1858 from Franklin and
Habersham Counties. It was named
for Dr. Richard Banks (1784–1850),
whose reputation as physician and
surgeon extended over north Ga. and

S. C. Especially noted for treating
Indians for smallpox, he practiced
medicine in Gainesville from 1832
until his death. First officers of Banks
County, commissioned March 19,
1859, were: William P. Richards, Sher-
iff; James Anderson, Clk. Sup. Ct.;
William H. Means, Clk, Inf. Ct.;
Archibald McDonald, Coroner; Pierce
C. Key, Surveyor; Fountain G. Moss,
Ord.; Thomas Ausburn, Tax Col;
Elijah Owens, Tax Rec.

(Located at Main Street/US 441/ GA
51 and Silver Shoals Road in front of
the old courthouse. GHM 006-7B,
1956.)

MT. PLEASANT CHURCH

In 1780 a group of people, Garrisons
and Wilmonts, met on top of the hill
behind the church, built a platform
between two trees, and held a religious
meeting. This small gathering, and the
statement that it was pleasant to worship on the mountain, led to the
building of the first Mt. Pleasant
Church, a log structure. The present
one, built in 1883, is on land given by
John Wilmont. A large wooden arbor
with small cabins around, used until
1885, was erected on the church
grounds for annual camp meetings.
Many outstanding people have gone
out from this church – teachers, doc-
tors, preachers, merchants, bankers,
nurses.

(From Homer take US 441 north 1.4
miles to GA 51, follow GA 51 east
2.7 miles to marker at the church.
GHM 006-7C, 1956.)

NAILS CREEK
BAPTIST CHURCH

Nails Creek Baptist Church, the first Baptist Church in Banks County, was established February 11, 1787. It was the Mother Church of Middle River, Grove Level and Indian Creek. Many descendants of its charter members are active in the work of the church. The first building burned in 1864 and was rebuilt in 1868. In 1881 a larger church was erected and that was replaced by the present brick structure in 1908. From 1836 to 1922 28 ministers filled the pulpit. Membership in 1922 was 457.

(Located on GA 51 near the junction with GA 63 at the church. From Homer, take US 441 north 1.4 miles to GA 51, follow GA 51 east 5.1 miles to marker. GHM 006-5, 1954.)

REVOLUTIONARY
BATTLEGROUND

Col. Elijah Clarke, distinguished Revolutionary soldier, in charge of American troops stationed on the mountain, fought a battle with the British and Indians in the valley across Broad River. The river, since straightened by a canal, then flowed by the foot of the mountain.

The river bridge, known as the Line Bridge is on the survey line of the "Last Four Mile Purchase Tract" bought from the Cherokee Indians by the government. General Wofford and a party appointed by the State Legislature rode horseback to Washington to intercede with the government to buy this land.

(From Homer take US 441 north 1.4 miles to GA 51, follow GA 51 2.8 miles, turn left on Homer–Toccoa Road/Old GA 184 and follow 5.8 miles to marker. GHM 006-7A, 1954.)

LINE BAPTIST CHURCH

The Line Baptist Church was constituted Sept. 13, 1802, by Rev. Moses Sanders, Thomas Maxwell and Daniel White.

This church was just over the line between Georgia and Cherokee lands. Meetings couldn't be held at night, because all white people had to be off Indian lands by sundown.

Thirteen churches met here and formed the Tugalo Baptist Association in 1818. This Association met here in 1822 and 1842. The Liberty Baptist Association was formed here in 1867.

This building, about 70 years old, is the second one on this site. It has stood in Franklin, Habersham and Banks Counties.

(Located on US 441/GA 15, 7.1 miles north of Homer in front of the church. GHM 006-3A, 1953.)

INDIAN BOUNDARY

The boundary between the State of Georgia and the Cherokee Nation established by the Treaty of Augusta, May 31, 1783, ran along here. The line ran "from the top of Currahee mountain to the head, or source, of the most southern branch of the

Oconee river, including all waters of the same."

This boundary line was re-affirmed by the Treaty of Hopewell, Nov. 28, 1785. It was originally marked by a line of felled trees at least twenty feet wide, which became a sort of No Man's Land.

(Located on US 441/GA 15, 7.2 miles north of Homer. GHM 006-1, 1953.)

BATTLE OF NARROWS

This battle was fought, Oct. 12, 1864 between Confederate troops and Union cavalry in the nearby mountain pass.

A Confederate victory saved Habersham County from pillaging by Union troops and camp followers and also saved grain fields for Confederate troops. There was a (C) drill field near the site of the battle.

Some historians have called this the "Battle of Currahee" because it was fought in sight of Currahee mountain. Casualties were small and the wounded were cared for by neighbors.

(Located at US 441/GA 15 and GA 105, 12.1 miles north of Homer. GHM 006-3B, 1953.)

LEATHERWOOD BAPTIST CHURCH

Leatherwood Baptist Church was established in 1801 at Eastanollee in Franklin County. Many members moved near here, organized this church and named it Leatherwood. Members remaining in Eastanollee reorganized and named their church Eastanollee. Land for the first church here was given by Hudson Moss. His granddaughter, wife of Thomas Scales Wells, pastor for many years, gave the land for the present church building. Many landowners and their slaves were members of the church. Near here is the site of the Battle of the Narrows and the old Muster Ground.

(Located on GA 105. From Homer, follow US 441 north 12.1 miles, take GA 105 east 3.9 miles to marker. GHM 006-6, 1954.)

BARROW COUNTY

Named in honor of David Crenshaw Barrow, Chancellor of the University of Georgia for many years. County Seat: Winder.

AUBURN

PERRY–RAINEY INSTITUTE

Perry–Rainey Institute founded 1892 by Mulberry Baptist Assn. at Appalachee Baptist Church, Auburn.

Predecessors of Perry–Rainey Institute, Harmony Grove Academy, Mulberry High School and Perry–Rainey College.

Named for Reverend Hiram Rainey and Mrs. W. T. Perry, donors. Institute opened 1893, chartered in 1894, first graduation 1896.

Sold in 1915 to Christian Church and became SOUTHEASTERN CHRISTIAN COLLEGE until 1924. Sold to Barrow County in 1928 and Administrative Building became Auburn–Consolidated School. Building was torn down in 1958. Only girls dormitory remains owned by R & R Manufacturing Co.

(Located one block off GA 8 at 7th Street and 6th Avenue in front of Auburn Elementary School. BCHS 007-99, 1983.)

BETHLEHEM

BETHLEHEM UNITED METHODIST CHURCH

Oldest Methodist Church in Barrow County, organized in the 1780's. Services first held in log house two miles N. E. of present site. In 1790 a church was built nearby. The present site was originally a camp ground with an arbor, tents & cottage for camp meetings. Arbor used as mobilization center during War Between the States. Exact date church moved to this site unknown. Land deeded by Rev. John W. B. Allen to trustees in 1847. First church here torn down in 1878 and another erected. Present church was built in 1949 as a memorial to Guy Lee Thompson. Church School building added in 1967. Narthex and steeple added in 1970.

(Follow GA 324/Star Street 0.8 mile, turn right on Bethlehem Church Road and follow 0.4 mile to marker and church. BCHS 007-98, 1977.)

KILGORE MILL COVERED BRIDGE

Located 1.5 miles west across Apalachee River; constructed by D. J. Thompson in 1874, replacing older bridge. Constructed by the Town Truss Design patented in 1820 by Ithiel Town of Conn.; the bridge consists of a web of planks crisscrossed at angles of 45° to 60° like lattice fastened with wooden pegs, extending 117 feet with one span, 16.5 feet wide and 15.5 feet high.

In 1833, Joseph James sold the land to Willis Kilgore, Sr. and it remained in his family over 75 years. He built a saw mill and grist mill at the dam. In 1924 E. M. & G. R. Brisco purchased the land and mills, and remained owners until 1940. It became known as Brisco Mills. Land on Barrow Co. side owned by Mrs. Ola Sims, and Walton Co. side by Mr. & Mrs. H. D. Kinsey. Only the bridge remains.

(Located on GA 11, 2 miles south of junction with GA 324. BCHS 007-97, 1977.)

STATHAM

STATHAM HOUSE

Built circa 1850. Owned by M. John C. Statham. He provided homes for widows of Civil War Veterans; donated

COURTESY, GEORGIA DEPARTMENT OF ARCHIVES AND HISTORY

KILGORE MILL COVERED BRIDGE

land for right-of-way of railroad; streets for town, and a lot for a Methodist Church – now the city cemetery.

Statham, incorporated Dec. 20, 1892, named in honor of its founder M.J.C. Statham. First Post Office known as Barber's Creek, 1846; then Delay 1854 and changed to Statham in 1892.

Statham was originally known as Calamit Village, part of the Talasee Colony on the Ocoloco Trail, inhabited by Creek and Cherokee Indians. In 1784, white settlers paid Indian Chief Umausauga 14 pounds of beads for land from Calamit to Snodon and Poganip calling it Beadland.

(Located on Broad Street near the junction with Jefferson Street. BCHS 007-89, 1977.)

STATHAM HIGH SCHOOL
IN HONOR – PAUL T. BARRETT

Educator: 52 years service in education. Born Feb. 12, 1900, Ila, Ga. Graduate of University of Georgia. Taught: Maysville, Cornelia, Buford 1921–1933. Principal – Coach

Statham School 1933–1957. Supt. Barrow County Schools 1957–1965. Professor of Education Brenau College 1965–1973. Barrow County Educator of the year 1978. Married Weebie Jones Dec. 17, 1922. Baptist: deacon, Sunday School Supt. and teacher 42 years. His influence touched the lives of many students and he will be remembered always with love and profound respect.

(Located on Broad Street at the Elementary School. BCHS 007-88, 1978.)

First Georgia Chapter
Future Farmers of America

was located at Statham Consolidated High School, Statham, Georgia. Organized October 1928 and chartered by State Association January 16, 1929.

Officers were:
William R. Bowdoin, President,
Ernest L. McLocklin, Vice President,
Dewey Nixon, Secretary,
Glenn Segars, Treasurer,
Robert Langford, Reporter,
A.P. Lewis, Adviser and Teacher of Voc. Ag.

Other members were: James Carruth, James Delay, Clarence Dunahoo, Leslie Finch, Lester Greenway, Lewis Grizzle, Thurmon Hale, Sam Hale, Samuel Hardigree, Marvel Hunter, Walter Jones, Joseph Kinney, Marion Kinney, Lewis Langford, Willie McGee, Eucephus Sims, Hill Winn Steed, and Aubry Savage.

(Located on Broad Street at the Elementary School Gymnasium. An identical marker is located on GA 8 at The Peoples Bank. FFA 007-87.)

WINDER

BARROW COUNTY

Barrow County was created by Act of July 7, 1914 from Gwinnett, Jackson and Walton Counties. It was named for David Crenshaw Barrow, Chancellor of the University of Georgia for many years. Born in Oglethorpe County, October 18, 1852, he died in Athens, January 11, 1929. Affectionately known to thousands as "Uncle Dave," he spent most of his life teaching. First officers of Barrow County, commissioned January 11, 1915, were: H. G. Hill, Ordinary; Geo. N. Bagwell, Clk. Sup. Ct.; H. O. Camp, Sheriff; J. A. Still, Tax Receiver; Alonzo N. Williams, Tax Collector, J. W. Nowell, Treasurer; R. L. Griffith, Surveyor; Tom McElhannon, Coroner; W. M. Holsenbeck, Co. School Supt.

(Located at Broad and Athens Streets on the courthouse lawn. GHM 007-2, 1956.)

THE STONEMAN RAID
BATTLE OF KING'S TANYARD

Closing in on Atlanta in July 1864, Maj. Gen. W. T. Sherman found it "too strong to assault and too extensive to invest." To force its evacuation, he sent Maj. Gen. Geo. Stoneman's cavalry (F) to cut the Macon railway by which its defenders were supplied. At the Battle of Sunshine Church (19 miles NE of Macon), Stoneman surrendered with 600 men to Brig. Gen. Alfred Iverson, Jr., (C) after covering the escape northward of Adams' and Capron's brigades. Both units retreated via Athens, intending to resupply their commands there and to "destroy the armory and other government works," but were stopped at the river bridge south of Athens by Home Guard units with a battery of guns. Unable to cross, they turned west; Capron on the Hog Mountain road through Jug Tavern (Winder), and Adams on roads farther north by which he reached the Union lines near Marietta without further losses.

Capron passed through Jug Tavern late that night and marched to King's Tanyard (5 miles NW on State 211) where he halted for two hours to rest his exhausted command. Before dawn on August 3rd, he was surprised by Williams' Kentucky brigade (C). About 430 of his men were captured and sent to Athens, a few escaping through the woods. Capron himself, with six men, reached the Union lines near Marietta four days later – on foot.

This action, known also as the Battle of Jug Tavern, was the final event of the Federal fiasco called the Stoneman Raid.

(Located at Broad and Laura Streets on the courthouse lawn. GHM 007-4, 1957.)

BUILDER OF THE NATION

This steam locomotive was presented to the City of Winder and Barrow County in 1959 by the Seaboard Air

BUILDER OF THE NATION

Line Railroad Company. It was placed here as a permanent exhibit in memory of the important service engines of this type rendered to the country. Built in 1930, it operated for a number of years on the Gainesville Midland Railroad. At the time of its retirement in 1959, No. 208 was one of the last steam locomotives in service in this section of the country.

(Located at Broad and Porter Streets at the railroad station. GHM 007-96.)

FORT YARGO

This remarkably preserved log blockhouse was built in 1793, according to historians. There are several references to Fort Yargo as existing prior to 1800. Its location is given as three miles southwest of "Jug Tavern," original name for Winder.

Early historians say Fort Yargo was one of four forts built by Humphries Brothers to protect early settlers from Indians. The other three forts were listed as at Talassee, Thomocoggan, now Jefferson, and Groaning Rock, now Commerce.

Fort Yargo is now a State Park with recreational facilities.

(Located on GA 81 at Carson Wages Road, 2.8 miles south of the junction with GA 8. GHM 007-1, 1954.) **Note:** The fort is 0.1 mile down Carson Wages Road.

FORT YARGO

COURTESY, GEORGIA DEPARTMENT OF ARCHIVES AND HISTORY

RICHARD RUSSELL, SR. (1861–1938)

COURTESY, GEORGIA DEPARTMENT OF ARCHIVES AND HISTORY

RICHARD RUSSELL, JR. (1897–1971)

RUSSELL HOUSE

The Russell House was built in 1912 by Richard Brevard Russell, Sr., B. 1861 – D. 1938, and his wife Ina Dillard, B. 1868 – D. 1953, who were married June 24, 1891. Fifteen children were born to this marriage. Judge Russell was elected Chief Justice, Supreme Court of Georgia, in 1922, and served in this capacity until his death. Mrs. Russell was Georgia's Mother of the year in 1950. In 1954, the late Senator Richard B. Russell, Jr., the oldest son, became the owner of the house and made it his home until his death in 1971.

Russell Memorial Park and Cemetery is located to the South of the house.

(Located on GA 8, 1.4 miles east of the junction with GA 81. BCHS 007-95, 1977.)

CONCORD METHODIST CEMETERY

In 1836, Byrd Betts, Pioneer Steward of the Concord Methodist Church, later to become the First Methodist Church of Winder, gave 10 acres land for the church and cemetery. Those known buried here.

Susan, wife of S.E. Beddingfield, 1829 – March 1851, J. B. Betts, Jan. 26, 1847 – June 19, 1886, O. G. Betts, Dec. 23, 1844 – Jan. 1884 – C.S.A., Margaret Betts, May 4,----; 1872 – Leila and Wade Bush, Malinda F. Coker, Aug. 22, 1859 – Sept. 13, 1871, T. C. Hardegree, May 25, 1825 – May 18, 1885 – C.S.A., A. S. Crossley, Oct. 4, 1881 – Jan. 28, 1885, C. W. Crossley, Apr. 29, 1883 – Jan. 30, 1885, Samuel Harrison, Jan. 8, 1809 – Dec. 17, 1886, Peter Kilgore, Mar. 13, 1828 – Apr. 8, 1860, William Saunders Kilgore, May 18, 1856 – Oct. 28, 1860, John A. Smith, May 7, 1861 – June 16, 1887, Dorinda T. Wills, Oct.

21, 1824 – May 24, 1885, Maruon C. Wills, May 18, 1884 – June 28, 18., Randolph Wills, October 20, 1808 – Apr. 1868 – C.S.A.

(Located on GA 211/Athens Street near the junction with Church Street. BCHS 007-94, 1977.)

WINDER'S MOST HISTORICAL SITE

For years inestimable, the CREEK INDIAN VILLAGE of SNODON stood here. In 1793 ALONZO DRAPER, HOMER JACKSON and HERMAN SCUPEEN and their families became the first white people to establish homes in SNODON. This same year SNODON became JUG TAVERN.

In 1862 BYRD BETTS gave a portion of land for JUG TAVERN'S first church, the First Methodist.

In 1880, HILLMAN D. JACKSON, DR. JAMES SAUNDERS and REV. D. FRANK RUTHERFORD purchased 11½ acres and built JUG TAVERN'S FIRST SCHOOL on this spot known as the ACADEMY LOT. These three men served as Board of Trustees until 1887, at which time they transferred the school to a new board consisting of: ROBERT L. CARITHERS, C. W. HARRIS, HILLMAN D. JACKSON, J. H. KILGORE and Z. F. STANTON.

JUG TAVERN became WINDER in 1893 and the ACADEMY LOT remained the site of WINDER'S Public School until 1938.

(Located on GA 211/Athens Street at Church Street. BCHS 007-93, 1979.)

BATTLE OF KING'S TANYARD

On July 31, 1864, at the Battle of Sunshine Church (19 miles NE of Macon), Maj. Gen. Geo. Stoneman (F) surrendered with 600 men to Brig. Gen. Alfred Iverson, Jr. (C), after covering the escape of Adams' and Capron's brigades of his cavalry command. Both units retreated via Athens, intending to resupply their troops there, but were stopped early on August 2nd at the river bridge south of Athens by Home Guard units with artillery. Unable to cross, they turned west; Capron on the Hog Mountain road to Jug Tavern (Winder), and Adams on roads farther north by which he reached the Union lines near Marietta without further loss.

Late that night, Capron halted briefly at Jug Tavern, fed and watered his horses, then marched to King's Tanyard (about 300 yards E) and halted again for two hours to rest his exhausted command. A large body of runaway negroes, who had followed the column, crowded in between the rear pickets and the main body.

Before dawn on August 3rd, Williams' Kentucky brigade (C), in pursuit from Sunshine Church, charged over his pickets and into the panic-stricken negroes "driving and scattering everything before them." Thrown into confusion, Capron's men soon gave way and stampeded toward Mulberry River. About 430 were captured and sent to Athens; others escaped into the woods. Capron himself, with six men, reached Marietta four days later – on foot.

This engagement, called also the Battle of Jug Tavern, was the final event of the Federal fiasco known as the Stoneman Raid.

(Located on GA 211, 5 miles north of the courthouse. GHM 007-3, 1957.)

BETHABRA BAPTIST CHURCH

Clayborn Dalton built an arbor for public Worship across Mulberry River in Jackson County in the early 1800's. It was called "Dalton's Stand." In 1813 the church was moved on this side of Mulberry River near the Maynard Cemetery. Rev. Anslem Anthony was the first Pastor serving from 1813 to 1855. He donated 2 ½ acres of land for the present church with buildings and improvements April 15, 1857. Another building was built about 1880, and stood until the present building was built in 1962.

(Located on Old Thompson Mill Road, off GA 211, 7 miles north of the courthouse. BCHS 007-92, 1977.)

WILLIAM PENTECOST
Born Nov. 4, 1762
Died Jan. 27, 1839

Served 3 years in Revolutionary War from Dinwiddie Co., Va. in Buford's Detachment. Lost an arm at the Waxhaws, May 29, 1780.

Remembered as successful business man, educator and civic worker, but most outstanding as devout Methodist minister. Is credited with establishing five churches. He established Pentecost Methodist Church in 1785. William

and Delilah Pentecost were buried in family plot. In 1909 their bodies were re-interred in a single grave in the Pentecost Church cemetery.

(From the courthouse, follow GA 53 north for 0.6 mile, turn right on GA 82 and follow 4.1 miles to marker and church. BCHS 007-91.)

ROCKWELL
UNIVERSALIST CHURCH

Organized 1839 – Second oldest Universalist Church in Georgia. Located here near original site of Rockwell School, oldest school in this section, and Rockwell Masonic Lodge. Confederate soldiers enlisted and drilled here in 1861–1865.

Church reorganized in 1867 by Dr. L. F. W. Andrews as first Universalist Church of then Jackson County, and called Mulberry Church. Voting precinct and Justice Court, known as House's District, were located here until 1900. Present building erected 1881, and name changed to Rockwell Church. Paul Hill deeded the land to the church.

ROCKWELL UNIVERSALIST CHURCH

(Located on GA 53 north, at Rockwell Church Road, 3.5 miles north of the courthouse. BCHS 007-90, 1978.)

BARTOW COUNTY

Named in honor of General Francis S. Bartow (1816–1861) who was the first Confederate general to be killed in the Civil War. County Seat: Cartersville.

ADAIRSVILLE

FEDERAL ARMIES AT ADAIRSVILLE

May 18, 1864. The 4th, 14th & 20th Corps (Army of the Cumberland) (F), together with the 15th & 16th corps (Army of the Tennessee) (F), reached Adairsville, from Resaca, at noon.

Sherman, convinced that all of Johnston's forces (C) had gone to Kingston & Etowah River crossings S. of it, directed his forces to converge there.

McPherson's Army of the Tennessee moved to Barnsley's; the 4th & 14th by direct road to Kingston; the 23d (F) (at Mosteller's Mills, 5 mi. E.) & the 20th, were shifted S.W. across the Gravelly Plateau.

(Located on US 41, 0.8 mile south of junction with GA 140 in front of cemetery. GHM 008-28, 1953.)

JOHNSTON'S ARMY AT ADAIRSVILLE

May 18, 1864. The three corps of the Confederate Army, on reaching Adairsville from Resaca, moved by two roads to Cassville. Hood's and Polk's corps marched S. on old U.S. 41 Highway; Hardee's corps took direct road to Kingston, W. and parallel to the R. R.

Units of Maj. Gen. S. G. French's div. and Brig. Gen. W. H. Jackson's Cavalry joined Polk's corps (C) here & at Cassville.

The march by 2 roads was to facilitate troop movement & to divide Sherman's forces (F) during his advance.

(Located On US 41 , 0.8 mile south of junction with GA 140 in front of cemetery. GHM 008-27, 1953.)

MOSTELLER'S MILLS

Five miles NE on State Highway 140 – a notable plantation and manufacturing center of the 1860's.

The Federal 23rd Corps, left wing of Sherman's forces (F) marching southward from Resaca having crossed at Field's Mill, Coosawattee River, enroute to Cassville, camped at Mosteller's, May 18, 1864.

Butterfield's Div., of the 20th Corps (F), having crossed at Field's also marched by Mosteller's. Geary's and Williams' Divisions, 20th Corps, were joined at Adairsville by Butterfield.

COURTESY, NATIONAL ARCHIVES

GENERAL JOSEPH EGGLESTON JOHNSTON
(1807–1891)

(Located on US 41, 0.8 mile south of the junction with GA 140 in front of the cemetery. GHM 008-2, 1959.)

HISTORIC
TRIMBLE HOUSE

About 2 miles N. is the plantation home of Augustus Crawford Trimble, pioneer settler, member of the Home Guard, and businessman of Adairsville. A son, serving in the 1st Georgia Cavalry under Gen. Joe Wheeler, engaged the enemy on the plantation. Confederates under Wheeler fought Federals north of the house and many of the wounded were carried to the Trimble house which was used as a hospital by Confederates and Federals. Two members of Wheeler's cavalry died in the house and are buried nearby. The house was not burned because it was used as a hospital and

did not lie in the direct path of the Federal advance.

(Located on GA 140. 0.7 mile east of junction with US 41 **or** 0.4 mile west of I–75. GHM 008-48, 1956.)

MOSTELLER'S PLANTATION

May 18, 1864: Butterfield's (3d) div., 20th A.C. and Maj. Gen. Hooker, (F) in person, from Field's Mill, reached this rd. ¾ mi. W., enroute to the J. McDow house 2 mi. S. of Adairsville.

Schofield's 23d. A.C., (F) having marched from Field's, camped here until dawn of the 19th, then moved S.W. by mill and spring. The route led through Little Prairie (possibly Pleasant Valley) and joined old 41 Highway at the McDow house, arriving there shortly after the 20th A.C. had moved southward.

(Located on GA 140 near Mostella Branch, 3.9 miles east of I–75 or 5.1 miles east of US 41. GHM 008-26, 1989.) ♦

ORIGINAL SITE
ADAIRSVILLE – 1830's

May 17, 1864, Johnston's (C) forces retreating S. from Resaca, paused here on an E.–W. line, the intention being to make a stand against the federals in close pursuit.

Finding the position untenable due to width of Oothcalaloga Valley, Johnston withdrew at midnight. Hardee's Corps (C) was astride the road at this point.

WILBUR G. KURTZ

JONATHAN McDOW HOUSE

In rear-guard action, (C) detachments from Hardee's Corps held the stone residence of Robt. C. Saxon, 0.2 mi. N. of the County line, until midnight.

(Located on US 41 near the Bartow–Gordon county line. GHM 008-1, 1952.) ♦ ★

SITE
JONATHAN McDOW HOUSE

A two-story brick residence of the 1840's used as h'dq'rs by Maj. Gen. Joseph Hooker, 20th A. C., & Maj. Gen. John M. Schofield, 23d A.C. (F), May 18, 19, 1864.

Both Corps were ordered by Sherman to concentrate at Kingston & were enroute there in the mistaken belief

that Johnston's forces had marched directly from Adairsville to Kingston.

By late afternoon, May 19, Hooker's & Schofield's corps, moving S. from McDow's, discovered Johnston's Army (C) at Cassville.

(Located on Old US 41/41st Street/Old Dixie Highway, 3.2 miles south of junction with GA 140. GHM 008-18, 1953.)

McPHERSON'S TROOPS
MARCH TO BARNSLEY'S

May 18, 1864. Logan's 15th A.C. of the Army of the Tennessee (F) left Adairsville in afternoon, following the 4th & 14th A.C. (F) as far as this point, where it turned S. W. to

Barnsley's Gardens, where it joined K. Garrard's Cavalry (F).

Dodge's 16th A.C. (F) followed the 15th from Adairsville after dark, & reached Barnsley's at midnight.

The Army of the Tennessee formed the right flank of the Federal Armies moving S. on a wide front toward the Etowah River.

(Located on Hall Station Road/ Adairsville–Kingston Road, 2.3 miles south of junction with GA 140. GHM 008-29, 1953.)

ALLATOONA

RAILROAD BLOCK–HOUSE

On Allatoona Creek, in this vicinity, a Federal block-house, guarding State R. R. Bridge, was garrisoned by Companies E,.F. and I. of the 18th Wisconsin Regt. (F).

Oct. 5, 1864, while retreating from Allatoona, 2 mi. N., French's Div. of Stewart's A. C. (C), burned the bridge and block-house, capturing 84 officers and men.

The State R. R. was shifted N. in 1949 and in 1950, Allatoona Creek was flooded by the impounded waters of Allatoona Dam.

(Located on Old US 41/GA 293 at the bridge between Emerson and Acworth. GHM 008-7, 1992.)

RUINS OF THE OLD IRON FURNACE
AT COOPER'S IRON WORKS

MARK ANTHONY COOPER'S IRON WORKS

These ruins of an old iron furnace built by Moses Stroup are all that remain of Cooper's Iron Works, developed by Mark Anthony Cooper, pioneer industrialist, politician, and farmer.

Cooper was born in 1800 near Powelton, Ga. Graduating from S. C. College (now the University of S.C.) in 1819, he was admitted to the bar in 1821 and opened a law office in Eatonton. A member of the Ga. Legislature in 1833, he later served in the 26th Congress, filled a vacancy in the 27th, and was reelected to the 28th. Resigning to run for Governor in 1843, Cooper was defeated by George W. Crawford and retired from politics.

Cooper bought an interest in the furnace then owned by Stroup, and in 1847 he and LeRoy M. Wiley bought Stroup out. Cooper's plants, including a nail factory, rolling-mill, and flour mill, were destroyed by Sherman's army. Cooper and Stroup were incorporators of the Etowah Railroad, completed to the rolling-mill in 1858. A

THE "YONAH" AT ETOWAH STATION AS THE
"GENERAL" STEAMS NORTHWARD

yard engine of this road, the "Yonah," was involved in the famous chase of the "General" in April, 1862.

Cooper, the first president of the Ga. Agricultural Society, a trustee of Mercer University, the University of Ga., and the Cherokee Baptist College, died in 1885 at his home, "Glen Holly."

(From US 41 south of Cartersville take Allatoona Dam Road east 1.8 miles to the Dam and Powerhouse parking lot. GHM 008-50, 1962.) **Note:** To locate the ruins of the furnace, from US 41 take the exit to GA 293 and follow 2.8 miles. The ruins are located across the river from the marker.

ALLATOONA PASS

Allatoona was in pioneer days a travel hub, because ridges from east and south met here where it was fairly easy to cross the Allatoona Mountain range by winding over a low ridge, or pass.

The Sandtown or Tennessee Road from the south, and the Old Alabama Road from the east, joined here to cross the pass, then separated, the Sandtown to cross the Etowah and aim for Tennessee, and the Alabama Road to run west on the south side of the Etowah.

(Located on the Emerson–Allatoona Road, 1.5 miles east of I–75, exit #122. GHM 008-44, 1956.)

BATTLE OF ALLATOONA
October 5, 1864

After artillery firing & repeated assaults by French's troops (C), the Federals made a final stand in the star fort W. of rock cut. Failing to dislodge the defenders, French retreated to New Hope Church in Paulding County.

French's Division consisted of Young's, Cockrell's & Sear's Brigades, (C) 3,276; losses 799. Corse's command: Alexander's & Rowett's Brigades, (F) 2,137; losses, 706.

This battle inspired the gospel hymn: "Hold the fort for I am coming."

(Located on Emerson–Allatoona Road, 1.6 miles east of I–75 exit #122. GHM 008-6, 1952.)

BATTLE OF ALLATOONA
October 5, 1864

Lt. Gen. John B. Hood, Army of Tenn., (C) while enroute N. from Palmetto, Ga., sent Lt. Gen. A. P. Stewart's Corps to destroy the State R. R.

GEORGE N. BARNARD

THE ALLATOONA PASS, LOOKING NORTH

from Big Shanty to the Etowah River. Stewart seized Big Shanty and Acworth on the 3d., and French's Div. was sent, on the 4th, to capture Allatoona.

Daylight, the 5th, French (C) deployed his troops around the Federal garrison, commanded by Gen. John M. Corse (F), posted on high ground E. and W. of the rock cut.

(Located on the Emerson–Allatoona Road, 2 miles east of I–75 exit #122, at entrance to Allatoona Landing. GHM 008-5, 1989.)

BATTLE OF ALLATOONA

After the fall of Atlanta, hoping Sherman would follow, Hood moved his Confederate army north, sending French's Division to fill the railroad cut at Allatoona, and burn the railroad bridge over the Etowah River, to hamper Sherman's movement.

French found Corse with 2,000 men entrenched on the ridge guarding military stores, and with his 3,000 he attacked on October 5, 1864. The fight was costly but indecisive. French lost 799, Corse 706 men. French, not risking an all-out attack, withdrew before aid reached Corse.

(From Cartersville take Center Road 3 miles, turn right on Right Bank Access Road/GA 294N and follow 2.6 miles to Overlook. or From I–75, Exit 125, take GA 20 east for a short distance and follow GA 294N 3.9 miles to Overlook. GHM 008-41, 1956.)

ETOWAH AND THE WAR

The Confederacy sought iron and munitions eagerly, which quickly brought prosperity to Etowah. Patriotic key workers, though exempt from army duty, enlisted, and loss of their skill hampered production.

Mark Cooper sold the works in 1862. In 1863, the Confederacy took over the firm seeking to increase production. As Sherman marched by in 1864, mindful of the war value of iron, he sent troops, who, after a brisk skirmish, burned the plant on May 22. This ended an era – the works were not rebuilt after the War, as cheaper and better production methods had been found.

(From Cartersville take Center Road 3 miles, turn right on Right Bank Access Road/GA 294 North and follow 2.6 miles, to Overlook. or From I-75, Exit 125, take GA 20 East for a short distance and follow GA 294N, 3.9 miles to Overlook. GHM 008-47, 1956.)

FRIENDSHIP MONUMENT

The nearby marble shaft has the unique distinction of having been erected by a debtor in honor of his creditors. Losses during the panic of 1857 forced Mark A. Cooper, proprietor of the Etowah Iron Works, to offer this property for sale to satisfy a $100,000 debt. Thirty-eight friends signed notes totaling that amount to save the enterprise.

When the debt was repaid in 1860, Cooper erected this monument on which the names of his benefactors are inscribed.

(From Cartersville take Center Road 3 miles, turn right on Right Bank Access Road/GA 294 North and follow 2.6 miles, follow signs to Overlook. Or From I–75, Exit 125, take GA 20 East for a short distance and follow GA 294N 3.9 miles to Overlook. GHM 008-51, 1963.)

CARTERSVILLE

BARTOW COUNTY

Originally Cass, Bartow County was created by Act of Dec. 3, 1832 from Cherokee County. The name was changed Dec. 6, 1861 to honor Gen. Francis S. Bartow (1816–1861), Confederate political leader and soldier, who fell mortally wounded at the First Battle of Manassas, while leading the 7th and 8th Ga. Vols. of his brigade. His last words were said to be, "They have killed me, boys, but never give up." First officers of this county, commissioned March 9, 1833, were: Benjamin F. Adair, Sheriff; Chester Hawks, Clerk Superior Court; Leathern Rankin, Clerk Inferior Court;

COURTESY, GEORGIA DEPARTMENT OF ARCHIVES AND HISTORY

FRANCIS S. BARTOW (1816–1861)

Nealy Goodwin, Surveyor; John Pack, Coroner.

(Located at South Erwin Street and Cherokee Avenue on the courthouse lawn. GHM 008-43, 1956.)

HOME OF SAM P JONES

Sam P. Jones was born October 16, 1847, in Oak Bowery, Alabama; he moved to Cartersville with his parents in 1856. After his admission to the Georgia Bar in 1868 he married Laura McElwain. In 1872 he was licensed as a Methodist minister. His national career of evangelism, begun in 1884, covered the U.S. and Canada. Dedicated on Christmas Day, 1885, this house was occupied for twenty-one years by Sam Jones. His public speaking was famous for its pathos and humor while his gospel was loved for

its appeal. He died on October 15, 1906.

(Located on Cherokee Avenue/GA 293 between Fite and North Bartow Streets. WPA 008-D8.)

SITE OF SAM JONES' TABERNACLE

For 20 years, thousands came annually to this site, attracted by the magnetic personality and forceful eloquence of Sam Jones, renowned Evangelist and Christian crusader.

Here he built, in 1886, at his own expense, a large open-air structure, called "The Tabernacle," for the interfaith meetings begun in 1884.

Until his death in 1906, he held services here each September, bringing to his hometown the co-workers who assisted him in the great revivals he held throughout the country.

(Located at West Main and School Streets, GHM 008-12B, 1953.)

HOME OF SAM P. JONES

SAM P. JONES (1847–1906)

REBECCA LATIMER FELTON (1835–1930)

PETTIT CREEK
Camp Site, Federal 23d Corps.

Johnston's forces (C) retreated southward from Cassville along this road, to Allatoona Mountains, south of the Etowah, May 20, 1864.

They were immediately followed by Schofield's 23d Corps, (F) which encamped in this vicinity. While, here, troops of Cox's Div. (F) were sent to destroy the Cooper Iron Works (site of Allatoona Dam), May 21, 22.

From this camp-site, the corps marched to the Etowah at Milam's Bridge, on 23d.

(Located on Cassville Road near junction with Goodyear Avenue. GHM 008-3, 1952.)

FELTON HOME

Dr. William H. Felton and his wife, Rebecca Latimer, lived from 1853 until 1905 in the house east of this marker.

A physician, minister and noted orator, Dr. Felton was the leader of the Independent Revolt from the State Democratic Party in the 1870's and won three spectacular Congressional campaigns.

Mrs. Felton's appointment in 1922 at the age of 87, as the first woman U.S. Senator climaxed a long career in which she had gained wide recognition as an author, newspaper columnist, and crusader for women's rights.

(Located at US 411 north and Old Tenn Highway, 0.4 miles north of the junction with US 41. GHM 008-14, 1953.)

"BILL ARP"

The Georgia philosopher – humorist of the War Between the States and Reconstruction era, "Bill Arp," in real life Maj. Charles H. Smith, in 1877 moved from Rome into a house which occupied the crest of the hill here. On this farm which he called "Fontaine-bleau," occurred many of the incidents of family and farm life he related to the delight of his readers.

Typical of his good-natured wit was his remark on returning from the Confederate Army: "I killed as many of the Yankees as they killed of me." He died in Cartersville in 1903, aged 77.

(Located on US 441 north, 2.3 miles north of junction with US 41. GHM 008-16, 1953.)

COURTESY, GEORGIA DEPARTMENT OF ARCHIVES AND HISTORY
BILL ARP (1826–1903)

ETOWAH

Four miles east, in the gorge of the Etowah River, are the picturesque ruins of the once flourishing town of Etowah, developed by Mark Cooper around his iron furnace and rolling mill. The furnace was built in 1844, following one built in 1837 on Stamp Creek. Later five others operated nearby.

In 1864, Etowah reached its peak with 2,000 inhabitants, iron furnace, foundry, and rolling mill, flour mill, corn mills and saw mills, and was destroyed for its munitious importance by Sherman's Army.

(Located on U.S. 41 just south of the Cartersville. city limit or 0.7 mile north of the Etowah River. the marker is located about 100 yards east of the highway in a no trespassing area. WPA 008-D13.)

FEDERAL FORT

Atop the hill to the east is a fort built by Sherman to protect the river bridge, part of the rail line which enabled him to supply his army during the Atlanta campaign. The rail line has been moved downstream, but piers in the river mark the site of the bridge in 1864. Troops here passed much time in swimming, hiking, picking berries, and they played baseball in the field to the west – doubtless some of the first games in this section.

Often the men went out seeking food, and sometimes were fired upon or captured. There was no major battle in the fort area.

(Located on US 41 at the Etowah River, 1.5 miles south of Cartersville. GHM 008-45, 1956.) ◆

GEORGE N. BARNARD

THE ETOWAH BRIDGE

CARTERSVILLE
MINING DISTRICT

You are crossing a district 9 miles long and 3 miles wide famous for production of these minerals: Limestone – first mined about 1835. Iron ore – 1837. Ocher – 1877. Manganese – 1866. Barite – 1887. On the surrounding hillsides are scars of present and past mining.

(Located on U S 41 about 2 miles south of Cartersville. WPA 008-D12.)
♦ ★ – not standing.

APPALACHIAN VALLEY

You are now leaving the Appalachian Valley, underlain by ancient sandstones, shales, and limestones, and entering the Piedmont Plateau, underlain by much older crystalline rocks. This gently rolling plateau, 150 miles in width, represents the beveled-off roots of the once mighty Appalachian Mountains, from which thousands of feet of rocks have been removed by the erosion during hundreds of millions of years. Granite, gold, and mar-

ble are among the valuable minerals mined in this region.

(Located on U S 41 about 6 miles south of Cartersville, at North Pumpkin Vine Bridge. WPA 008-D14.)
♦ ★ – not standing.

CASSVILLE

ATLANTA CAMPAIGN
CASSVILLE

On May 19, 1864, Johnston entrenched on the ridge east of this marker, planned to give battle but Sherman threatened his flank and his Corps commanders objected to the position. He therefore withdrew to Allatoona Pass. Rather than attack this strong position Sherman moved past it toward New Hope Church.

(Located on U S 41 at Cassville Road in a small park. NPS 008-99.)

SITE – CHEROKEE
BAPTIST COLLEGE

On Chapman Hill; a school for boys established Jan. 1854. A large three-story brick bldg. flanked by two-story wings. Burned 1856; rebuilt 1857, destroyed by Federal forces Oct. 12, 1864.

This, & the Methodist Female College ¾ mi. N. E., were the first chartered institutions of higher education in Cherokee Georgia.

Their destruction, together with the burning of Cassville, marked the passing of a notable educational center in this section of the state.

(Located at US 41 and Fire Tower Road. GHM 008-22, 1953.)

SITE – CASSVILLE FEMALE COLLEGE

A large brick structure erected 1853.

May 19, 1864: Skirmishers of Polk's A. C. (C) withdrew from this ridge E. to Cassville when pressed back by Butterfield's (3d) Div., 20th A.C. (F), from the Hawkins Price house.

Battery C, 1st Ohio Lt. Art., supported by 73d Ohio, 19th Mich., & 20 Conn. Reg'ts. (F) occupied ridge & shelled the town as Johnston's Army (C) withdrew to ridge E. of it.

At night, Cassville was seized by the 19th Mich. & 20th Conn. Female College & town were burned by Federal forces, Nov. 1864.

(Located at US 41 and Fire Tower Road. GHM 008-21, 1953.)

CONFEDERATE ARMY OF TENN. AT CASSVILLE

Gen. Joseph E. Johnston's forces (C), reaching Cassville May 18,1864, from Resaca, 30 m. N., took positions on ridge W. of the town & prepared to withstand the advancing Federals.

May 19: Pursuant to this intention, Hood's corps (C) moved N. of the town to oppose the Federal 20th and 23rd corps marching S. from Adairsville.

But Hood's corps diverted by an attack on its right by McCook's cavalry (F), changed front & was ordered, with the rest of the Army (C) to withdraw to ridge E. & S. of the town.

(Located at US 41 with Willow Lane. GHM 008-20, 1953.)

GRAVELLY PLATEAU & TWO RUN CREEK

May 19, 1864: Butterfield's (3d) Div., 20th A.C. (F), moving S. E., from McDow's, left the road here & marched to the Hawkins Price house, enroute to Kingston.

The 1st & 2nd Divs. (F), on roads W., had the same objective – an erratic move by Sherman, who assumed that Johnston's Army (C) had retreated on Kingston.

Butterfield's march disclosed that Johnston's Army was at Cassville – not Kingston. The 23rd A.C. (Schofield) (F) marched on this road from McDow's, reaching Cassville at dark.

(Located at US 41 and Cassville Road, north of Cassville. GHM 008-19, 1953.)

TOWN OF CASSVILLE

In this valley was once situated the proud town of Cassville, begun in July, 1833, as the seat of justice for Cass County and soon the center of trade and travel in the region recently comprising the Cherokee Nation. Both the county and town were named in honor of Gen. Lewis Cass, Michigan

CASS STATION, BUILT IN 1858

statesman and Secretary of War in the Cabinet of President Andrew Jackson.

A decade after its founding Cassville lost its preeminence as a trading center due to the location of the state-owned Western and Atlantic railroad two miles west of its limits. It continued to flourish, however, and in 1860 was a community of some 1300 persons. Two four-year colleges located here and its newspaper. The Cassville Standard, gave weight to its claims of being the educational and cultural center for all northern Georgia.

In 1861 the name of the county was changed by action of the Georgia Legislature to Bartow in memory of Gen. Francis S. Bartow, a native Georgian killed at the First Battle of Manassas, and the name of the town became Manassas.

The entire town was destroyed by fire on Nov. 5, 1864 at the hands of the

Fifth Ohio Cavalry (F). Only three houses and three churches were left standing. So complete was the destruction that no rebuilding of the town was attempted.

(Located on Cassville Road east of US 41. GHM 008-17, 1952.)

SITE OF CASSVILLE
NAMED FOR LOUIS CASS

County Seat, Cass County 1832–1861. First Decision, Supreme Court of Georgia, 1846. Name changed to Manassas, 1861. Town burned by Sherman 1864 and never rebuilt.

(Located on Old US 41 in Cassville Park. WPA 008-97.)

CONFEDERATE DEAD

In this cemetery are buried about 300 unknown Confederate soldiers who died of wounds or disease in the several Confederate hospitals located in Cassville. These hospitals operated from late 1861 until May 18, 1864, then moved south out of the path of the invading Federal forces. In May 1899, the Cassville Chapter of the United Daughters of the Confederacy, to honor these unknown soldiers, placed headstones at each of their graves.

(From Cassville Road, follow Cass–White Road to the cemetery. GHM 008-39B, 1956.)

GRAVE OF GEN. WILLIAM TATUM WOFFORD

Gen. William Tatum Wofford (June 28, 1824–May 22, 1884), Cav. Capt. in the Mexican War, Col. and Brig. Gen. in the Confederate Army, is buried here. After Fredericksburg he succeeded to the command of Gen. Thomas R. R. Cobb, who was mortally wounded there. He served with distinction at Manassas, South Mountain, Antietam, Fredericksburg, Chancellorsville and the Wilderness. Jan. 23, 1865, the Confederate War Department placed him in charge of forces in North Georgia to protect citizens against "bushwhackers" and "guerrillas" and finally to arrange the surrender of Confederates in Georgia.

(From Cassville Road, follow Cass–White Road to the cemetery. GHM 008-40B, 1956.)

CONFEDERATE LINE
5 P. M. MAY 19, 1864.

The three corps of Gen. Joseph E. Johnston's Army (C) were withdrawn from N. & W. of Cassville to this ridge, E. & S. of the town.

Hardee was posted astride the R. R. near Cass Station on the S.; Polk centered here & Hood's line skirted the cemetery N.

This shift from an aggressive to a defensive position resulted in a Council of War at Polk's hd'q'rs. where it was claimed the line was untenable, whereupon Johnston ordered a retreat to the Etowah River that night.

(Located on Mac Johnson Road, 0.2 mile from the junction with Cassville Road. GHM 008-23, 1953.)

GEN. LEONIDAS POLK'S HEADQUARTERS

The William Neal McKelvey residence – 1864. A Council of War held here May 19, discussed the advisability of holding the position E. & S. of Cassville by the Confederate army.

Present were: Gen. Joseph E. Johnston; Lt. Gen. Polk; Lt. Gen. John B. Hood; Maj. Gen. S. G. French; & Capt. W. J. Morris, Chief Engineer, Polk's A.C.

After hearing the statements of the Council, Johnston ordered the withdrawal of the army at midnight. This decision stemmed from a failure to make an opportune attack on the Fed-

LIEUTENANT GENERAL LEONIDAS POLK
(1806–1864)

erals, & alleged inability to hold a defensive line as it was then situated.

(Located on Mac Johnson Road, 1.2 miles from junction with Cassville Road. GHM 008-38, 1954.)

HISTORIC PRICE HOUSE

2.5 mi. N. E. is the ante-bellum house of Col. Hawkins F. Price; State Senator 1857–1865; Mem. Ga. Secession Convention.

A landmark of military operations near Cassville, where both Gen. Daniel Butterfield & Gen. Hooker (20th A.C.) (F) had hdqrs May 19, 1864.

Hooker had been ordered from Adairsville to Kingston, on false reports that Johnston (C) had retreated there. S. of the Price house, Hooker discovered that Johnston had gone to Cassville.

(Located on GA 293/Old US 411 towards Kingston, east of Two Run Creek. GHM 008-8, 1952.) ♦ ★

EMERSON

EMERSON

Named for Joseph Emerson Brown, Gov. of Ga., 1857–1865, U. S. Senator, 1880–1891. Known as Stegall's Station prior to 1889, site of the Bartow Iron Works.

May 20, 1864: Gen. Joseph E. Johnston's forces (C) camped here after retreating from Cassville and burning the highway and R. R. bridges over the Etowah. Having heard that Sherman's forces (F) had moved southward from Kingston toward Dallas, Johnston resumed his march on roads that converged there, May 23d, 24th.

Allatoona, scene of Oct. 5, 1864, battle, is 2 mi. E.

(Located on GA 193 in Emerson. GHM 008-4, 1952.)

EUHARLEE

MILAM'S BRIDGE

The covered structure over the Etowah here, was burned by Jackson's (C) Cav., May 21, 1864, the day after Johnston's (C) passage of the river at State R. R. Bridge.

May 23d, the 2 pontoon bridges intended for the passage of Schofield's 23d A.C. (F) were usurped by the 20th A.C.(F) (mistakenly diverted from Gillem's bridge) and the 23d A.C. did not cross until the 24th.

This and crossings lower down were on Federal routes from Kingston & Cassville toward Dallas, Paulding Co. Sherman (F) called the Etowah "The Rubicon of Georgia."

(Located at Euharlee and Milam Roads. GHM 008-9, 1952.)

GILLEM'S BRIDGE

In 1864, a covered structure spanned the Etowah at this point.

On May 23d, the 20th Corps (F), moving from Cassville, having been ordered to cross here, was diverted through error, to Milam's Bridge 5 mi. upstream. The 4th Corps (F), moving from Cassville, crossed here and the 14th Corps (F), moving from Kingston, crossed at Island Ford, 2 mi. west.

The three Corps camped that night near Stilesboro – a movement that was part of Sherman's advance southward from Cassville and Kingston toward Dallas, Paulding County.

(Located on the Kingston–Euharlee/ Hardens Bridge Road near the north end of the bridge over the Etowah River. GHM 008-10, 1992.)

OLD MACEDONIA CHURCH ORGANIZED 1847

In 1864, a road southward from Wooley's Bridge (Etowah River), crossed the road near this point and ran to Van Wert (Rockmart) and Dallas.

This was the route of McPherson's Army of the Tennessee, (15th and 16th Corps) (F) right wing of forces under Sherman moving from Kingston to the Dallas front, May 23, 24.

The church stood at the N.W. angle of the crossroads until another edifice was erected on the site of the present structure, ¾ mile eastward.

(Located at Macedonia and Euharlee Roads, 3.5 miles west of Euharlee. GHM 008-12A, 1984.)

KINGSTON

HOME OF DR. FRANCIS GOULDING

This home was built by Dr. Francis Goulding in 1852. Dr. Goulding was born in Liberty County, GA., Sept. 28, 1810. As a teacher, author and inventor, he had a distinguished career. Graduate University of GA., 1830, ordained Presbyterian minister, 1833. In 1833, he married Mary Howard of Savannah, who died here, 1853. His famous book, *The Young Marooners* was published in 1852. He

COURTESY, GEORGIA DEPARTMENT OF ARCHIVES AND HISTORY

DR. FRANCIS GOULDING (1810–1881)

married Matilda Rees of Darien, 1855. He died in Roswell, Georgia 1881.

(Located on GA 293, 0.6 mile east of Kingston. WPA 008-C12.) ♦ ★ – not standing.

CONFEDERATE MEMORIAL DAY

First Decoration, or Memorial Day, was observed in Kingston in late April of 1865, and has been a continuous observance here since that day, the only such record held by any community in this Nation. The first Memorial, or Decoration Day, was observed while Federals still occupied this town, flowers being placed on both Confederate and Federal graves that day. Much credit is due the Dardens and other patriotic citizens of this town for their untiring efforts to keep alive memories of the gallant Confederates – greatest fighting men of all time.

(Located at Park and Railroad Streets. GHM 008-39A, 1956.)

THE ANDREWS RAIDERS AT KINGSTON

April 12, 1862. James J. Andrews with 18 Ohio soldiers (F) in disguise, & 1 civilian, having seized the locomotive "GENERAL" at Big Shanty (KENNE-SAW), intending to wreck the State R.R., were forced to side-track here and wait for S. bound freights. After long delay, the "GENERAL" continued N.

Pursuing from Big Shanty, Capt. W. A. Fuller (Conductor), Jeff Cain (Engineer), & Anthony Murphy (C), – using a push-car – reached the Etowah, where the engine "YONAH" brought them to Kingston; pursuit was resumed on the Rome R.R. locomotive "WM. R. SMITH."

(Located on Johnson Street between Railroad and Main Streets. GHM 008-34, 1953.)

WILBUR G. KURTZ

THE "WILLIAM R. SMITH" AT KINGSTON

HOUSE - SITE
THOMAS V. B. HARGIS

Maj. Gen. W. T. Sherman's
Headquarters, May 19–23, 1864.

Sherman (F) occupied the Hargis
house for three days of reorganization
of forces in the campaign that ended
at Atlanta.

Assuming that Johnston's army (C)
had moved, from Adairsville, directly
on Kingston & the river crossings S.,
May 18, led Sherman to concentrate
his forces here – only to discover that
Johnston had gone directly to Cassville where, without making a stand,
he retreated to Allatoona, May 20th.
Sherman countered May 23, by moving due S.

(Located at Johnson and Main Streets.
GHM 008-35, 1953.)

SURRENDER OF
CONFEDERATE TROOPS
May 12, 1865.

Brig. Gen. Wm. T. Wofford (C)
arranged with Brig. Gen. Henry M.
Judah, U.S.A. for the surrender of
some 3000 to 4000 Confederate soldiers, mostly Georgians, not paroled
in Virginia, N. Carolina and elsewhere.

During final negotiations, Gen. Wof-
ford's h'dq'rs were at the McCravey–
Johnston res., on Church St., Gen.
Judah's h'dq'rs were at Spring Bank,
the home of the Rev. Charles Wallace
Howard, 2 mi. N. of Kingston.

Rations were supplied to the Confederate soldiery by the Federal Commissary.

(Located at Church and Main Streets.
GHM 008-36, 1953.).

KINGSTON
METHODIST CHURCH

The original church, with another
name and at another location, was
built in 1845, rebuilt in Kingston in
1854, and dedicated by Rev. Lovick
Pierce, a leading preacher of the
nation and father of Bishop George F.
Pierce. The only church remaining
after Sherman's march through here, it
opened its doors freely to all denominations, creating such a spirit of fellowship that children of the
generation grew up feeling there was
only one church. It was Kingston's
schoolhouse, too. For many years Confederate Memorial Day services were
held at the church. Among its ablest
pastors have been Gen. Clement A.
Evans, Simon Peter Richardson,
Lovick Pierce. Bishop George F.
Pierce, Dr. W. H. Felton, Sam P. Jones
have preached here, while Mrs. Lem
Gilreath and Mrs. Mary Harris Armor
have held temperance rallies.

The large, handsome bell in this
church, a gift of John Pendleton King.
U.S. Senator, president of the W. &
A. Railroad, for whom Kingston is
named, for 100 years has been the
town fire alarm and has announced
the return of peace after four wars. It
can be heard over a radius of four
miles.

In 1906 the church was rebuilt on its present location.

(Located at Main and Elliott Streets in front of the church. GHM 008-49, 1958.)

UNKNOWN CONFEDERATE DEAD

Here sleep, known but to God, 250 Confederate and two Federal soldiers, most of whom died of wounds, disease and sickness in the Confederate hospitals located here – 1862–1864.

These men were wounded in the battles of Perryville, Chickamauga, Missionary Ridge, and in the Dalton-Kingston Campaign.

Surgeon B. W. Avent was in charge of these hospitals. Hospitals were moved to Atlanta in May of 1864 to avoid capture by Federals. These hospitals later used by the Federals.

(Located on the south end of Johnson Street at the cemetery. GHM 008-40A, 1956.)

HARDEE'S CORPS AT KINGSTON

May 18, 1864. Lt. Gen. Wm. J. Hardee's A.C. marched from Adairsville on the road parallel to the State R. R. – turning E. on this rd. to join Polk's & Hood's corps (C) at Cassville, which had moved on the direct Adairsville – Cassville road.

Sherman's (F) error in assuming that all of Johnston's army (C) had marched from Adairsville, as Hardee had, to Kingston, caused him to order his forces concentrated here – discovering later that the Confederate Army

CONFEDERATE CEMETERY

COURTESY, LIBRARY OF CONGRESS

GENERAL WILLIAM J. HARDEE (1815–1873)

was 5.5. miles E. at Cassville & not at the river S. of Kingston.

(Located at GA 293 north/Howard Street and Martin Circle. GHM 008-37, 1953.)

THE FEDERAL ARMY AT KINGSTON

May 19, 1864. The 4th, followed by the 14th A.C. (F), reached Kingston, 8 a.m. The 4th turned E. to Cassville; a div. of the 14th went to Gillem's bridge, Etowah River, finding no retreating Confederates. Johnston's forces (C) were at Cassville, 5.5. mi. E.

McPherson's 15th & 16th A.C. (F), moving S. from Barnsley's, camped on Woolley's plantation 2 mi. W; 4th, 20th & 23d A.C. at Cassville.

Sherman's forces in camp to May 23, when advance across the Etowah began. Of the 3 bridges, Milam's, Gillem's & Woolley's, only Milam's was burned by the Confederates.

(Located at GA 293/Howard Street and Hall Station Road. GHM 008-33, 1953.)

SPRING BANK

Ante-bellum plantation and residence of the Rev. Charles Wallace Howard, where he established a private school.

May 18, 1864. Hardee's A.C. (C) moved from Adairsville to Kingston on this road enroute to Cass Station. May 19, the 4th & 14th A.C. (F) followed, occupying Kingston, to which point all the rest of the army had been directed by Sherman under the false impression that Johnston's forces had retreated there.

The stirring events of the locality are ably set forth by Frances Thomas Howard in her book: "In and Out of the Lines."

(Located on Hall Station Road/ Adairsville–Kingston Road, 1.5 miles north

COURTESY, WOODLANDS/BARNSLEY GARDENS

SPRING BANK

of junction with GA 293 north. GHM 008-32, 1986.)

4TH & 14TH A. C. MARCH TO KINGSTON

May 18, 1864. Howard's 4th Corps leading & two divs. of Palmer's 14th (F), moved from Adairsville on this direct road to Kingston. They were halted just outside of Adairsville to await the support of the 15th A.C. of McPherson's Army of the Tennessee (F), which had not yet arrived.

The 4th & 14th began the march at 1 p.m. They traveled both the wagon road & R.R. right-of-way, reaching this point on E. fork of Conesena Creek at 6 p.m.

May 19th. The march was resumed at 5 a.m., Kingston was reached at 8 a.m.

(Located on Hall Station Road/ Adairsville–Kingston Road, 3.7 miles north of junction with GA 293 north. GHM 008-31, 1953.)

BARNSLEY'S

A unique, ante-bellum plantation, established by Godfrey Barnsley in the 1850's.

Maj. Gen. J. B. McPherson's H'dq'rs. (F), May 18, 1864.

K. Garrard's cav. (F), via Hermitage, arrived at noon. A detachment (Minty's brigade) sent S. toward Kingston was driven back by Ferguson's cav. (C). During the fighting near the house, Col. R.G. Earle, 2d

COURTESY, WOODLANDS/BARNSLEY GARDENS

BARNSLEY BOXWOOD GARDENS ABOUT 1896

COURTESY, WOODLANDS/BARNSLEY GARDENS

BARNSLEY MANOR HOUSE ABOUT 1890

COURTESY, WOODLANDS/BARNSLEY GARDENS

BARNSLEY MANOR HOUSE RUINS
BEFORE STABILIZATION

BARNSLEY MANOR HOUSE
AFTER STABILIZATION

Ala. cav. (C), was killed. McPherson, & Logan's 15th A.C., arrived at evening – Harrow's 4th div. camping on the plantation. Midnight, Dodge's and the 16th A.C. (F), camped in vicinity. These troops moved S.on 19th and camped on the Woolley plantation 2 mi. W. of Kingston.

(Travel 4.7 miles north on Hall Station Road/Adairsville–Kingston Road from junction with GA 293 north, turn west on Barnsley Gardens Road and follow 2.5 miles to marker. GHM 008-30, 1985.)

WOOLLEY'S BRIDGE

In 1864, this covered structure spanned the Etowah River on the plantation of Andrew F. Woolley, 0.5 mi. S. Next to the river was the Rome–Kingston R. R. discontinued, 1943.

May 19, McPherson's Army of the Tenn. (15th & 16th Corps) (F) marched from Barnsley's and camped on the Woolley Plantation. This right wing of Sherman's advance, Kingston to Dallas, – crossed the river, May 23rd.

October 11, while encamped on the Woolley Plantation, the Ohio soldiers of the 23d Corps (F), voted in a State Election.

(Located at GA 293 and Robertson Road, 2.7 miles north of Kingston. GHM 008-11, 1952.)

PINE LOG

CORRA HARRIS

Author of "A Circuit Rider's Wife" and many other books and articles lived from 1913 until her death in 1935 at "In the Valley" four miles west of here.

The most productive years of her career were spent in a picturesque log cabin which, according to legend, was once the home of a Cherokee Indian Chief.

Born at Elberton in 1869, she married the Rev. Lundy Howard Harris at the age of 17. From her experiences as the wife of an itinerant Methodist minister she later drew her literary material.

(Located on US 411 between the junction with GA 140 east and GA 140 west. GHM 008-13, 1953.) ♦

STILESBORO

THE ARMY OF THE CUMBERLAND AT STILESBORO

May 23–24, 1864: The 4th, 20th & two divisions of the 14th corps (F) converged here, from Etowah River crossings at Island Ford, Gillem's & Milam's bridges, & moved S.E. up the valley of Raccoon Cr. to Burnt Hickory P.O. (Huntsville).

The Army of the Ohio (23d A.C. & Stoneman's Cavalry), (F) crossing at Milam's, moved E. & S. to Burnt Hickory, via Sligh's Mill.

COURTESY, CORRA HARRIS PAPERS, HARGRETT RARE BOOK AND MANUSCRIPT LIBRARY, UNIVERSITY OF GEORGIA

CORRA HARRIS (1869–1935)

These troops composed center & left of Sherman's advance to New Hope Church.

(Located at GA 113 and Old Stilesboro Road near the Georgia Power Plant, **or** 4.4 miles west of the junction with GA 61. GHM 008-24, 1953.)

RACCOON CREEK

Geary's (2d) Div., 20th A.C., (F), having crossed the Etowah, May 23, drove Ross' cavalry (C) beyond the creek, May 24, 1864. This covered the march of the rest of the corps S. to Burnt Hickory P.O., in which Geary's troops joined – being relieved here by Schofield's 23d. A.C. (F) at noon.

Schofield moved E. on this, the Alabama rd., enroute to Sligh's Mill – these troops being the left of Sherman's (F) flanking march around the Allatoona Mountains.

The 20th A.C. route to Burnt Hickory was the road next W. of Raccoon Creek.

(Located on GA 113 between Stilesboro and Cartersville, 2.4 miles west of junction with GA 61. GHM 008-25, 1953.)

CATOOSA COUNTY

The county name is thought to have derived from an Indian chief who lived at Catoosa Springs. County Seat: Ringgold.

RINGGOLD

CATOOSA COUNTY

Created December 5, 1853, the county has an Indian name. Ringgold bears the name of Major Samuel Ringgold, who died of wounds received at the Mexican War battle of Palo Alto in 1846.

Taylor's Ridge, visible for miles, is named for the Indian chief Richard Taylor.

Catoosa Springs, four miles to the east, and Gordon Springs, ten miles south, were colorful antebellum summer resorts.

The bloody Chickamauga battle was fought seven miles to the west, the battlefield now being a National Military Park.

(Located on US 41/76/Nashville Street between Maple and Jail Streets cn the courthouse lawn. GHM 023-1, 1953.)

CONFEDERATE HOSPITALS

Here in 1862–1863 were located several Confederate hospitals – The Foard, The General, The Bragg and

COURTESY, LIBRARY OF CONGRESS

GENERAL BRAXTON BRAGG (1817–1876)

The Buckner. The Court House, Napier's Hotel, two Churches, several warehouses, and temporary buildings were also used as hospitals. More than 20,000 sick and wounded Confederates passed through these hospitals, men from every Confederate State. After the Battle of Chickamauga food became so scarce that mule meat was fed to these sick and wounded men. Gallant women of this community served in these hospitals. To avoid capture, the hospitals moved south from here early in October 1863.

(Located on US 41/76/Nashville Street between Maple and Jail Streets on the courthouse lawn. GHM 023-14, 1956.)

BATTLE OF CHICKAMAUGA

Nine miles west of here on Saturday and Sunday, September 19th and 20th, 1863, the bloody Battle of Chickamauga was fought. Here, Federal forces of about 60,000 under Major-General William S. Rosecrans, U.S.A., fought the two day battle with Confederates, numbering about 66,000, under General Braxton Bragg, C.S.A. Federal losses were about 16,179. Confederate losses were about 17,804. It was a bloody victory for the Confederacy from which it never recovered.

(Located at Tennessee and LaFayette Streets in a small park. GHM 023-15, 1956.)

THE WHITMAN HOUSE

This house of handmade brick was built about 1863 by Mr. William L. Whitman, prominent merchant of Ringgold. After the Battle of Ringgold General U.S. Grant established his headquarters here. When he and his staff were leaving he offered Mrs. Whitman pay for lodging in $50.00 U.S. greenbacks but she asked for Confederate money instead. Gen. Grant is said to have remarked, "She certainly is not whipped yet," and his soldiers cheered her as they left. The Whitman family watched the fiercest part of the fight around the depot from upstairs windows.

(Located at Tennessee and High Streets, 2 blocks off US 41/76. GHM 023-10, 1955.)

THE WHITMAN HOUSE

WESTERN & ATLANTIC DEPOT

WESTERN & ATLANTIC DEPOT

This is the only depot between Atlanta and Chattanooga that has been in continuous use since May 9, 1850, when the first train ran over this end of the line. Previous to the coming of the W & A to "Cherokee Georgia," the nearest market was Augusta, 3 weeks away by ox wagon. In the early 1850's Ringgold was a bigger market than Chattanooga and large quantities of wheat were shipped from this depot. Built in 1849 of local sandstone, with walls 14 inches thick, the building was badly damaged by Hooker's guns during the Battle of Ringgold, November 27, 1863. It was, as may be seen, repaired with limestone blocks.

(Located on US 41/76, GA 2/3 at Depot Street. GHM 023-8, 1955.) **Note:** The depot is not in use at this time.

CHEROKEE SPRINGS CONFEDERATE HOSPITAL

One half mile east is the site of Cherokee Springs Confederate Hospital, located here in 1862–1863. Hundreds of sick and wounded Confederate soldiers were sent to the hospital to rest and recuperate, being benefitted by the healing waters of the springs. General and Mrs. Braxton Bragg were patients in August 1863. Bishop Quintard preached the first sermon at the opening of the religious chapel at the hospital on August 21, 1863. Early September 1863 the hospital moved south out of the path of the invading Federals. Federals and Confederates skirmished here February 23, 1864.

(Located south of Ringgold on Cherokee Valley road, 0.3 miles east of junction with US 41/76. GHM 023-12, 1955.) ♦ ★

RINGGOLD GAP
November 27, 1863

After the Battle of Missionary Ridge, Bragg's Confederate Army retreated in disorder toward Dalton. Brig. Gen. Patrick R. Cleburne was ordered to take position in the gap, hold back the Federals, and save the trains and artillery from capture.

Exercising his only major independent command, Cleburne utilized the terrain and his well– trained troops to hold up Federal pursuit for five precious hours. The trains and artillery were saved. By Joint Resolution the Confederate Congress thanked Cleburne for his achievement.

(Located on US 41/76, GA 2/3 in a small park just south of Ringgold. GHM 023-16, 1959.)

ATLANTA CAMPAIGN
RINGGOLD GAP
MAY 7, 1864.

Here, through Ringgold Gap, a Federal advance position, Sherman and his army moved forward to begin the campaign against Atlanta and the heart of the South. The Confederate defense, well conceived and ably executed delayed the March to the Sea and the eventual division of the Confederacy.

Here a Federal advance position was maintained during the winter 1863–1864 with the main force concentrated at Chattanooga. Sherman moved south through this gap, May 7, 1864 to begin the Atlanta Campaign. He captured Atlanta four months later, Sept. 2, and reached the coast at Savannah, December 21. This movement split the Confederacy in two, destroyed military resources, centers of supply, and hastened the end of the war.

(Located on US 41/76, GA 2/3 in a small park just south of Ringgold. NPS 023-99.)

COURTESY, LIBRARY OF CONGRESS

GENERAL PATRICK R. CLEBURNE (1828–1864)

OLD FEDERAL ROAD

The highway bearing left is the Old Federal Road, an early thoroughfare that linked Georgia and west Tennessee across the Indian Country. It began on the southeast boundary of the Cherokees, in the direction of Athens, Georgia and led toward Nashville via Rossville. Another branch ran from Ramhurst, Georgia toward Knoxville. Formal permission to open this road was granted by the Cherokees in the 1805 Treaty of Tellico. Prior to its use by the Whites, the route was an Indian trading path to Augusta.

This thoroughfare became the earliest vehicular way of northwest Georgia, the first postal route of this section, and an important emigrant trace to the West.

(Located on GA 2 just east of junction with US 41. GHM 023-7, 1954.)
♦ ★

OLD STONE PRESBYTERIAN CHURCH WAR TIME HOSPITAL

This Church, organized September 2, 1837, before the Cherokee Indians were removed from this area, was the first church organized by white settlers in the bounds of the present Catoosa County, according to available records. The organizers were a group of Scotch Irish Presbyterians from Tennessee or the Carolinas and the Charter Members were: Robert Magill, James H. McSpadden, Robert C. Cain, Sarah Black, Alfred McSpadden, Fanny Magill, Susan McSpadden, Winifred Cain, Margaret Cain and Nancy Tipton. This building of sandstone quarried nearby, was erected in 1850 and following the Battle of Ringgold, November 27, 1863, was used as a hospital. Blood stains are still visible on the floor. It remained a Presbyterian Church until about 1920 when it was sold to a Methodist congregation which maintained it for some years. It then passed into private hands and to save it from destruction a group of descendants of the early members raised a fund and purchased it, deeding it to a board of trustees to be used for religious purposes. In recent years it has been used by various denominations.

(Located at US 41/76 and GA 2, 2.5 miles south of Ringgold. GHM 023-9, 1955.)

OLD STONE PRESBYTERIAN CHURCH
NOW KNOWN AS OLD STONE BAPTIST CHURCH

CATOOSA SPRINGS CONFEDERATE HOSPITALS

In 1862–1863 several Confederate hospitals were located here. The sick and wounded Confederate soldiers drank of the health-giving waters of the several mineral springs in this area. Drinking this mineral water and bathing in it enabled many sick soldiers to return to duty. Early in October 1863 these hospitals were abandoned to prevent capture by Federal forces. A skirmish took place here May 3, 1864. Part of the 4th Army Corps., (F) under General Howard camped here May 4th, 5th, and 6th, 1864.

(From US 41/76 and Ga 2, follow GA 2 1.3 miles east. Turn left on Keith Road and follow 0.7 mile to marker. GHM 023-13, 1987.)

CAMPAIGN FOR ATLANTA BEGAN HERE

The 4th A.C., marching from Cleveland, Tenn., reached Catoosa Springs May 4, 1864. The 23d A.C., via Cleveland & Red Clay, camped in this vicinity. Both corps moved S. from these positions toward Dalton, May 7.

COURTESY, LIBRARY OF CONGRESS

MAJOR GENERAL JOSEPH WHEELER (1836–1906)

The 4th A.C. went by direct rd. to Tunnel Hill; the 23d, to Crow Valley, E. of Rocky Face.

The elevated ground N. is the site of the Dr. Lee house. Observing the initial troop movements from the yard of the Lee house, were officers of the Federal high command: Sherman, Thomas, Schofield, Howard, Newton, Stanley & Cox.

(Located at GA 2 and Tunnel Hill Road, 3.5 miles south of junction with US 41/76. GHM 023-4, 1954.)

4TH CORPS' ROUTE TO TUNNEL HILL

May 7, 1864. The 4th A.C., marching from Catoosa Springs, moved S. on this road to Tunnel Hill–Stanley's div. in advance, followed by Wood & Newton; Maj. Gen. O. O. Howard, commanding.

The march was opposed by outposts of Wheeler's cav. – the road obstructed by felled timber.

This move, together with the march of Palmer's 14th A.C. on direct rd. from Ringgold to Tunnel Hill, was the beginning of hostilities in the Campaign for Atlanta. Wheeler's cav., driven from Tunnel Hill, withdrew to Mill Creek Gap. During the next 5 days, Federal attempts to take Dalton were without success.

(Located on Tunnel Hill Road, 0.6 mile off GA 2, 3.5 miles south of junction with US 41/76. GHM 023-5, 1954.)

OLD FEDERAL ROAD

For the last eight miles this highway has followed closely the course of the Old Federal Road, northwest Georgia's earliest vehicular thoroughfare and first postal route. It led this way from the southeast Cherokee boundary, in the direction of Athens, Georgia, via Tate, Talking Rock, Spring Place and Ringgold, running toward Nashville, Tennessee. The Indians granted formal rights to open the trace in the 1805 Treaty of Tellico, Tennessee. Another prong of the route led from Ramhurst, toward Knoxville, Tenn.

At this point the old route bore left toward Rossville, passing just south of the road intersection ahead.

(Located on US 41, north of Ringgold. GHM 023-6, 1992.)

THE NAPIER HOUSE

Thomas Thompson Napier built this house in 1836 of heavy local timber prepared by slaves and finishing lumber brought by oxwagon from Augusta. During the Battle of Chickamauga 20 wounded soldiers were cared for in the house by Mrs. Martha Harris Napier and Mrs. Debbie Thedford, assisting an Army nurse. Water was hauled to the battlefield from the Blue and Sweet Springs on the Napier place. In early days there was a race track on the property where Indians and early settlers were said to gather for races and chicken fights.

(From I–75 follow GA 151 south 1 mile, turn right on Poplar Springs Road and follow for 3.5 miles, turn left on Three Notch Road and follow for 3.4 miles to marker. GHM 023-11, 1955.).

LEET'S TANYARD

Residence and Tanyard of the Rev. Arthur I. Leet, (native of Monaghan, Ireland), 1812–1892. A noted landmark of the Chickamauga Campaign; was Gen. Braxton Bragg's H'dq'rs., (C) Sept. 17, 18, 1863.

May 6, 1864. H'dq'rs. Maj. Gen. Joseph Hooker (20th A.C.) (F) and Maj. Gen. Daniel Butterfield. Williams' (1st) Div. was at Pleasant Grove Ch., 4.5 mi. N.E.; Geary's (2d) Div. at Peavine Ch., 2 mi. N.W., and Butterfield's (3d) at Leet's Tanyard.

These troops had marched from Chattanooga enroute to the valley E. of Taylor's Ridge – an initial move by Sherman's forces against the Confederate army at Dalton, under Gen. Joseph E. Johnston.

(From I–75 follow GA 151 south 5.3 miles, turn right on Yates Spring Road for 2.7 miles, turn left on Mt. Pisgah Road for 0.4 mile. GHM 023-3, 1986.)

NICKAJACK GAP

The road E. ascends Taylor's Ridge & via Nickajack Gap, crosses E. Chickamauga Cr. Valley.

May 7, 1864. Brig. Gen. Judson Kilpatrick's (3d) Div., Elliott's Cav. Corps (Army of the Cumberland), (F) moving from Ringgold, crossed Taylor's Ridge at Nickajack Gap, followed by Williams' (1st) Div., 20th Corps.

The 2d & 3d Divs. crossed the ridge 4.5 mi. S. at Gordon Springs Gap, the same day. Kilpatrick's Cav. masked the advance of the 20th A. C. into E. Chickamauga Valley, enroute to Mill Cr. Gap & Dug Gap, in Rocky Face Ridge – outposts of the Confederate forces at Dalton commanded by Gen. Joseph E. Johnston.

(Located on GA 151 at Nickajack Road, 7.6 miles south of the junction with I–75. GHM 023-2, 1953.)

CHATTOOGA COUNTY

Named for the Chattooga River which flows through the middle of the county. County Seat: Summerville.

MENLO

LAST INDIAN AGENT

Hugh Montgomery, born in S.C., Jan. 8, 1769, is buried here. He was employed in 1786 to survey the line between Franklin Co. and the Cherokee Nation. He represented Jackson Co. in the Ga. legislature in 1807–11 and in the State Senate, 1812–18 and 1823–35.

A religious man, he is said to have financed the first missionary to the Cherokees. He was appointed U. S. Indian Agent to the Cherokees by President Monroe, Mar. 3, 1825 and served until the Cherokees were driven out of Georgia. For his services he was granted 3,000 acres of land in Chattooga county.

(Located on GA 337, 1.7 miles south of junction with GA 48 at the Alpine Church. GHM 027-1, 1953.)

COURTESY, LIBRARY OF CONGRESS

SEQUOYAH (C.1770–1843)

river which flows through the county, called Chattooga by the Cherokee Indians. Sequoyah (George Guess or Gist), inventor of the Cherokee Alphabet, was born and lived for some time near Alpine in Chattooga County. First County Officers, commissioned February 5, 1839, were: G. T. Hopkins, Clerk Superior Court; I. N. Bibb, Clerk Inferior Court; W. T. Gellet, Sheriff; I. McNeally, Coroner.

(Located at Commerce and West Washington Streets on the courthouse lawn. GHM 027-2, 1956.

SUMMERVILLE

CHATTOOGA COUNTY

Chattooga County was created by Act of Dec. 28, 1838 from Floyd and Walker Counties. It was named for the

CHEROKEE COUNTY

Named in honor of the Cherokee Indian Tribe. County Seat: Canton.

BALL GROUND

BATTLE OF TALIWA

Two and one-half miles to the east, near the confluence of Long-Swamp Creek and the Etowah River, is the traditional site of Taliwa, scene of the fiercest and most decisive battle in the long war of the 1740's and 50's between Cherokee and Creek Indians.

There, about 1755, the great Cherokee war-chief, Oconostota, led 500 of his warriors to victory over a larger band of Creeks. So complete was the defeat that the Creeks retreated south of the Chattahoochee River, leaving to their opponents the region later to become the heart of the ill-fated Cherokee Nation.

(Located on GA 372/Gilmer Ferry Road in a small park next to the railroad tracks. GHM 028-1, 1953.)

CANTON

CHEROKEE COUNTY

Created December 3, 1832 from Cherokee Indian lands, and named in memory of the Cherokees. Early settlers tried to start silk production, but were not successful, and today there remains no trace of this except Canton, hopefully named for the Chinese silk center.

The Marietta and North Georgia Railroad reached Canton in 1879, providing a considerable stimulus to development.

The locally financed and managed textile mill, which began operations in 1900, has provided a payroll of much local importance.

(Located on North Street across from the courthouse in a small park. GHM 028-2, 1953.) ◆

CHEROKEE COUNTY GOLD

Cherokee County, located along Georgia's gold belt, figured prominently in the gold rush of the 1830's and 40's. Several mines operated along a five mile area near the Etowah River in the northeastern part of the county, including the Franklin–Creighton, Sandow, and Latham Mines. More than 30 other small placer mines extended southwesterly across the county and included the Sixes Mine, worked earlier by the Cherokees. After the 1860's, most gold mining operations in the county either slowed of ceased. The most successful, the most sophisticated, the Franklin–Creighton, continued operations until 1913, when a shaft collapsed and the mine was flooded.

(Located on North Street in front of the courthouse. GHM 028-4, 1988.)

JOSEPH EMERSON BROWN (1821–1894)

JOSEPH EMERSON BROWN

Born April 15, 1821, in Pickens District, South Carolina, he grew up in Union County, Georgia. He taught to pay for his education, and while teaching in Canton he read law at night, being admitted to the bar in August, 1845.

He graduated from the Yale Law School and practiced law in this city. He was elected State Senator in 1849; Judge of the Superior Court, Blue Ridge Circuit, in 1855; Governor in 1857, serving during the trying years of the War Between the States until 1865.

He was Chief Justice of the Georgia Supreme Court from 1868 to 1870, resigning to become manager of the Western and Atlantic Railroad.

He was President of the Dade Coal Company, and had other large mining interests, and owned several farms. He was elected United States Senator in 1880; then elected for a second term.

In memory of his son, Charles McDonald Brown, he established a $50,000 scholarship at the University of Georgia.

Governor Brown died November 30, 1894. His Canton home stood near this marker. After his death his heirs presented this tract to the city for a park fittingly named Brown Park.

(Located at Marietta and Jarvis Streets in Brown Park. GHM 028-3, 1953.)

CRESCENT FARM ROCK BARN

The Crescent Farm Rock Barn was constructed in 1906 by Augustus (Gus) Lee Coggins. One of a rare number of rock barns constructed in Georgia. the Rock Barn, together with the nearby Georgian Revival style main house, constitutes the core of the original Crescent Farm.

Originally a race horse stable, the rock barn was one of three barns on Cog-

CRESCENT FARM ROCK BARN

COURTESY, THE UNITED STATES TROTTING ASSOCIATION

ABBEDALE 2:00¼ (1917–1950)
GRAND CIRCUIT WINNER
SIRE OF SIX 2:00 PACERS

gins' cotton and horse farm. It was built to replace a wooden barn destroyed in a fire which killed valuable race horses. The Rock Barn is made of rock quarried on the original farm from the banks of the Etowah River.

Coggins bred and raised horses for harness racing. Crescent Farm was widely known in the racing circle because of Abbedale, its world class racehorse. Abbedale brought fame to Crescent Farm and is listed in the Harness Racing Hall of Fame in Goshen, N.Y. Abbedale sired six pacers with two-minute mile records.

(Located on GA 5 Business near South Etowah Drive across from the Canton Elementary School. GHM 028-5, 1990.)

CLARKE COUNTY

Named in honor of General Elijah Clarke (1733 or 1742–1799), a distinguished soldier of the Revolution and Georgia legislator. County Seat: Athens.

ATHENS

UNIVERSITY OF GEORGIA

Endowed with 40,000 acres of land in 1784 and chartered in 1785, the charter was the first granted by a state for a government controlled university. After Louisville and then Greensboro were first selected, the current site, was chosen.

The first president, and author of the school's charter, Abraham Baldwin, resigned when the doors opened, and was succeeded by Josiah Meigs. The University first began to thrive under Moses Waddel, who became president in 1819. Alonzo Church was president 1829–1859.

During the War for Southern Independence, most of the students entered the Confederate Army. The University closed its doors in 1864, and did not open again until January, 1866. After the War many Confederate veterans became students.

Famous pre-war profs. were John and Joseph LeConte and Charles F. McCay, while famous students were Robert Toombs, Alexander H. Stephens, Howell Cobb, and Crawford W. Long.

Plans for a modern university were first developed by Walter B. Hill and realized under Harmon W. Caldwell. The best known of the post-war presidents (now chancellors) was David C. Barrow. The builder of the modern plant was Chancellor Steadman V. Sanford.

(Located at East Broad and College Streets, next to the arch at the entrance to the campus. GHM 029-1, 1992.)

ROBERT TOOMBS OAK

A majestic oak tree once stood on this spot and one of the University's most endearing legends also flourished here.

Robert Toombs (1810–1885) was young, and boisterous when he was dismissed from Franklin College in 1828. Five decades later it was said that Toombs returned on the next commencement day after he was expelled and spoke so eloquently under the tree that the entire audience left the chapel to hear him. Later, it was said, that the tree was struck by lightning on the day Toombs died and never recovered. The tree finally collapsed in 1908 and the remains were cut into mementos that have since been handed down by alumni.

Robert Toombs was a lawyer, planter and statesman. He served in the Georgia House 1837–1840, 1842–1845, in the U.S. Congress 1845–1853, the U. S. Senate from 1853 until he resigned in 1861. Toombs was Secretary of State of the Confederacy then a brigadier general in the C.S.A. He also played a major role in Georgia's Constitutional Convention of 1877.

Marker erected at direction of General Assembly resolution approved March, 1985.

(Located between the Chapel and Demosthenian Hall near the Arch on the University of Georgia campus. GHM 029-15, 1987.)

THE STONEMAN RAID

Closing in on Atlanta in July, 1864, Maj. Gen. W. T. Sherman found it "too strong to assault and too extensive to invest." To force its evacuation, he sent Maj. Gen. Geo. Stoneman's cavalry (F) to cut the Macon railway by which Atlanta's defenders were supplied. At the Battle of Sunshine Church (19 miles NE of Macon), Stoneman surrendered with 600 men to Brig. Gen. Alfred Iverson, Jr., (C), after covering the escape of Adams' and Capron's brigades. Both retreated via Athens, intending to resupply their commands here and to "destroy the armory and other government works."

At the bridge over Middle Oconee River (4 miles SW), they were stopped by Home Guard units with artillery. Unable to cross, they turned west; Capron on the Hog Mountain Road through Jug Tavern (Winder), and Adams on roads farther north by which he reached the Union lines near Marietta without further loss.

While resting his exhausted command briefly at King's Tanyard (NW of Winder), Capron was surprised before dawn on the 3rd by Williams' Kentucky brigade (C). About 430 men were captured, Capron himself and a few others escaping through the woods. The prisoners were brought to Athens by Col. W. C. P. Breckinridge, 9th Kentucky Cavalry, and held under guard on the college campus until they could be sent to the prison at Andersonville.

(Located on East Broad Street near South Lumpkin Street. GHM 029-6, 1984.)

1891
FIRST GARDEN CLUB

Founders' Memorial Garden which commemorates the founders of America's first garden club. The Ladies Garden Club organized in 1891, Athens, Georgia. This garden was developed on University of Georgia campus by university's Landscape Architecture Department and the Garden Club of Georgia.

Presented by Ladies Garden Club 1950.

(Located at South Lumpkin and Bocock Streets. LGC 029-97, 1950.)

BIRTHPLACE OF MILDRED LEWIS RUTHERFORD, LIT. D.

Born July 16, 1851. Died August 15, 1928 in Athens. Historian for life of the Georgia Division, 1896–1928. Historian General, 1911–1928 of the United Daughters of the Confederacy.

(Located at 1234 South Lumpkin Street in front of the Treanor House. UDC/WPA 029-96, 1936.)

LUCY COBB INSTITUTE
(1858-1931)

Lucy Cobb Institute, a College for Girls, was established in 1858 through the effort of T. R. R. Cobb and named for his daughter Lucy. Later, three of his nieces taught here: Miss Mildred Rutherford, Principal, Mrs. Mary Ann Lipscomb, Mrs. Bessie Rutherford Mell. Closed as a school in 1931, it serves as a dormitory for girls attending the University of Georgia.

Nearby is Seney–Stovall Chapel, named for George I. Seney who contributed the funds to build it and Miss Nellie Stovall who solicited his help. He also gave a pipe organ and paintings for the walls of Lucy Cobb.

"Her Alumnae Rise Up and Call Her Blessed."

(Located on North Milledge Avenue, 1½ blocks north of West Broad Street. GHM 029-8, 1958.)

DR. WILLIAM LORENZO MOSS
BIRTHPLACE

William Lorenzo Moss, medical researcher and physician, was born in this house at 479 Cobb Street in Cobbham on August 23, 1876. Crawford W. Long was the attending physician. Dr. Moss received his B.S. degree from the University of Georgia in 1897 and the M.D. degree from the Johns Hopkins University in 1905. He taught at the latter school, at Yale, and at Harvard. In 1926 Dr. Moss was Acting Dean at Harvard's School of Public Health Medicine. In 1931 he was named Dean of the Medical

COURTESY, SPECIAL COLLECTIONS, GREENBLATT LIBRARY, MEDICAL COLLEGE OF GA

DR. WILLIAM LORENZO MOSS (1876–1957)

Department of the University of Georgia (now the Medical College of Georgia).

It is as a researcher in the fields of immunology, blood types, and tropical diseases that Dr. Moss is best remembered. His most noted single contribution lay in the development of the Moss System, a classification of blood groupings which he labeled I through IV. This system was widely used throughout the world until modified during World War II. Dr. Moss headed numerous international medical research expeditions in the Caribbean, South America, and the South Pacific from 1914 to 1937.

Dr. Moss died in Athens on August 12, 1957.

(Located on Cobb Street between North Chase and Franklin Streets off North Milledge Street. GHM 029-14, 1983.)

OLD STATE NORMAL SCHOOL

Here at the old State Normal School, now part of the University of Georgia, stands Gilmer Hall, once known as Rock College. Built in 1860 by the University to house classrooms for freshmen and sophomores, it was never so used but was opened in 1862 as University High School. From 1866 to '68 disabled Confederate veterans were educated here except for a short period when the school was closed by order of Gen. Pope, military governor of Georgia. It was taken over in 1872 by the State College of Agriculture & Mechanical Arts. When the Normal School was established by Act of 1891 the building and land were given by the University and it was shortly named Gilmer Hall for the Gilmer Fund. On January 1, 1895, Captain S. D. Bradwell became first President of the Normal School which opened on April 17. First graduation exercises were held on November 26, 1896. In its early years vitally needed financial assistance was received by the Normal School from both Clarke County and the City of Athens, helping to make possible short summer sessions in 1892, '93 & '94, before the regular opening in 1895. At the 1892 session there were 112 students enrolled representing thirty two counties. In 1897 enrollment had increased to the point where students were living in tents erected upon the campus, until new dormitories could be built.

(Located off Prince Avenue on the campus of the U. S. Navy Supply Corps School in front of the Carnegie Library. GHM 029-3, 1955.)

U.S. NAVY
SUPPLY CORPS SCHOOL

Commissioned on this site 15 January 1954, The U.S. Navy Supply Corps School is the "Home" of the Navy Supply Corps. At this school newly commissioned Navy Supply Corps officers receive basic training in leadership, retail operations, disbursing, food service, data processing, and inventory management to prepare them for their roles as "The Navy's Business Managers" afloat and ashore. The school also provides specialized advanced logistics training not only to U. S. Navy personnel, but also to military officers from many foreign nations. Although the history of the Supply Corps dates back to 1795 it was not until 1921 that the first Supply Corps School opened in Washington D.C. In 1924 the school was discontinued and reopened in 1934 as the Naval Finance and Supply School in Philadelphia, PA. In 1941 the school was merged into the Harvard University Graduate School of Business Administration. In 1945 the school was moved to Bayonne, NJ, where it operated until 1954 when it was relocated to this site. Also located on this site is the Supply Corps Museum which depicts the history, heritage and traditions of the Supply Corps.

(Located on Prince Avenue at the entrance to the U.S. Navy Supply Corps School. USN 029-99.) **Note:** See other side of marker.

FORMER SITE OF GEORGIA
STATE NORMAL SCHOOL

In February 1860 the University of Georgia purchased 93 acres surrounding this site and later sold all but 30 acres to finance the construction of Rock College, a preparatory school for the University of Georgia. Between 1862 and 1891 the school served the educational needs of Georgia in a variety of roles. In 1891 the Georgia General Assembly established the State Normal School on this site to train Georgians to be rural teachers. The nearby commercial area soon adopted the name "Normal Town." The oldest remaining academic building on campus, Winnie Davis Hall, was erected in 1902 as a memorial to the daughter of Jefferson Davis. In 1910 the Carnegie Library was erected with a grant from the Andrew Carnegie Foundation. Because of its historical and educational significance, it is listed on the National Register of Historic Places. In 1929 the institution's name was changed to The Coordinate College. During WW II, the campus was used by the U.S. Army as a training site and after WW II the school was again occupied by women students attending the university. In 1953 the site was purchased by the U.S. Navy as a permanent location for its Supply Corps School.

(Located on Prince Avenue at the entrance to the U. S. Navy Supply Corps School. USN 029-98.) **Note:** See other side of marker.

AMERICA'S FIRST GARDEN CLUB

In 1891 at this site, the Ladies Garden Club was founded by twelve Athens ladies in the home of Mrs. E. K. Lumpkin, Mrs. Lamar Cobb was the first president. Beginning as a small neighborhood group, the club extended membership to all Athens ladies interested in gardening in 1892.

In the spring of 1892 the group presented its first flower and vegetable exhibition. By 1894 a set of standards, similar to those of today, had been drawn up to make the shows as professional as possible.

In 1936 the National Council of State Garden Clubs recognized the Ladies Garden Club as America's first garden club.

(Located on Prince Avenue near Prince Place and North Chase Street. GHM 029-9, 1963.)

THE TAYLOR–GRADY HOUSE

General Robert Taylor (1787–1859), a planter and cotton merchant, built this Greek Revival home as a summer residence in 1839. Shortly thereafter he moved his family here permanently from Savannah in order for his sons to attend the University of Georgia.

Henry Woodfin Grady (1850–1889) lived in this house from 1865 to 1868 while a student at the University. His father, William S. Grady, bought the house in 1863 and it remained in the family's possession until 1872. Henry Grady often referred to this house as

THE TAYLOR–GRADY HOUSE

"an old Southern home with its lofty pillars, and its white pigeons fluttering down through the golden air." The 13 Doric columns are said to represent the 13 original states.

As managing editor of the *Atlanta Constitution*, Henry W. Grady became the spokesman of the New South. An impressive orator, he stressed the importance of reconciliation between North and South after the Civil War. The South today, with an economy balanced between industry and diversified agriculture, has made a reality of Grady's dream for his native region.

(Located at 634 Prince Avenue. GHM 029-13, 1970.)

CAMAK HOUSE:
LANDMARK IN GEORGIA RAILROADING

On March 10, 1834, a group of Athens men met in this house, then the home of Mr. James Camak, to accept the charter of the Georgia Railroad Company and to organize the corporation. At this meeting Mr. Camak was elected its president, and he soon began a tour of the State building up interest in the railroad and explaining its purpose. Camak served

COURTESY, GEORGIA DEPARTMENT OF ARCHIVES AND HISTORY

JOSEPH HENRY LUMPKIN (1799–1867)

as president for two years and played an important part in blazing the way for the future success of the company.

The Georgia Railroad Company was incorporated by an act of the legislature of 1833 and empowered "to construct a Rail or Turnpike Road" from Augusta to Eatonton, Madison, and Athens. It was during Camak's administration, in 1835 that the charter was amended to change the name to Georgia Railroad and Banking Company and to authorize the company to conduct a banking business. The Georgia is the oldest railroad in the State operating under its original charter.

By 1874 the main line from Augusta to Atlanta, as well as a branch line to Athens, had been completed. The company continued its banking activities until 1892, at which time a subsidiary, the Georgia Railroad Bank & Trust Company, was formed to conduct the banking business.

(Located at Meigs and Finley Streets, one block off Prince Avenue. GHM 029-10, 1963.)

HOME OF JOSEPH HENRY LUMPKIN GEORGIA'S FIRST CHIEF JUSTICE

Joseph Henry Lumpkin, born in Oglethorpe County, Georgia, Dec. 23, 1799, entered the University of Georgia at fifteen, completing his college education at Princeton, New Jersey, in 1819. Lumpkin passed the bar in 1820 and began practicing law in Lexington, Georgia. He served in the State Legislature, 1824 and 1825, and helped frame the Georgia Penal Code, 1833.

When the Georgia Supreme Court was formed in 1845, the General Assembly elected Lumpkin, Hiram Warner, and Eugenius Nisbet to the bench. His colleagues chose Lumpkin Chief Justice, and he held that position until his death, June 4, 1867. When the University added a school of law, it was given Lumpkin's name, and he lectured there until the outbreak of the Civil War. The eloquent opinions of Georgia's first Chief Justice, who revered the spirit as well as the letter of the law, were of ines-

HOME OF JOSEPH HENRY LUMPKIN

timable importance in firmly establishing the Supreme Court as part of the State's legal system.

Lumpkin's beautiful Greek Revival home was built in 1842. After his death in 1867, the house was used by Madame Sophie Sosnowski as her "Home School" for young ladies. It is now the home of the Athens Woman's Club.

(Located at 248 Prince Avenue. GHM 029-12, 1964.)

DR. MOSES WADDEL
NOTED EDUCATOR AND
PRESBYTERIAN MINISTER

Dr. Moses Waddel, educator and minister, was born in 1770 in N.C. At fourteen he began teaching pupils near his home. Moving to Ga. in 1786, he taught in the Greensboro area until 1787, opening another school at Bethany, Greene County, in 1788. While at Bethany Waddel decided to enter the ministry. He studied at Hampden–Sydney College and graduated in less than nine months in 1791, thereafter combining the careers of teacher and minister.

Establishing his most famous academy at Willington, S. C., in 1804, Waddel continued his work there until 1819 when he became President of Franklin College, now the University of Ga. One of the most prominent ante-bellum leaders of that institution, he served until 1829. Unwilling to divorce education from religion, Waddel stimulated the religious life of the campus. In 1820 he organized and was pastor of the first Presbyterian

congregation in Athens, which became the First Presbyterian Church. The present church building was erected in 1855.

Waddel died in 1840 at his son's home in Athens. His pupils during a lifetime of teaching included John C. Calhoun, William H. Crawford, George R. Gilmer, Augustus B. Longstreet, and George McDuffie.

(Located at 185 East Hancock Avenue across from city hall and in front of the First Presbyterian Church. GHM 029-11, 1963.)

THE ATHENS DOUBLE-BARRELLED CANNON

This cannon, the only known one of its kind, was designed by Mr. John Gilleland, a private in the "Mitchell Thunderbolts," an elite "home guard" unit of business and professional men ineligible because of age or disability for service in the Confederate army. Cast in the Athens foundry, it was intended to fire simultaneously two balls connected by a chain which would "mow down the enemy somewhat as a scythe cuts wheat." It failed for lack of a means of firing both barrels at the exact instant.

It was tested in a field on the Newton's Bridge road against a target of upright poles. With both balls rammed home and the chain dangling from the twin muzzles, the piece was fired; but the lack of precise simultaneity caused uneven explosion of the propelling charges, which snapped the chain and gave each ball an erratic and unpredictable trajectory.

CARROLL PROCTOR SCRUGGS

THE DOUBLE-BARRELLED CANNON

Lacking a workable firing device, the gun was a failure. It was presented to the City of Athens where, for almost a century it has been preserved as an object of curiosity, and where it performed sturdy service for many years in celebrating political victories.

(Located at College and East Hancock Avenues on the city hall lawn. GHM 029-5, 1957.)

CLARKE COUNTY

Clarke County, created by Act. of Dec. 5, 1801, from Jackson County, originally contained Oconee and part of Madison and Greene Counties. It was named for Gen. Elijah Clarke who came to Wilkes County, Ga., from N.C. in 1774 and fought through Ga. and S.C. during the Revolutionary War. He engaged in several battles with the Indians and signed treaties with the Cherokees in 1783 and Creeks in 1783 and 1785. He died

Dec. 15,1799. First officers of Clarke County, commissioned Dec. 31, 1801, were: Abner Bankston, Sheriff; Bedford Brown, Clk. Sup. Ct.; Gabriel Hubert, Clk. Inf. Ct.; Stephen Nobles, Surveyor; Daniel Conner, Coroner.

(Located at North Jackson and East Washington Streets next to the courthouse. GHM 029-4, 1956.)

COOK & BROTHER CONFEDERATE ARMORY

To this building in 1862 was brought the machinery of the armory established in New Orleans at the outbreak of the War by Ferdinand W. C. and Francis L. Cook, recent English immigrants, the former a skilled engineer, for the manufacture of Enfield rifles, bayonets and cavalry horse shoes. Said to be the largest and most efficient private armory in the Confederacy, it produced a rifle declared by an ordnance officer to be "superior to any that I have seen of Southern manufacture." Under contract to supply 30,000 rifles to the Confederate Army the armory operated until its employees, organized as a reserve battalion under Major Ferdinand and Captain Francis Cook, were in 1864 called to active duty upon the approach of Sherman's army. The battalion took part in the battles of Griswoldville, Grahamville, Honey Hill and Savannah where Maj. Cook was killed. After Griswoldville Gen. P. J. Phillips reported that Maj. Cook and his men "participated fully in the action, deported themselves gallantly and ... suffered much from wounds and death." Leased by the Confederacy in 1865 the armory was operated until the close of the War. The property was bought by the Athens Manufacturing Co. in 1870.

(Located on East Broad Street near the river. GHM 029-2, 1955.)

GEORGIA'S PIONEER AVIATOR BEN T. EPPS 1888–1937

Ben T. Epps – Georgia's First in Flight – designed, built and in 1907 flew the first airplane in the State of Georgia. He was born in Oconee County, educated in Clarke County, and attended Georgia Tech. A self-taught aviator, aircraft designer, and builder, Epps built the 1907 Monoplane in his shop on Washington Street in Athens and designed and flew new airplanes in 1909, 1911, 1916, 1924, and 1930.

The 1924 Epps Monoplane weighed only 350 pounds, had a wingspan of 25 feet, and was powered by a two-cylinder motorcycle engine. Designed for the average man, easy to fly, and inexpensive to operate, it would get 25 miles per gallon at 60 miles per hour.

Epps began operation of an airport at this location in 1917, and operated a flying service for the next 20 years. In 1937, he died of injuries incurred here after engine failure and the crash of his light biplane on take-off.

(Located off US 78 in front of the Athens/Clarke County Airport. GHM 029-16, 1987.)

BEN EPPS WITH HIS 1907 AIRPLANE

THE STONEMAN RAID

On July 31, 1864, at the Battle of Sunshine Church (19 miles NE of Macon), Maj. Gen. Geo. Stoneman (F) surrendered with 600 men to Brig. Gen. Alfred Iverson, Jr., (C), after covering the escape northward of Adams' and Capron's brigades of his cavalry command. Adams moved via Eatonton and Madison and Capron via Rutledge, rejoining north of Madison late the next day.

Early on August 2nd, Adams, intending to resupply his command and to "destroy the armory and other government works" in Athens, reached

this point and found the planks removed from the bridge over Middle Oconee River (on the old road) and guns emplaced on the hill above Princeton Factory (0.3 miles N), supported by the "Mitchell Thunderbolts" and other Home Guard units, commanded by Capt. Edward P. Lumpkin, CSA, son of the first Chief Justice of Georgia, and home on convalescent leave. Unable to cross, Adams turned west and, avoiding towns, reached the Union Lines near Marietta on August 4th, his brigade almost intact.

Capron, who had waited in reserve near Watkinsville, attempted to follow him but found himself on the Hog

Mountain road to Jug Tavern (Winder) instead. Passing through Jug Tavern late that night, he marched to King's Tanyard (5 miles NW of Winder) and halted for two hours rest. Before dawn on August 3rd, he was surprised by Williams' Kentucky brigade (C). About 430 of his men were captured, a few escaping through the woods. Capron himself, with six men, reached Marietta four days later – on foot.

(Located on US 129/441 south at the bridge over the Middle Oconee River. GHM 029-7, 1957.) ♦ ★ – not standing.

COLUMBIA COUNTY

Named in honor of Christopher Columbus (c.1446–1506). County Seat: Appling.

APPLING

COLUMBIA COUNTY

Columbia County, named for Christopher Columbus, was created by Act of Dec. 10, 1790 from Richmond County. Originally, it contained parts of McDuttie and Warren Counties. Settled by Quakers before the Revolution, it has been the home of many prominent Georgians. Here were Carmel Academy and Kiokee Baptist Church, "Mother Church" of Baptists

in Georgia. First Officers of Columbia County, commissioned Dec. 15, 1790, were: Peter Crawford, Clk. Sup. and Inf. Ct.; John Pearre, Coroner; John Walton, Surveyor; Daniel Marshall, Tax Col.; Anderson Crawford, Tax Rec.; Edmund B. Jenkins, Sheriff.

(Located on US 221/GA 47 on the courthouse lawn. GHM 036-4, 1956.)

FIRST BAPTIST CHURCH IN GEORGIA

Kiokee Church, the first Baptist Church to be constituted in Georgia, was organized in the Spring of 1772, by the Rev. Daniel Marshall, one of the founders of the Baptist denomination in Georgia. A meeting house was built, and the Rev. Daniel Marshall became the first pastor, ministering from his headquarters at Kiokee to an ever increasing number of Baptists in the area.

In October, 1784, the preliminary meeting for the organization of a Georgia Baptist Association was held at Kiokee Church. The Rev. Daniel Marshall died November 2, 1784, and some time later the church was moved

KIOKEE – FIRST BAPTIST CHURCH IN GEORGIA

to Appling and a new brick edifice erected.

Kiokee Baptist Church was incorporated December 23, 1789, as "The Anabaptist Church on Kiokee," with Abram Marshall, William Willingham, Edmund Cartledge, John Landers, James Simms, Joseph Ray and Lewis Gardener as Trustees.

(From Appling, follow US 221/GA 47 north 2.8 miles, turn right on Tubman Road and follow 0.4 mile to church which is well off the road. GHM 036-7, 1956.) ◆ ★

DAMASCUS
BAPTIST CHURCH

Damascus Baptist Church, organized July 29, 1820, was constituted by Samuel Cartledge and Widner Hilman. First members were Jeremiah Blanchard, James Ramsey, Jeremiah Roberts, Sara Blanchard, Sara Reid, Dilly Swan and Margaret Wilkins. James Ramsey was the first clerk of the church. Jeremiah Blanchard was the first deacon, elected Sept. 9, 1820.

The first pastor, Samuel Cartledge, served from 1820 to 1839. He was the officer who arrested Rev. Daniel Marshall, founder of the Kiokee Church in 1772, who was hauled into court in Augusta for "holding religious services not in accord with the rites and ceremonies of the Church of England." Cartledge was said to have been so impressed by the exhortation by Mrs. Marshall upon the arrest of her husband that he was converted, baptized by Rev. Marshall, served as a deacon for several years and was ordained in

1789. He preached for the rest of his long life.

For a time after the War Between the States the church did not meet but, under the leadership of Mrs. Jane Hardin Eubank, it was reactivated in 1875. The present building was constructed in 1901. Several additions have been made since that time.

(From Appling follow US 221/GA 47 north 6 miles to Pollards Corner. Turn left onto GA 104 and travel 4.2 miles, turn right on Ridge Road and follow for 1 mile to marker and church. GHM 036-6, 1956.)

HARLEM

OLIVER NORVELL HARDY

Harlem became the birthplace of the rotund member of one of Hollywood's greatest comedy teams when Oliver Hardy was born January 18, 1892. After his father died and was buried in the Harlem Cemetery the year of Oliver's birth, Mrs. Hardy took the family to Milledgeville where she became the manager of the Baldwin Hotel. Young Oliver was enthralled by the visiting troupes of performers who stayed there. Later, as manager of the town's first movie theater, Hardy performed regularly.

After attending Georgia Military Academy, the Atlanta Conservatory of Music, and, for a short time, the Univ. of Georgia, Hardy left Georgia in 1913 for the newly established film colony in Jacksonville, Florida. After

STAN LAUREL (1890–1965) WITH OLIVER NORVELL HARDY (1892–1957)

working at various studios on the east coast, he left for Hollywood in 1918.

"Babe," as Hardy became known to his friends, worked for several years as a supporting actor until he was accidentally teamed with a young Englishman, Stan Laurel. Laurel and Hardy remained partners and friends until Hardy's death in Hollywood in 1957.

(Located on US 221/Louisville Street at the railroad crossing. GHM 036-9, 1989.)

FAMOUS INDIAN TRAIL

For the last 20 miles this highway has followed the course of the noted Upper Trading Path that led from present Augusta to Indian tribes as far away as the Mississippi River. By various connections the trail reached the Cherokees of North Georgia; the Muscogees or Creeks of Eastern Alabama; and the Choctaws and Chickasaws of North Mississippi.

The Oakfuskee Path, main branch of the route, led past Warrenton, Griffin and Greenville to Oakfuskee Town, an early Upper Creek center, on the Tallapossa River in Alabama.

White traders began using this trail in the early 1700s.

(Located on US 78/278 and Verdery Street. GHM 036-1, 1954.)

WINFIELD

SHARON BAPTIST CHURCH

Sharon Baptist Church was founded in 1799. The first pastor, Abraham Marshall, who served the church until his death in 1819, probably constituted the church. This building, the second on the site, was erected in 1869. Many names prominent in Georgia are found in Sharon cemetery. Three men, one a Negro, have been ordained in this church. Two, W. P. Steed and L. G. Steed, served this church. Ephraim White, Negro, owned by L. P. Steed, served the Mt. Carmel Negro Church across the road until his death. Ground for the Mt. Carmel Church was deeded by Sharon Church.

(Located at GA 150 and Mistletoe Road. GHM 036-5, 1956.)

BASIL NEAL – SOLDIER OF '76

"Happy Valley," homesite and burial place of Basil Neal, Revolutionary soldier, lies one-half mile off this highway in the direction the arrow points.

Basil Neal, or O'Neal, was born in Maryland in 1758. When he was 17 years old his family moved to Virginia. There he grew to manhood and married Miss Ellen Briscoe daughter of an eminent Virginia physician, granddaughter of Colonel Stuart of New York, and great-granddaughter of Lord Bromfield of England.

Basil Neal fought heroically against the Indians and British, before, during and after the Revolutionary War. In 1780 he came to Georgia and set-tled in Columbia County on this plantation, where he built his home and called it "Happy Valley." After the death of his first wife, who had borne him six children, Basil Neal married Miss Sarah Hull Green, daughter of Captain McKeen Green, who also had served in the Revolutionary War under the command of General Nathanael Greene, to whom he was related. Six children also were born of the second marriage, including Basil Llewellyn Neal, who served in the Confederate Army as a flag bearer, was captured and imprisoned at Pt. Lookout, Md. He is buried near his father.

(Located on GA 150, 1 mile north of junction with Mistletoe Road. GHM 036-2, 1956.)

WILLIAM FEW
SIGNER OF THE
U. S. CONSTITUTION

On this site stood the home of William Few, one of Georgia's two signers of the United States Constitution. Built in 1781, the house burned in 1930.

William Few was born near Baltimore, Maryland, June 8, 1748. In 1776, he moved to Augusta, Georgia, and began to practice law. Among the positions he held during the next twenty years were the following: Lieutenant-Colonel of the Richmond County Militia during the Revolution; member of the State House of Assembly from original Richmond County; member of the Executive Council; presiding judge of the Richmond County Court; surveyor general of Georgia; member of the Continental Congress;

WILLIAM FEW (1748–1828)

original trustee for establishing the University of Georgia; delegate to the convention which drafted the Federal Constitution; signer of the Constitution; delegate to the Georgia convention which ratified the Federal Constitution; United States Senator; and judge of the Superior Court of Georgia, Middle Judicial Circuit.

In 1799 Colonel Few moved to New York City, where he served as a member of the New York Assembly; State prison inspector; city alderman; United States commissioner of loans; director of Manhattan Bank; and president of the City Bank. Colonel Few died at the home of his son-in-law, Major Albert Chrystie, in Fishkill, New York, July 16, 1828.

(Located on GA 150, 0.4 mile south of junction with Mistletoe Road. GHM 094-8, 1966.) **Note:** This marker will be renumbered.

SHILOH METHODIST CHURCH

Shiloh Methodist Church, the outgrowth of the earliest known Methodist place of worship in this community, has had a church building on this site for over 125 years. Originally, services started by a local hermit "who lived by a spring," were held in a "brush arbor" about a mile west of here. A short time later a church was built on this site. In Sept. 1825, after the church was completed, two plots of land were deeded to the four commissioners of the Methodist meetinghouse. One, including the hermit's spring, was from Waters Briscoe, the other, including the site of Shiloh Church, was from Green Dozier. The present church building was erected in 1859.

(Located on GA 150, 1.5 miles south of junction with Mistletoe Road. GHM 036-3, 1956.)

DADE COUNTY

Named in honor of Major Francis Langhorne Dade (1793–1835) who was killed while fighting the Seminoles. County Seat: Trenton.

TRENTON

DADE COUNTY

Often called the "State of Dade" because, as legend has it, the county seceded from the Union ahead of Georgia, and only returned to the Union, July 4, 1945.

Created December 25, 1837, and named for Major Francis Langhorne Dade, killed by Indians in Florida, December, 1835. The county seat was first named Salem, then changed to Trenton in 1840.

Outstanding picturesque mountain scenery accounts for the creation of Cloudland State Park. Rich coal and iron deposits have been worked since Ante-Bellum times.

(Located on Main Street on the court-house lawn. GHM 041-1, 1953.)

CHIEF WAUHATCHIE'S HOME

Just East of the railroad from here and 200 yards North of Wauhatchie Spring and Branch, stood the home of Wauhatchie, Chief of the Cherokees. In the War of 1812 he served in a company of Cherokees under Capt. John Brown, Col. Gideon Morgan and Maj. Gen. Andrew Jackson, fighting the Creeks from Jan. 27 to April 11, 1814. Old records say "Wauhatchie, severely wounded March 27th, lost his horse." He was a signer of the Hiawassee Purchase of July 8, 1817, is listed in the U. S. Census of the Cherokee Nation in 1835 and fol-lowed the "Trail of Tears" westward, when the Cherokees were moved from Georgia.

(Located on US 11/GA 58 at GA 299, 9.7 miles north of Trenton. GHM 041-2, 1955.)

NICKAJACK CORNER

The corner where Georgia, Alabama, and Tennessee meet, 12 miles, was established June 1, 1818, by joint com-missioners from Tennessee and Geor-gia. A permanent stone marker was erected on Nickajack Mountain, a mile south of the Indian Village of Nickajack, then standing on the banks of the Tennessee River. This point was supposed to have been placed on the 65th parallel, but a recent survey shows it to be about half a mile south of this latitude.

(Located on US 11/ GA 58 just south of the Georgia – Tennessee state line. WPA 041 -A2.) ♦ ★ – not standing.

COURTESY, GEORGIA DEPARTMENT OF ARCHIVES AND HISTORY

MARKING THE APPALACHIAN TRAIL

DAWSON COUNTY

Named in honor of William Crosby Dawson (1798–1857) who was known as a soldier, lawyer and U.S. Senator. County Seat: Dawsonville.

DAWSONVILLE

DAWSON COUNTY

This County, created by Act of the Legislature Dec. 3, 1857, is named for William C. Dawson who died in 1856, having served in Congress from Dec. 1836 to Nov. 1842, and in the U.S. Senate from 1849 to 1855. He also commanded a brigade in the Creek Indian War of 1836. Among the first County Officers were: Sheriff Samuel R. Fendley, Ordinary Henry K. Mikel, Clerk of Superior Court Daniel P. Monroe, Clerk of Inferior Court John Matthews, Tax Receiver David H. Logan, Tax Collector John Bruce, Treasurer James B. Gordon, Surveyor Andrew I. Glenn and Coroner John W. Beck.

(Located at GA 53 and GA 9 on the courthouse lawn. GHM 042-1, 1954.)

AMICALOLA FALLS

Amicalola Falls, 12 miles to the north, is the highest in Georgia. The streams descend 722 feet in a series of beautiful cascades, with one clear drop of over 100 feet. The part of the stream above the falls once drained Westward into the Cattecay River at the higher

AMICALOLA FALLS

level. The swifter, lower Amicalola pushed back its headwaters divide until it beheaded the other stream, forming the present falls.

(Located at GA 53 and GA 183, 2 miles west of Dawsonville. WPA 042-E7.) ◆ ★ – not standing.

THE APPALACHIAN TRAIL

Here begins the approach trail to Springer Mountain, the southern terminus of the Appalachian Trail, a continuous footpath extending more than

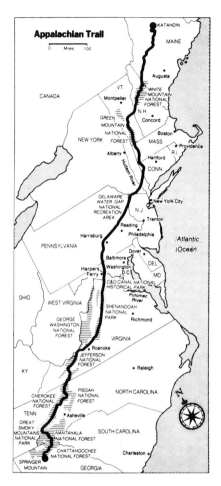

COURTESY, MENASHA RIDGE PRESS, BIRMINGHAM, AL.
PROVIDED BY THE APPALACHIAN TRAIL CONFERENCE.

THE APPALACHIAN TRAIL

2,000 miles to Mt. Katahdin, Maine. The Appalachian Trail was conceived by Benton MacKaye, forester, philosopher, dreamer, who in 1921 envisioned a footpath along the crest of the Appalachian Mountains. The Trail is maintained by volunteer hiking clubs, the U. S. Forest Service, and the National Park Service, coordinated through the Appalachian Trail Conference.

"Remote for detachment, narrow for chosen company, winding for leisure, lonely for contemplation, it beckons not merely north and south, but upward to the body, mind, and soul of man." Harrold Allen

(Located off GA 52 in Amicalola Falls State Park in front of the visitors center. GHM 042-2, 1976.)

DOUGLAS COUNTY

Named in honor of Stephen A. Douglas, a Vermonter who was a congressman from Illinois. He was the Democratic candidate for president in 1860 on the ticket with Governor Herschel V. Johnson of Georgia.

DOUGLASVILLE

DOUGLAS COUNTY

This County, created by Act of the Legislature October 17, 1870, is named for Stephen A. Douglas, the "Little Giant," a Vermonter who was Congressman from Illinois 1843 to '47, Senator from '47 to '61, and Democratic candidate for President in 1860 on the ticket with Gov. Herschel V. Johnson of Georgia for Vice President. Among the first County Officers were: Sheriff T. H. Sellman, Clerk of Superior Court A. L. Gorman, Ordinary Wm. Hindman, Tax Receiver Jno. M. James, Tax Collector M. D. Watkins,

STEPHEN A. DOUGLAS (1813–1861)

Treasurer C. P. Bower, Coroner S. W. Biggers and Surveyor John M. Hughey.

(Located at West Broad Street and Court House Square on the courthouse lawn. GHM 048-1, 1954.)

BLUE STAR MEMORIAL HIGHWAY

A Tribute to the Armed Forces that have defended the United States of America.

Sponsored by The Garden Clubs of Georgia, Inc. in cooperation with the Dogwood District and Town and Country Club, Douglasville, Georgia.

(From I-20, Exit #11, follow Lee Road north 0.6 miles, turn right on Mt. Vernon and follow 2.4 miles to Sweetwater Creek State Park. Turn left into park and follow 0.3 mile to marker. GCG 048-99, 1965.)

ELBERT COUNTY

Named in honor of General Samuel Elbert (1740–1788), Revolutionary War hero and governor of Georgia. County Seat: Elberton.

ELBERTON

ELBERT COUNTY

Created from Wilkes County by Act of Dec. 10, 1790, Elbert County was settled in 1784 by Gen. George Mathews and a group from Virginia and Carolina. The site of Petersburg, the original settlement and third largest town in Georgia in its day, is covered by the Clark Hill Reservoir. Nancy Hart, celebrated Revolutionary patriot, lived in this county. Elbert County was named for Gen. Samuel Elbert, Revolutionary soldier and Governor of Georgia (1785–1786). A native of South Carolina and resident of Savannah, he was a member of the Council of Safety and fought at Savannah (1778) and Brier Creek (1779).

On Jan. 20, 1791, the first session of Elbert County Superior Court was held at the home of Thos. A. Carter on Beaverdam Creek, some 5 miles NW of here. George Walton, Georgia signer of the Declaration of Independence, was presiding judge. The Carter plantation house stands today. Nearby is the family cemetery.

First officers of Elbert County were: Matthew Talbot, Clerk; Robert Middleton, Sheriff; Robert Cosby, Collector of Taxes; W. Higginbottom,

COURTESY, GEORGIA DEPARTMENT OF ARCHIVES AND HISTORY

COLONEL SAMUEL ELBERT (1740–1788)

Register of Probate; Thos. Burton, Receiver of Tax Returns; Richardson Hunt, Surveyor; James Tate, Coroner.

(Located on GA 77/South Oliver Street at the Public Square on the courthouse lawn. GHM 052-13, 1959.)

OLD POST ROAD

This road is older than Elberton. Mail was carried over it by Post Riders before Falling Creek Church was built in 1788 and during Washington's Administration. Later a stage coach ran between Elberton & Lexington three times a week, stopping at the old Globe Hotel which stood on the site of the present court house in Elberton. Stocks for local merchants were brought over this road until 1878 when the first railroad came to Elberton. With the coming of Rural Free Delivery Mr. Giles made the first delivery in Elbert County over this road on horseback.

(Located on GA 77/South Oliver Street at the Public Square on the courthouse lawn. GHM 052-3, 1955.)

GRAVE OF GENERAL WILEY THOMPSON

General Wiley Thompson, considered the ablest and most humane of the agents to the Seminole Indians of Florida, was ambushed and killed near the agency at Fort King, Florida, December 28, 1835, by Osceola and a band of warriors who opposed removal to the West. Some months later his body was brought to Elberton and reburied in the garden of his home, 4 blocks east of here (now Heard Street).

Born in Virginia, September 25, 1781, General Thompson was reared in Elbert County. A militia officer in the War of 1812, in 1817 he was elected major general of the 4th Division of the Georgia Militia. A State Senator from 1817 to 1819, General Thompson resigned and served on the commission to determine the boundary between Georgia and Florida. After serving six consecutive terms as a member of Congress where he supported President Jackson's policy of Indian removal, he was appointed agent in September, 1833.

(Located on GA 77/South Oliver Street at the Public Square on the courthouse lawn. GHM 052-14, 1959.)

GOV. HEARD'S HOME

Off this road lies the site of Heard-mont, home of Governor Stephen Heard, 1740–1815, and "God's Acre," the family cemetery where he lies buried. A ten acre park surrounding the site is owned and maintained by the Stephen Heard Chapter, D.A.R. A Virginian of Irish descent, Heard came to Georgia, establishing Heard's Fort, now Washington, Ga., in 1773, and fighting with Gen. Elijah Clarke at the Battle of Kettle Creek where he was captured. As President of the Council, he was de facto Governor for a period in 1781. After moving to Heardmont he was one of three who selected the site of Elberton.

(From the courthouse follow GA 17/72 2.1 miles, turn left on GA 72 east, and follow 6.6 miles to marker at Pearl Mill Road. GHM 052-4, 1955.)

"OLD DAN TUCKER"

Rev. Daniel Tucker owned a large plantation on the Savannah River and is buried near his old homesite, "Point Lookout," six miles from here. Born in Virginia, February 14, 1744, Daniel Tucker came here to take up a land grant. A Revolutionary soldier, planter and minister, he owned and operated Tucker's Ferry near his home. He died April 7, 1818 – but not "of a toothache in his heel." Esteemed by his fellow planters, he was loved by the Negroes who composed the many verses of the famous ditty, "Old Dan Tucker," a favorite song at corn shuck-ings and other social gatherings.

(From the courthouse follow GA 17/72 2.1 miles, turn left on GA 72 east and follow 6.6 miles to Marker at Pearl Mill Road. GHM 052-12, 1957.)

OLD DAN TUCKER

Old Dan Tucker was a fine ole man,
He washed his face in a fryin' pan;
Combed his hair with a wagon wheel,
Died with a toothache in his heel

Old Dan Tucker, he got drunk,
Fell in the fire, kicked up a chunk;
Red hot coals in his shoe,
Laws a-mussy, hoe de ashes flew.

GOV. HEARD'S GRAVE

Stephen Heard, Governor of Georgia in 1781, lawyer, planter, surveyor and soldier of the Revolution, lies buried in this family cemetery. With a price on his head he was captured by the British at the Battle of Kettle Creek and condemned to die. On the eve of his execution he was rescued by his servant "Mammy Kate" with the aid of her husband "Daddy Jack," both of whom lie buried near him. Heard's home "Heardmont" once stood nearby in the 10 acre park established by the Stephen Heard Chapter, D.A.R. Com-ing to Georgia from Virginia, Heard, an Irishman, established Heard's Fort, now Washington, Ga. in 1773.

(From the courthouse follow GA 17/72 2.1 miles, turn left on GA 72 east and follow 6.6 miles, turn left onto Pearl Mill Road. At 2.9 miles take right fork and follow 1.7 miles to marker. GHM 052-5, 1955.)

COURTESY, GEORGIA DEPARTMENT OF ARCHIVES AND HISTORY

STEPHEN HEARD (1740–1815)

BETHLEHEM METHODIST CHURCH

Bethlehem Methodist Church, second oldest Methodist Church in Georgia and formerly known as Thompson's Meeting House, sponsored the First Methodist Annual Conference in Georgia, on April 9, 1788. Bishop Asbury and his party, delayed by weather and illness, held the meeting, scheduled for the church, in the home of Judge Charles Tait. Richard Ivey, Thomas Humphries, Moses Parks, Hope Hull, James Conner, Bennett Maxey, Isaac Smith, Matthew Harris, Reuben Ellis, John Mason attended the conference. Several Revolutionary soldiers are buried near the church.

(From the courthouse follow GA 17/72 2.1 miles, turn left on GA 72 east and follow 10.4 miles to marker and church off to the right. GHM 052-7, 1955.)

COLONISTS' CROSSING

"The Point," where early settlers crossed into Georgia, is eight miles

COURTESY, SPECIAL COLLECTIONS DEPT., ROBERT W. WOODRUFF LIBRARY, EMORY UNIV.

BISHOP FRANCIS ASBURY (1745–1816)

east of here. As soon as this area was ceded, Governor Wright opened a post at the confluence of the Broad and Savannah Rivers, known as Fort James. "The Point" became the gateway for settlers from Virginia, North Carolina and South Carolina who registered there and secured their tracts of land. A land court at Dartmouth, which grew up around the fort, was held from September 1773 through June 1775 to open this section. In 1777 all this ceded land was, by the State Constitution created into Wilkes County.

(From the courthouse follow GA 17/72 2.1 miles, turn left onto GA 72 east and follow 12.3 miles to marker. GHM 052-8, 1957.)

SITE OF PETERSBURG

In 1784, Gen. George Mathews brought a number of Virginians and

Carolinians, large tobacco planters, to settle this section. Dionysius Oliver laid out the town of Petersburg, on the site of the earlier settlement of Dartmouth, at the union of the Broad and Savannah rivers, and built a large tobacco warehouse. Among the early settlers were Gov. Wm. Wyatt Bibb and Judge Charles Tait, who served together in the U. S. Senate (1813–17), the Shackelfords and other prominent Huguenot families. Both Petersburg and the old road from Petersburg to Augusta are now under water.

(Located off GA 72 in Bobby Brown State Park. GHM 052-9B, 1956.)

REVEREND DOZIER THORNTON (1754–1843)

VAN'S CREEK BAPTIST CHURCH

Van's Creek Baptist Church, established early in 1785 by Rev. Dozier Thornton, Revolutionary soldier and Virginian, was named for an Indian convert, David Vann, famed Chief of the Cherokees. Though the 6th Baptist Church in Georgia, it is the oldest in continuous service. Rev. Thornton was its pastor for 43 years. Original members were Rev. Dozier Thornton, his wife Lucy Elizabeth Thornton, Elizabeth Thornton, William Arnold, first Deacon and Clerk. Susan Arnold, Nathan Morgan, Elizabeth Morgan, Thomas Gilbert, John White, Milly White.

(From GA 77, 1.3 miles north of the courthouse, follow New Ruckersville Road 6.2 miles, turn left on Ruckersville Circle for 0.1 mile to marker. GHM 052-6, 1955.)

COLDWATER METHODIST CHURCH

In the late 1770's, a large caravan of Virginians, including a Methodist preacher, traveling south in search of a new home, settled in this neighborhood. In the company were the Adams, Alexander, Banks, Cunningham, Fleming, Anderson, Gaines, Johnson, Teasley, Tyner, Stower and Brown families. At once they built a place of worship with loopholes for defense against Indians. In this "Meeting House," Bishop Francis Asbury, leader of early American Methodism, preached from time to time. His remark – "This is indeed cold water" – after drinking from the nearby spring gave the church its name.

The second house of worship was of lumber sawed on Coldwater Creek by Ralph Gaines. The three Adams brothers–Hiram, James, and Lawrence –joined him in erecting the building.

Destroyed by fire in 1883, it was replaced by an exceptionally beautiful rural church. The fourth building, started in 1947, was dedicated August 29, 1947 by Rev. Horace Smith, District Superintendent.

Of ten memorial windows in this church, two are dedicated to Howell Gaines Adams and Nick Drewry Carpenter, who fell in battle in World War II.

(From GA 77, 6.2 miles north of the courthouse, turn right on Coldwater Creek Road and follow for 4.5 miles until dead end, turn left and travel 0.8 mile to marker. GHM 052-10, 1957.)

FALLING CREEK BAPTIST CHURCH

In 1788, Thomas Maxwell founded the Falling Creek Baptist Church. A Virginian, he was born September 8, 1742, and died December 12, 1837. Imprisoned a number of times for preaching the Baptist faith, he was able, once, to convert the jailer and his family. According to tradition, he rubbed away part of his prominent nose by preaching through the bars of the jails, and was defended by Patrick Henry when jailed in Culpeper County, Va.

In 1835 at Falling Creek Church, the Sarepta Baptist Association voted to join the State Baptist Convention, after 15 years consideration.

(Located on GA 77, 2.7 miles south of Elberton. GHM 052-11, 1957.)

STINCHCOMB METHODIST CHURCH

STINCHCOMB METHODIST CHURCH

About a mile from here is the Stinchcomb Methodist Church, one of the first in this section of the state. On Dec. 30, 1794, Middleton Wood granted to Absalom Stinchcomb, John Gatewood and John Ham the "privilege to erect a meeting house on his land on waters of Dove Creek." The first building was a log structure. By 1850's the church acquired surrounding property. The present building has been in continuous use for over 100 years. The sills are handhewn, 14 inches square. Among old graves in the churchyard cemetery is that of Dionysius Oliver, Revolutionary soldier.

(Located on GA 17, 4.6 miles north of Elberton. GHM 052-8B, 1956.)

NANCY HART (C.1735–C.1830) CAPTURING A BAND OF TORIES

NANCY HART

On Wahatche (War Woman) Creek, in Revolutionary times, lived Nancy Morgan Hart, her husband, Benjamin, and their children. Six feet tall, masculine in strength and courage, Nancy Hart was a staunch patriot, a deadly shot, a skilled doctor and a good neighbor. A spy for the colonists, she is credited with capturing several Tories. Later, with her son, John, and his family, she joined a wagon train to Henderson County, Kentucky, where she is buried. Hart County, the Nancy Hart Highway, and schools in Elbert and Hart Counties are named for her. A replica of her log home, with chimney stones from the original, is in the Nancy Hart State Park.

(Located on GA 17, 10.7 miles south of Elberton. GHM 073-5, renumbered 052-9A, 1957.)

FANNIN COUNTY

Named in honor of Colonel James W. Fannin (1809–1836) who died in the War of Texas Independence. County Seat: Blue Ridge.

BLUE RIDGE

FANNIN COUNTY

This County, created by Act of the Legislature Jan. 21, 1854, is named for Col. J. W. Fannin who was killed in the massacre at Goliad, Mar. 27, 1836. He had been captured with about 350 Georgia Volunteers under his command while fighting for the Republic of Texas in its successful War of Independence with Mexico. The first County Site was at Morganton but it was moved to Blue Ridge Aug. 13, 1895 by vote of a public election. The greater part of this County, which contains the Noontootly National Game Refuge, lies in the Chattahoochee National Forest.

(Located at East Main and Summit Streets on the courthouse lawn. GHM 055-1, 1954.)

FLOYD COUNTY

Named in honor of General John Floyd (1769–1839) who with the Georgia Militia fought the Creek and Choctaw Indians. He also served as a member of the Georgia legislature and was elected to Congress for one term. County Seat: Rome.

ARMUCHEE

FARMER'S BRIDGE
ARMUCHEE CREEK

May 15, 1864. Minty's Brigade of Garrard's Cav., scouting toward Rome in advance of the infantry column, Davis' div. (14th A.C.)(F), encountered Brig. Gen. L. S. Ross' Texas brigade (Jackson's Cav. div.) (C) at Farmer's Bridge.

Ross was driven to within 3 mi. of Rome, where he was supported by infantry & artillery. Minty, driven back to the bridge, returned to Lay's Ferry, (near Resaca) May 16.

May 17. Davis' div. (F), enroute from Resaca, reached bridge at noon. Davis

advanced toward Rome, 2 p.m., driving Ross' Cav. back to DeSoto Hill, this side of the Oostanaula River.

(Located on US 27/GA 1 at the bridge over Armuchee Creek. GHM 057-5, 1984.)

CAVE SPRINGS

GEORGIA
SCHOOL FOR THE DEAF

In 1833, a deaf man, John Jacobus Flournoy, of Jackson County, great grandson of Jacob Flournoy, a French Huguenot, urging education for the deaf, interested Governor Wilson Lumpkin and the Georgia Legislature in this educational movement. At first the pupils, few in number, were sent to the American Asylum for Deaf and Dumb in Hartford, Conn. Distance, weather and the youth of the pupils made that unsatisfactory. On May 15, 1846, with four pupils in a log cabin, with O. P. Fannin, teacher, this school began as a part of the Hearn Manual School at Cave Spring, Georgia. This school grew rapidly and, in 1847, a brick building was erected and dedicated. Later, other additions were made. The school was closed during the War Between the States and used as a hospital by both Confederate and Union forces. It resumed operations in February 1867 and is still supported by the State of Georgia. In 1955 this school had 82 teachers and employees and an income of more than $500,000.

(Located on the campus of the Georgia School for the Deaf. GHM 057-11, 1956.)

EVERETT SPRINGS

SITE OF
MOUNTAIN SCHOOL

Everett Springs Seminary, antecedent of the famous Martha Berry Schools, was chartered in 1889 in Floyd County. The school, which was in existence until 1908, was the first mountain school in Georgia which had boarding facilities for its students.

The pupils at Everett Springs Seminary were expected to do their own cooking and housekeeping in the little cottages which surrounded the schoolhouse. The schoolhouse and cottages were built by the community of Everett Springs for the school.

In 1892 Professor W. J. Moore of Tennessee was elected Principal of Everett Springs Seminary. The following year he was reelected Principal and made President of the Board of Trustees. His brother Issac Moore was elected Assistant. For many years the brothers ran the school and won the love and admiration of the mountain children whom they taught. The pupils of W. J. Moore, who meet annually for a reunion at the old schoolhouse, remember that their professor commanded such respect that a word of disapproval was often discipline enough for the high spirited pupils of Everett Springs Seminary.

(From GA 156 (New Rosedale Road) and Everett Springs Road proceed north on Everett Springs Road 4.2 miles until the stone church is reached at the junction with Floyd Springs Road. Proceed 100 yards beyond the church, turn left on dirt road by old school site and proceed 0.1 mile. GHM 057-13, 1963.)

FLOYD SPRINGS

FLOYD SPRINGS

Garrard's Cavalry (F), having left Villanow, May 14, 1864, passed Floyd Springs May 15, enroute to Farmer's Bridge & Rome. After scouting toward Rome, the Cav. withdrew & camped here.

May 16. Returning toward Lay's Ferry (near Resaca), Garrard met Davis' (2d) div. 14th A.C. (F), enroute S. to Rome. Garrard informed Davis that Farmer's Bridge, 8 Mi. N. of Rome, was an Armuchee Cr., not an Oostanaula River crossing. This was news to Davis, who had been informed otherwise – due to confusing reports at headquarters.

Davis' march from Resaca to Rome was predicated on a river crossing at Farmer's Bridge.

(Located at Floyd Springs and Rosedale Roads. GHM 057-4, 1953.)

LINDALE

MEDORA FIELD PERKERSON
Author – Newspaper Columnist

Medora Field (1892–1960) was born nearby on the site of the present Lindale Baptist Church. In her early twenties she became a member of *The Atlanta Journal-Constitution Magazine* staff, and later was married to Angus Perkerson, its editor. For many years, troubled people sought the sympathetic and sound counsel she gave in her weekly column as "Marie Rose." She was the friend of the friendless. Through offices held in her Church, in the Child Service Association of Atlanta and in organizations of writers, she became an influence for good throughout Georgia and beyond its borders.

Mrs. Perkerson's most notable book, *White Columns in Georgia*, tells the story of her state through its historic houses. Her two other books, *Who Killed Aunt Maggie?* and *Blood on Her Shoe*, have Georgia settings.

(Located on Park Avenue at the railroad crossing in front of the Baptist Church. GHM 057-12, 1961.)

ROME

FLOYD COUNTY

Floyd County was created by Act of Dec. 3, 1832 out of Cherokee County. Originally, it included parts of Chattooga, Polk and Gordon Counties. Early settlers came from Tenn., S. C., and older parts of Ga. The county was named for Maj. Gen. John Floyd (1794–1829), Legislator, Congressman, Gen. of Ga. Militia, Commander of Ga. troops against the Creeks in 1813 and Commander of troops at Savannah. First officers of Floyd County, commissioned March 18, 1833, were: Andrew H. Johnston, Sheriff; Edwin G. Rogers, Clerk Superior Court; Philip W. Hemphill, Clerk Inferior Court; John Smithwicke, Surveyor; Lemuel Milligan, Coroner.

(Located on Fifth Avenue on the courthouse lawn. GHM 057-10, 1956.)

GEORGIA'S PAUL REVERE

Along this road John H. Wisdom rode from Gadsden, Ala. to warn that a Federal force of over 2,000 men was approaching Rome to occupy the town, destroy foundries making ammunition for the Confederates and to cut Confederate communications (May 2, 1863).

On Wisdom's arrival in Rome the bridge over the Oostanaula river was fortified and made ready for burning as a last resort. Wisdom's warning and the plans for defense played a big part in the surrender of Colonel Streight (F) with 1,500 men to Gen. Nathan Bedford Forrest (C) with only 425 men.

(Located at South Broad and Myrtle Hill Cemetery. GHM 057-1, 1953.)

DAVIS' MARCH TO ROME

May 16, 1864. Brig. Gen. J. C. Davis' div. (14th A.C.(F) left Sugar Valley via roads west of the Oostanaula River to outflank Johnston's forces (C) retreating from Resaca.

Davis had been informed that Farmer's Bridge on Armuchee Cr. was an Oostanaula crossing. Learning otherwise at Floyd Springs, he reported same to Thomas, who ordered Davis to return to Lay's Ferry; instead, Davis kept on toward Rome, reaching DeSoto Hill, May 17.

The river was crossed under fire, May 18, & the Federals occupied Rome where they remained until May 24, when their march to Dallas, Paulding County, began.

(Located on North 2nd Street near Floyd Medical center. GHM 057-6, 1953.).

FRENCH'S DIV. AT ROME

May 16, 1864. Maj. Gen. S. G. French, in person, reached Rome from Ala., enroute with his div. (Polk's A. C.), to join Johnston's army (C) at Cassville. Sear's brigade was sent to Kingston that night.

May 17. Ector's, resisting Davis' approach on the Armuchee rd., was sent across the Oostanaula with Ross' & J. T. Morgan's cav. Cockrell's brigade arrived at dark & went on to Kingston. Ector was withdrawn at midnight – leaving a small force to defend the city.

HERNANDO DE SOTO (C.1500–1542)

French made a token defense only, as he was under strict orders to reinforce Johnston's army, confronted by five corps of the Federal army under Sherman, at Cassville.

(Located on US 27/GA 1/Martha Berry Boulevard near junction with Little Dry Creek north of the railroad underpass. GHM 057-8, 1953.)

FEDERAL OCCUPATION OF ROME

May 18,1864. Davis' div., (14th A.C.)(F), moving from Resaca via. W. bank of the Oostanaula, forced passage of the river against Confederate opposition & captured the city.

Davis' seizure of Rome was incident to a move E. toward Kingston upon the flank of Johnston's forces (C) retreating from Resaca, but the military situation having changed by May

23, Davis' column was diverted to Dallas in support of McPherson's troops on that front.

Davis div. left Rome for Dallas (Paulding Co.) May 24 (via State Highway 101), camping that night at Peek's Spring (Aragon, Polk County).

(Located off US 27/Turner-McCall Boulevard at Civic Center Hill next to the Visitor Center. GHM 057-7, 1953.)

DE SOTO IN GEORGIA

In May, 1539 Hernando de Soto landed in Florida with over 600 people, 220 horses and mules, and a herd of swine reserved for famine. Fired by his success in Pizarro's conquest of Peru, De Soto had been granted the rights, by the King of Spain, to explore, then govern, southeastern North America.

After wintering in Tallahassee, the De Soto expedition set out on a quest for gold which eventually spanned four years and crossed portions of nine states. This was the first recorded European exploration of the interior of the Southeast. Over 300 members died on the expedition, including De Soto in 1542. This tremendous effort forever changed the lives of the Indians who were infected with old world diseases, killed in battle, enslaved, made destitute and sometimes befriended.

Many scholars believe that De Soto visited this general area on August 31, 1540. He visited several towns on a large river, probably the Coosa, trav-

MARTHA BERRY (1866–1942)

eling westward and left Georgia about September 5, 1540.

(Located off US 27/Turner-McCall Boulevard at Civic Center Hill next to the Visitor Center. GHM 057-16, 1990.)

MARTHA BERRY'S BIRTHPLACE

Martha Berry, founder of the Berry Schools, was born and lived here at "Oak Hill." Daughter of Capt. Tom Berry, wealthy plantation owner, she devoted her life to providing educational opportunities for the children of her less fortunate neighbors in the mountains. The school grew under her direction from a small log cabin on the plantation in 1900 to a 30,000 acre campus. More than 15,000 students have received their educations in the day school at Possum Trot, the Girls School, Boys School and Berry College. Martha Berry died in 1942 leaving a deathless monument.

(Located at US 27 and GA 57 Spur near the Martha Berry Museum at Oak Hill. GHM 057-9, 1954.)

ORIGINAL CABIN

This cabin, birthplace of The Berry Schools, (now Berry College and Berry Academy) was built as a playhouse for Martha Berry and her brothers and sisters shortly after the Civil War. Here, in the late 1800's, three small boys from Lavender Mountain received Martha Berry's first Sunday School lesson. Word of her kindness and interest spread and soon the cabin was overflowing with people. In the evolution from this modest beginning to a day school at Possum Trot, a boarding school and finally a college, the Cabin was outgrown but not forgotten. Martha Berry chose the Cabin to represent simplicity on the school seal, along with the Bible for religion, the lamp for learning and the plow for work. On this foundation she built a world renowned educational institution extensively copied in the U.S. and abroad.

(Located near US 27 and GA 57 Spur, on the grounds of Oak Hill near the Cabin. GHM 057-15, 1974.)

DR. ELIZUR AND ESTHER BUTLER MISSIONARIES TO THE CHEROKEES

Buried in the grave sixty feet south of this point is Esther Post Butler. Born in Connecticut on September 15, 1798, Esther Post married Dr. Elizur Butler, physician and minister, in October, 1820. The Butlers were sent by the American Board of Commissioners for Foreign Missions to Brainerd and then to Creek Path, before arriving at the Haweis Mission, near Rome, in 1826. Mrs. Butler died in 1829 after eight years of service to the Cherokees.

Two years later Dr. Butler was arrested for residing in the Cherokee Nation without taking an oath of allegiance to the State of Georgia and obtaining a license from the Governor. Sentenced, with Samuel Worcester, to four years of hard labor in the State penitentiary at Milledgeville, he was pardoned by Governor Wilson Lumpkin in 1833, almost a year after the United States Supreme Court nullified the law under which the missionaries were arrested.

COURTESY, GEORGIA DEPARTMENT OF ARCHIVES AND HISTORY

MINING BAUXITE

Upon his release, Dr. Butler returned to the Mission at Haweis, but was forced to move the following year. In addition to attending the Cherokees during the Removal, Dr. Butler served the missions at Red Clay, Park Hill, and Fairfield and the Cherokee Female Seminary prior to his death in Arkansas in 1857.

(Located 7.5 miles west of Rome City limits (1990) on GA 20, 0.4 mile west of junction with GA 100 south. GHM 057-14, 1967.)

BAUXITE ORE OF ALUMINUM

The first discovery of bauxite in North America was made at Hermitage, one mile east in 1887, by James Holland. For many years this section of Georgia furnished a large part of the domestic supply of bauxite.

(Located on the Old Calhoun Road/ Old GA 53, 7 miles north of Rome. WPA 057-H2, 1940.) ♦ ★ – not standing.

HERMITAGE

Home of Joseph Watters (1792–1866), pioneer settler in Floyd County; an admirer of Andrew Jackson, he named it "Hermitage." A settlement of that name is 1 mi. S.E.

May 17, 18, 1864, Brig. Gen. K. Garrard's (2d) div. of Elliott's Cavalry Corps. Army of the Cumberland (F), moved down this road from near Calhoun to strike the Rome R.R. west of Kingston.

Operating on the right wing of McPherson's Army of the Tennessee (F), Garrard turned S.E. here & reached Barnsley's – noon, May 18, in advance of McPherson's troops which had turned E. at McGuire's, 3 mi. N.E.

(Located on the Old Calhoun Road/Old GA 53, 2.5 miles off GA 53, at the family cemetery in Shannon. GHM 057-3, 1953.)

McGUIRE'S

Cited thus in McPherson's dispatches of May 17, 1864, & military maps; otherwise known as Nannie P. O., & Pinson's Store.

McPherson's 15th and 16th A.C. (F) marched from near Calhoun, camped here, night, May 17, enroute to Kingston via Barnsley's. There was no direct road to Barnsley's above Hermitage, & to avoid over-extending his right, Sherman directed McPherson to detour E. from McGuire's to Adairsville.

McPherson's troops constituted the right of Sherman's forces advancing on a wide front Southward, after a two-day battle at Resaca, May 14, 15.

(Located on GA 53 near junction with GA 140 several miles northeast of Rome. GHM 057-2, 1953.)

FORSYTH COUNTY

Named in honor of John Forsyth (1780–1841), a native of Virginia and famed Georgia diplomat, governor and statesman. County Seat: Cumming.

CUMMING

FORSYTH COUNTY

Forsyth County was created by Act of Dec. 3, 1832 from Cherokee County. It was named for Gov. John Forsyth (1780–1841), a native of Frederick Co., Va., a graduate of Princeton, and gifted Georgia lawyer. He was Attorney-General of Ga., Congressman, Senator, Minister to Spain, Governor, and Secretary of State under Presidents Jackson and Van Buren. First officers of Forsyth County, commissioned April 20, 1833, were: John Blaylock, Clerk of Superior Court; Thomas Burford, County Surveyor; Alston B. Wilborn, Coroner; Hubbard Barker was commissioned Sheriff, January 31, 1834.

(Located on Dahlonega Street between Main and W. Maple Streets, on the courthouse lawn. GHM 058-2, 1956.)

COURTESY, GEORGIA DEPARTMENT OF ARCHIVES AND HISTORY

JOHN FORSYTH (1780–1841)

COLONEL WILLIAM CUMMING

The town of Cumming (incorporated 1834) is named in honor of Col. William Cumming, distinguished Georgian, born July 27, 1788, son of Thomas Cumming and Ann Clay, daughter of Joseph Clay, of Savannah. William Cumming graduated from the College of New Jersey at Princeton and studied law at Gould's Law School, Litchfield, Connecticut. The War of 1812 brought him military prominence. Captain of the Augusta Independent Blues in 1812, he was commissioned Major, USA, in 1813, and appointed Adjutant General of the Northern Army the following year with the rank of Colonel. In 1815, however, he resigned from the Army and the Board of War, on which he served. Although in 1818 he was appointed Quartermaster General of the Army by President Monroe, and, in 1847, Major General by President Polk, he declined both appointments and spent the remainder of his life in Augusta, where he died February 18, 1863.

A series of duels in 1822 with Senator George McDuffie of South Carolina received nationwide attention and illuminated the larger political controversy between proponents of states' rights (Cumming) and those favoring a strong central government (McDuffie).

(Located on Dahlonega Street between Main and West Maple Streets, on the courthouse lawn. GHM 058-3, 1962.)

BLUE STAR MEMORIAL HIGHWAY

A tribute to the Armed Forces
that have defended the
United States of America

Sponsored by The Garden Club of Georgia, Inc. in cooperation with The Rose Garden Club of Cumming.

(Located on GA 9/Dahlonega Highway, 1.9 miles north of Cumming. GCG 058-99, 1977.)

OLD FEDERAL ROAD

The highway crossing east and west at this intersection is the Old Federal Road, first vehicular way and earliest postal route west of the Chattahoochee. Beginning to the east on the Hall–Jackson county line, it linked Georgia and Tennessee across the Cherokee Nation.

Rights to use the route were granted informally by the Indians in 1803 and formally in the 1805 Treaty of Tellico, Tennessee.

Prior to that time the trace served as a trading path from Augusta to the Cherokees of northwest Georgia and southeast Tennessee.

(Located at GA 9/Dahlonega Hwy and GA 369 in the Coal Mountain community, 5.2 miles north of Cumming. GHM 058-1, 1954.)

FRANKLIN COUNTY

Named in honor of Benjamin Franklin (1706–1790). County Seat: Carnesville.

CARNESVILLE

FRANKLIN COUNTY

This County, created by Act of the Legislature Feb. 25, 1784, is named for Benjamin Franklin, Revolutionary patriot and statesman. It was formed from lands obtained from the Indians by the Treaty of Augusta, 1783. Capt. James Terrell of the Revolution was an early settler. Volunteers from Franklin Co. under Capt. Morris distinguished themselves at the Battle of Pea River Swamp, Mar. 25, 1837, in the Creek Indian War. The present County Site was established by Act of Nov. 29, 1806, at Carnesville named for Thomas B. Carnes, member of the Third Congress, 1793–97.

(Located at Lavonia Road and Hill Street on the courthouse lawn. GHM 059-1, 1954.)

HEBRON PRESBYTERIAN CHURCH

Hebron Presbyterian Church was organized in 1796 by Rev. John Newton, a native of Pennsylvania. Rev. Thomas Newton, a younger brother, was the first pastor. First elders were John McEntire and Samuel Mackie, natives of Ireland, and Thomas Mayes and William Fleming, from Pennsylvania. Churches organized out of Hebron were: Carnell (Homer), Mount Hermon (Ila), Harmony, Hartwell, Carnesville, Mayesville, Commerce, Cornelia and Hopewell. Nine ministers have gone out from this church. The work of the church is still carried on by the descendants of its founders. The present building was erected in 1884.

(Located on GA 59, 9.6 miles south of Carnesville. GHM 059-6, 1957.)

CARROLL'S METHODIST CHURCH

Instituted in 1797, this church was named for the William Carroll family, among its first members. Families identified with the church through the years are McWhorters, Osborns, Starrs, Stones, Browns, Burtons, Sewells, Jacksons, Hemphills, Deans, Buffingtons, Cheeks, Mabrys, Turmans, Stricklands, Carsons, Hayes, Greens,

CARROLL'S METHODIST CHURCH

Millers and many others. The present building, erected about 1835, was restored in 1951–52 under the leadership of Bishop John H. Baker. Rev. Nelson Osborn (1797–1873) was a lifelong member and minister for many years. A number of other well-known Georgia ministers have served the church.

(Located on GA 145/Royston Road and Jackson Bridge Road, 1.7 miles south of Carnesville. GHM 059-3, 1957.) **Note:** To find the church, follow Jackson Bridge Road 1.9 miles, turn left on unimproved road for 0.6 mile.)

CARROLL'S METHODIST CHURCH

This church, instituted in 1797, was named for the Wm. Carroll family, among its first members. The present building, erected about 1835, was restored in 1951–52 under the leadership of Bishop John H. Baker. Rev. Nelson Osborn (1797–1873) was a life-long member and minister for many years. The renowned Bishop Francis Asbury wrote in his diary: "Friday, Nov. 21, 1799, we drove 16 miles to Carroll's Meeting House, a New

Log Cabin in the Woods. Some of the People of the Congregation are from the East and West Parts of Maryland. I felt the Lord was with them. We have the Kitchen, House and Chamber all in one and no closet but the woods."

(Follow GA 145/Royston Road 1.7 miles south of Carnesville, turn left on Jackson Bridge Road and follow 4 miles to junction with GA 327. Look to the left for the marker. GHM 059-4, 1957.) **Note:** The road to the church will be passed 1.9 miles after turning onto Jackson Bridge Road.

DOUBLE BRANCHES BAPTIST CHURCH

Constituted in 1801, this church had 19 charter members. First a member of the Sarepta Association, it was one of 13 churches to form the Tugalo Association in 1818. Some members came many miles in wagons and buggies to attend its services. Among the early pastors were John Sandridge, Francis Calloway, John A. Davis, Samuel B. Sanders, John G. York, and W. F. Bowers. Davis and Bowers "departed the Association because of ladies wearing jewelry and Free Masonry" to form the "Reformation Church," a short-lived group of churches in this area. This building was erected in 1911.

(Follow GA 145/Royston Road 1.7 miles south of Carnesville, turn left on Jackson Bridge Road and follow 4 miles, turn left onto GA 327 and follow 0.8 mile to marker. GHM 059-6B, 1957.)

POPLAR SPRINGS METHODIST CAMP GROUND

POPLAR SPRINGS
METHODIST CAMP GROUND

Camp meetings have been held here each year, from 1832, except four years during the War Between the States. The 50-acre plot, "extending one-half mile in every direction from the preacher's stand," was purchased from Daniel and Jacob Groover for $25 by William Hammons, John F. Wilson, George Shell, John B. Wade, Dennis Phillips, Thomas King and Rev. Nelson Osborne, Trustees. The first meeting, August 1832, was held under a brush arbor with 30 tents on the ground. Women were seated on one side of the arbor; men on the other. John W. Osborne, appointed usher, served at every meeting until his death in 1914.

(Follow GA 145/Royston Road 1.7 miles south of Carnesville, turn left on Jackson Bridge Road and follow 4 miles, turn right onto GA 327 and follow 2.3 miles to marker. GHM 059-5, 1957.)

FRANKLIN SPRINGS

THE FRANKLIN SPRINGS

For the first hundred years, Franklin Springs existed as a famous health resort. The Springs, as well as the County, was named for Benjamin Franklin. Three types of water flowed strongly from these springs, mineral, sulphur, and freestone.

Preceding the Civil War the area was a famous watering place. Into the 20th century it continued to be a gathering place for the sick and invalid who sought cure through its mineral water. Later, social life became more of an attraction than its healing waters. By 1917 there were two hotels, a skating rink, and two pavilions.

The nationally famous Methodist evangelist Lorenzo Dow spoke to large crowds under these trees in 1802 and 1803. On February 22, 1803, the subject of his sermon was The Trinity where he spoke using three large tree branches as an illustration. On March 1, 1918, the site was purchased by the Pentecostal Benevolent Association consisting of G. O. Gaines, Perry Sexton, Hugh Bowling, Josiah Allen, John W. Jordan, and Joseph C. Sorrow. It became the home of Franklin Springs Institute, now Emmanuel College.

(Located on US 29 next to city hall. GHM 059-9, 1981.)

LAVONIA

BLUE STAR MEMORIAL HIGHWAY

A tribute to the Armed Forces that have defended the United States of America

Sponsored by The Garden Club of Georgia, Inc. in cooperation with Department of Transportation of Georgia and Toccoa Garden Club of Toccoa, Georgia

(Located on I-85 southbound at the Georgia Welcome Center, just inside GA/SC State Line. GCG 059-99, 1980.)

POPLAR SPRINGS BAPTIST CHURCH

Established in 1805, Poplar Springs Baptist Church, "Mother Church" of the Tugalo Baptist Assn., began in May of that year. Some of the first members were Joseph Chandler, Thomas Wilkins, John Nail, John Mullins, and James Jackson. John Cleveland, Thomas Gilbert, Francis Calloway, Jr., were early pastors. Many landowners and slaves were members. The slave cemetery is to the right of the church on the Yow estate. On Sept. 12, 1818, delegates from 13 churches met here to form the Tugalo Baptist Assn. of the Southern Baptist Convention. The present auditorium was erected in 1873. The educational building was built in 1955.

(From GA 59 and 17, follow GA 59 north 1.1 miles, turn left on GA 328 (road to Tugaloo State Park) and fol-

COURTESY, GEORGIA DEPARTMENT OF ARCHIVES AND HISTORY

DR. STEWART D. BROWN, SR. (1881–1952)

low for 4.7 miles to church and marker. GHM 059-8, 1957.)

ROYSTON

DR. STEWART D. BROWN, SR.

Dr. Brown (1881–1952), Royston native, after years of the best training, returned home to practice surgery, bringing modern techniques and ingenious methods. He served his townspeople unfailingly for 40 years, performing 35,000 operations. With no hospital facilities, he pioneered, traveling from house to house, accompanied by his trained help, for 14 years. His territory stretched to seventy-five miles or more. He then opened a small hospital of his own, soon outgrown. Also active in educational and civic affairs he rendered a lasting service to his home town.

(Located on US 29 near Cobb Street. GHM 059-2, 1957.)

GILMER COUNTY

Named in honor of George Rockingham Gilmer (1780–1859), U.S. congressman and governor of Georgia. County Seat: Ellijay.

ELLIJAY

GILMER COUNTY

Gilmer County was created by Act of Dec. 3, 1832 out of Cherokee. Originally, it contained parts of Fannin, Dawson and Pickens Counties. The county was named for George Rockingham Gilmer (1790–1859), who served with distinction as a soldier, lawyer, legislator, Congressman and twice as Governor of Georgia, 1829–1831 and 1837–1839. First officers, commissioned March 9, 1833, were: Levi A. Hufsteller, Sheriff; Thomas M. Burnett, Clerk Superior Court; Henry K. Quillian, Clerk Inferior Court. Officers commissioned July 10, 1833 were Thomas Gutterry, Coroner, and Benjamin M. Griffith, Surveyor.

(Located on Dalton Street on the courthouse lawn. GHM 061-4, 1956.)

OAKLAND ACADEMY

The educational center for this section for years, Oakland Academy was established in 1867, following the War Between the States, by Nathan T. Tabor and John E. Robeson, first teacher. Originally a private school, it was operated for many years as a

COURTESY, ATLANTA HISTORICAL SOCIETY

GEORGE GILMER (1790–1859)

church school by the ME Church (South). Students attended the academy from this and surrounding counties. In 1920, when the private school was discontinued, the property was deeded to Gilmer County for a county school. Early teachers included John B. Robeson, W. F. Cruselle, Mary Lewis, Rev. Walter Dillard, Emma Tabor, Harriet E. Tabor, Mary Kirby and John S. Hudson.

(Located on GA 52, 2.2 miles east of Ellijay, GHM 061-2, 1957.)

CARTECAY METHODIST CHURCH

This church, Cartecay Methodist (South), was organized and a building erected in August 1834 on the property of Lewis D. Ellington. The first preacher was William Ellington, ordained in 1805 by Bishop Asbury. The first Sunday School was organized

April 20, 1851 and has operated continuously.

The present building, erected 1859, remains, in style and arrangement, as originally built. During the War Between the States, the building was guarded at night by groups of men to protect it from Union sympathizers who roamed the country-side.

Among the early preachers were: Rev. Bethel Quillian, Rev. John B. Robeson, Rev. A. J. Hughes, Rev. A. J. Hutchinson, Rev. C. M. Ledbetter, Rev. John W. Quillian, Rev. M. L. Underwood, Rev. C. A. Jamison, Dr. John Watkins, Rev. W. O. Butler, Rev. A. D. Echols, Rev. Walter B. Dillard, Rev. R.B.O. England, Rev. G. W. Griner, Rev. W. L. Singleton, Rev. J. N. Myers, Rev. W. C. Hunnicutt, Rev. John B. Pettit. As a young man, Bishop Warren Candler preached here.

(Located on GA 52, 3 miles east of Ellijay, GHM 061-5, 1957.)

EBENEZER BAPTIST CHURCH

This church was established August 24, 1839, by 7 people (Samuel B. West, his wife, Nancy; Jacob Bearden, his wife, Winey; Wm. Kimzey, his wife, Rebecca; John Pettit), while some Indians remained in this area. First officers were: Able Miles, pastor; J. D. Chastain, clerk; Robert Kincaid, treasurer; Samuel B. West, deacon. Attendance was stressed. At each service the clerk called the roll and any absence was checked carefully for cause. Among early pastors were Able Miles, Samuel B. West, William Kimzey, J. D. Chastain, James Adams,

Jacob Cantrell, D. Blythe, and R. Jordan.

(Located on GA 52, 9.7 miles east of Ellijay, GHM 061-3, 1957.)

GORDON COUNTY

Named in honor of William Washington Gordon (1796–1842), attorney, West Point graduate and first president of the Central Georgia Railroad. County Seat: Calhoun.

CALHOUN

GORDON COUNTY

This county was named for William Washington Gordon of Savannah (1796–1842). The first Georgian to graduate at West Point, he entered the practice of law and was a pioneer in the railroad field in this State.

He was the founder and first President of the Central Railroad and Banking Company, now the Central of Georgia System.

Gordon County was created by an act of the Georgia Legislature, February 13, 1850. Area 375 square miles. 1950 population 18,957.

(Located at North Wall and North Court Streets, on the courthouse lawn. GHM 064-14 A, 1953.)

CALHOUN, GA.
MAY 16, 1864

Gen. J. E. Johnston's three Corps (C), after 2 days of battle at Resaca – outflanked by superior Federal forces – withdrew S.

Hood's Corps marched by a road 1 mile E., Polk's & Hardee's on direct road to Calhoun – Polk continued to Adairsville.

Hardee's Corps shifted to the S.W. where, on the banks of Oothcaloga Creek, Bate's, Walker's & Cleburne's divisions in a rear guard action, delayed the advance of McPherson's Army of the Tennessee (F) for 24 hours to secure the passage of the wagon trains.

(Located on North Wall Street in front of City Hall. GHM 064-16, 1953.)

RICHARD PETERS'
PLANTATION

May 16, 1864 Williams' 1st & Geary's 2d divs., 20th A.C. (F) crossed the Coosawattee at McClure's Ferry near Pine Chapel, & night of the 17th, reached this cross-roads – Buschbeck's brigade of Geary's div. camping on the Peters plantation.

These troops, together with the 4th & 14th Corps (F) on the Atlanta road 1 mile W., were of the Army of the Cumberland & center of Sherman's advance S. from two days of battle at Resaca.

THE CHEROKEE PHŒNIX

The 4th & 14th Corps marched to Kingston; the 20th, to Cassville.

(Located at Plantation and East Belmont Drives. GHM 064-25, 1953.)

BLUE STAR MEMORIAL HIGHWAY

A Tribute to the Armed Forces that have defended the United States of America.

Sponsored by The Garden Club of Georgia, Inc. in cooperation with the Department of Transportation of Georgia and the Hillhouse and Sequoyah Garden Clubs, Calhoun, Georgia.

(Located on I–75 off exit #128 in the northbound rest area. GCG 064-99.)

CHEROKEE NATION

During the 1800's, northern Georgia was heart of the sovereign, indepen-

COURTESY, NEW ECHOTA HISTORIC SITE

THE OFFICE OF THE CHEROKEE PHŒNIX

dent Cherokee Indian Nation. By this time the Cherokees were the most progressive Indian Tribe in North America. In 1821, they became the first American Indians with a written form of their native language, invented by Sequoyah, an uneducated Cherokee.

New Echota, the Cherokee national capital, was located 10 miles north. There a constitutional government of executive, legislative, and judicial branches ruled the Nation. Once the largest town in the area, New Echota consisted of houses, stores, taverns, a Council house, Supreme Courthouse, and a printing office which published a national bilingual newspaper, the CHEROKEE PHOENIX.

Most of the 17,000 Cherokees were farmers and lived in small log cabins but some grew very wealthy and owned great plantations such as the Vann House, located 27 miles north.

In 1838, at gunpoint, the Cherokees were rounded up and imprisoned by state and federal armies. Later that year they were forced to what is now Oklahoma. Four thousand Cherokees died on the terrible march west known as the "Trail of Tears."

(Located on I–75 off exit #128 in the northbound rest area. GHM 064-32, 1983.)

OOTHCALOGA MISSION

The two-story portion of this house was the Oothcaloga Moravian Mission Station, serving this region of the Cherokee Nation from 1822 until 1833. John Gambold, whose grave lies 100 yards east, was first missionary here.

Built in 1821 by Joseph Crutchfield, and sold to the Moravians in 1822, this house was an active church and educational center for Cherokee adults and children. Gambold died Nov. 9, 1827. He was followed by J. R. Schmidt (1827–28), Franz Eder (1828–29), and Henry G. Clauder (1828–38). Clauder served Moravian Cherokees for 6 years after white people occupied this building in 1833, following the Georgia Land Lottery of 1832.

(From I–75, follow GA 53 east 0.3 mile, turn south on Belwood Road and follow 1.7 miles to marker. GHM 064-28, 1959.)

MORAVIAN MISSION

1.5 miles east is the old Oothcaloga Mission Station, operated by the Moravian Church 1822–1833 as a center of education and religious instruction for the Cherokee Indians.

John Gambold, first missionary here, taught many Indian children and built up an active Cherokee church congregation.

In 1832 Georgia distributed Cherokee lands by lottery; and by 1833 two white families had moved into the Oothcaloga Mission House.

(Located on US 41, 4 miles south of Calhoun. GHM 064-27, 1959.) ♦ ★

OOTHCALOGA VALLEY

During the advance of Sherman's forces So. from Resaca, May 16–17, the (F) 4th, followed by the 14th corps, marched by this and nearby roads, pursuing Johnston's forces (C) which had evacuated Resaca the night before. Newton's Div., leading 4th Corps (F), was aligned across the road, his right on hill to the West.

A spirited rear-guard action followed, in which Francis T. Sherman's Brigade assaulted detachments of Cheatham's Div. (C), at the Saxon house, near the County Line.

(Located on US 41/GA 3, 1.1 miles from the Bartow/Gordon County line. GHM 064-1, 1953.) ♦ ★

SITE OF THE
ROBT. C. SAXON HOUSE

Otherwise known as the Octagon or Gravel house – an eight-sided stone residence, built in 1856 on knoll E.

May 17, 1864, a rear-guard action between Cheatham's Div., Hardee's A.C. (C) and Newton's 2d Div., 4th A.C. (F) was fought along this road.

8 Tenn. Regts. of Wright's, Maney's & Vaughan's (C) brigades posted here, defended it during several hours of musketry & artillery fire, withdrawing at midnight. Burned by 73d Illinois regt. (F) next day.

(Located on US 41/GA 3 at Miller Ferry Road, 0.2 mile from the Bartow/Gordon County line. GHM 064-2, 1953.) ♦ ★

JOHNSTON'S REAR GUARD
STOPS McPHERSON

May 16, 1864. Walker's div. of Hardee's A.C. (C), having delayed McPherson's troops (15th & 16th A.C.) (F) at Lay's Ferry (3.25 mi. N.W.) the day before, was joined here by 2 divisions – Bate's and Cleburne's(C).

Deploying on both sides of Oothcaloga Creek, the left of the line covering the road to Adairsville, Hardee – facing N. & W. – held McPherson's forces throughout the day to enable the Confederate wagon trains to proceed to Adairsville.

This, the Battle of Rome Cross Roads, was an episode of the Atlanta Campaign.

(Located on GA 53 Spur at Oothcaloga Creek, west of the city. GHM 064-18, 1953.)

BATTLE OF
ROME CROSS ROADS

May 16, 1864. McPherson's two A.C. (15 & 16) (F), moving S. from Lay's Ferry (Oostanaula River), enroute to Kingston, were delayed 24 hrs. by Hardee's A.C. (C) in an action here.

Hardee's objective was to insure safety of his wagon-trains. This accomplished, he retreated S. on the road this side of Oothcaloga Creek toward Adairsville.

May 17. The Federal 15th & 16th A.C. resumed march toward Kingston, via the Rome Road to McGuire's, & Adairsville.

(Located on GA 53 Spur at Terrell Farm Road, west of Oothcaloga Creek and west of Calhoun. GHM 064-20, 1953.)

BATTLE OF LAY'S FERRY

May 14, 1864. A contingent from Sweeny's (2d) div., 16th A.C. (F) made a crossing here in pontoon boats, but on a rumor of Confederate crossings upstream, it withdrew.

May 15. The division, supported by Welker's Artillery (F), crossed in force & deployed to meet the immediate attack by Maj. Gen. W. H. T. Walker's div., Hardee's A.C. (C), in the area between the George W. Frix house & the Oostanaula River.

This Federal move on the Confederate left & rear forced Johnston (C) to evacuate his lines at Resaca.

(From GA 156 and GA 136 Conn, follow GA 156 west 1.2 miles, turn right by the Mt. Zion Church onto Herrington Bend Road. Travel (bearing right at the fork) 1.7 miles to marker. GHM 064-19, 1953.)

LAY'S FERRY

Lay's or Tanner's Ferry, Oostanaula River, was 1.5 mi. S.W. of this point – access road thereto no longer existing.

May 14, 1864, Sweeny's (2d) div. 16th A.C. (F) moved to Lay's Ferry & effected crossing by one brigade but a false rumor of Confederate crossings

above, caused the Federals to withdraw to this side.

May 15, Sweeny's div. made the crossing. He was at once assailed by Walker's div. of Hardee's Corps (C) – an affair known as the battle of Lay's Ferry. This move on Johnston's left rear caused him to abandon position at Resaca and retreat South.

(Located at GA 136 Spur/Sugar Valley Road and Hall Memorial Road, 2.0 miles north of the Oostanaula River. GHM 064-12, 1960.)

SNAKE CREEK GAP

May 8, 1864. McPherson's 15th & 16th Corps (F) seized Snake Creek Gap. On the 9th, attempting to destroy the R. R. at Resaca (defended by Cantey's Div. of Polk's Corps) (C), McPherson was forced to withdraw to the mouth of the gap where he intrenched.

This was the beginning of Sherman's (F) move to outflank Johnston's forces (C) at Dalton.

May 13–14, Sherman moved the 14th, 20th, & 23d Corps (F) through the gap & together with McPherson's troops, advanced toward Resaca – the 4th Corps (F) marching due S. from Dalton. On the 14th began the two-day battle of Resaca.

(Located at GA 136 and GA 136 Spur, 1.1 miles inside the Gordon/Walker County Line. GHM 064-8, 1953.)

NEW ECHOTA FERRY

The head of the Oostanaula River is formed 200 yards northeast by the confluence of the Coosawattee and the Conasauga Rivers. The passage of travelers and freight along the Tennessee Road was served at this point by a ferry operated by the Cherokee Indians, principally by Alexander McCoy from 1819 through 1835.

(Located east of Calhoun off GA 225 at the New Echota Historic Site. GHM 064-31, 1962.)

NEW ECHOTA
Cherokee National Capital

The sprawling town of New Town which had stood here since 1819 was designated the seat of government for the new Cherokee Nation in a legislative act of 1825 and it was renamed New Echota for a former principal town in Tennessee. In its short history New Echota was the site of the first Indian language newspaper office, a court case which carried to the U.S. Supreme Court, one of the earliest experiments in national self-government for an Indian tribe, the signing of a treaty which relinquished Cherokee claims to lands east of the Mississippi, and the assembly of Indians for the removal west.

(Located east of Calhoun off GA 225 at the New Echota Historic Site. GHM 064-29, 1962.)

TRAIL OF TEARS

The New Echota Treaty of 1835 relinquished Cherokee Indian claims to lands east of the Mississippi River. The majority of the Cherokee people considered the treaty fraudulent and refused to leave their homelands in Georgia, Alabama, North Carolina, and Tennessee. 7,000 Federal and State troops were ordered into the Cherokee Nation to forcibly evict the Indians. On May 26, 1838, the roundup began. Over 15, 000 Cherokees were forced from their homes at gunpoint and imprisoned in stockades until removal to the west could take place. 2,700 left by boat in June 1838, but, due to many deaths and sickness, removal was suspended until cooler weather. Most of the remaining 13,000 Cherokees left by wagon, horseback, or on foot during October and November, 1838, on an 800 mile route through Tennessee, Kentucky, Illinois, Missouri, and Arkansas. They arrived in what is now eastern Oklahoma during January, February, and March, 1839. Disease, exposure, and starvation may have claimed as many as 4,000 Cherokee lives during the course of capture, imprisonment, and removal. The ordeal has become known as the Trail of Tears.

(Located east of Calhoun off GA 225 at the New Echota Historic Site. GHM 064-33, 1989.)

NEW ECHOTA CEMETERY

On the hilltop, 100 yards to the south, is the cemetery for the village of New Echota. The marked graves are those of Pathkiller, Principal Chief of the

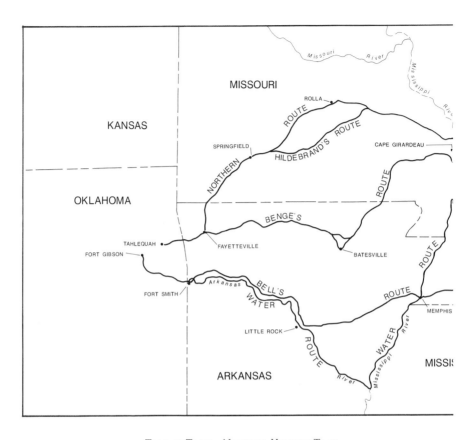

TRAIL OF TEARS – NATIONAL HISTORIC TRAIL

Cherokee Nation until his death in 1827 and a colonel in Morgan's regiment in the War of 1812, and Harriet Gold Boudinot, born in Connecticut in 1805, wife of Elias Boudinot, editor of the Cherokee Phoenix. One of the unmarked graves is that of Jerusha Worcester, infant daughter of Samuel and Ann Worcester, the mission family at New Echota.

(Located east of Calhoun off GA 225. Near the New Echota Historic Site, follow New Town Church Road 0.8 mile to marker. GHM 064-30, 1962.)

HARLAN'S CROSS ROADS

Maj. Gen. John M. Schofield's Headquarters
May 16, 1864

Hovey's 1st & Judah's 2d divs. of Schofield's 23d A.C. (F), enroute from Resaca battlefield, crossed the Conasauga River at Fite's Fy. intending to pass the Coosawattee at McClure's Ferry, 1.25 mi. east of here.

But the 20th A.C. (F) diverted from Newtown ferry by Gen. Hooker got ahead of Schofield & crossed at

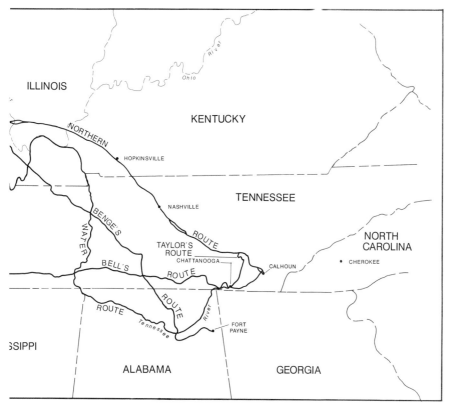

ILLINOIS

KENTUCKY

HOPKINSVILLE

NORTHERN

BENGE'S

WATER

NASHVILLE

TENNESSEE

TAYLOR'S ROUTE

ROUTE

CHATTANOOGA

BELL'S

ROUTE

CALHOUN

NORTH CAROLINA

CHEROKEE

ROUTE

ROUTE

Tennessee

River

FORT PAYNE

SSIPPI

ALABAMA

GEORGIA

UNITED STATES DEPARTMENT OF THE INTERIOR, NATIONAL PARK SERVICE

McClure's. This forced Schofield's 2 divs. 2 mi. S.E. to Field's Fy.

Cox's (3d) div. (F) crossed the Conasauga near Tilton, & via Holley, marched to Field's Fy.

(From New Echota, travel 3.6 miles on GA 225 east to junction with West Pine Chapel Road. GHM 064-21, 1953.)

McCLURE'S FERRY

May 16, 1864. Maj. Gen. Joseph Hooker (20th A.C.) (F) moving E.

from Resaca, with orders to cross at Newtown Fy., elected to usurp the crossing at McClure's, thereby forcing Schofield's 23d A.C. (F) to proceed E. to Field's Mill & Ferry.

Williams' (1st) & Geary's (2d) divs. (F) crossed at night on a temporary bridge. To hasten progress, Butterfield's (3d) div. (F) moved on to Field's – further complicating affairs by getting there ahead of Schofield.

The 23d A.C., with Stoneman's & McCook's Cavalry, constituted the left wing of Sherman's advance S. from Resaca.

(From New Echota, travel 3.6 miles on GA 225 east, turn right on West Pine Chapel Road for 1 mile to marker across from Pine Chapel Church. GHM 064-22, 1953.)

FIELD'S MILL & FERRY

May 16, 1864. Butterfield's (3d) div., 20th A.C. (F) instead of crossing at McClure's Ferry 2 mi. down stream, sought to gain time by moving to Field's – reaching here 11 p.m. Not until noon of the 17th was it across.

Schofield, prevented from crossing his corps (23d) (F) at McClure's, moved the 1st & 2d divs. to Field's, arriving here early the 17th – as did Cox's (3d) div., which had marched via Tilton & Holley.

With Butterfield at Field's, Schofield's A.C. (the left wing of Sherman's advance from Resaca) was held up 24 hours because of the erratic moves of the 20th corps.

(From New Echota travel 3.6 miles on GA 225 east, turn right on West Pine Chapel Road for 1 mile. Continue on Owens Gin Road for 2.4 miles to marker. GHM 064-23, 1959.)

BIG SPRING

May 17,1864: Butterfield's (3d) div., 20th A.C. (F), marched this way from Field's Mill, Coosawattee River, enroute to Kingston & camped at the Smith farm 2½ miles N. of Mosteller's Mills.

May 18: Schofield's 23d A.C. (F), marching from Field's, reached vicinity at 2 A.M. Cox's 3d div. camped at this cross-roads until 5 A. M., & via Sonora, moved to Mosteller's. Hovey's 1st & Judah's 2d divs. camped at Big Spring (at other end of Dew's Lake) & by evening reached Mosteller's.

These troops formed the left flank of Federal forces enroute to Etowah River.

(From GA 156 at Redbud take Cash Road south 3.2 miles, turn right 0.1 mile to marker. **Or**, from Sonoraville, take Cash Road north 3.1 miles, turn left 0.1 mile to marker. GHM 064-24, 1953.)

RESACA

BATTLE OF RESACA

May 13,1864. McPherson's 15th & 16th A.C. (F), moving from Snake Creek Gap, reached this cross-roads where his forces were deployed for advance toward Camp Cr.

Gen. Judson Kilpatrick's Cav. Div. (F) led advance; during a sharp engagement he was wounded by skirmishers of Polk's Corps (C).

Night found the 20th, 14th & 23d Corps (F) N. on Dalton–Calhoun road, & by noon May 14th, Federal forces W. of Resaca were deployed on ridges parallel to & overlooking Camp Creek. The battle began 2.5 mi. N. by attacks on left of Hood's & right of Hardee's lines (C).

(Located at Hall Memorial and Hall Roads, just off GA 136. GHM 064-9, 1953.)

BATTLE OF RESACA

May 13, 1864. The 15th & 16th A.C. (F) deployed astride road on ridges W. of those next to & this side of Camp Creek, where Polk's Corps (C) was posted.

May 14: The 15th & 16th A.C. drove Polk's troops across creek from this ridge and occupied it. Polk established a line on a chain of hills just E. of creek.

5:30 pm: the 15th & Veatch's (4th) Div. 16th A.C. (F) moved across creek & carried Polk's position, holding it against repeated attempts to regain it. Polk withdrew E. to a line near the Dalton–Resaca road (U.S. Highway 41).

(Located west of Resaca at GA 136 and Fain Brown Road. GHM 064-13, 1953.)

POLK'S LINE WITHDRAWN TO RESACA

May 14, 1864 after being driven from hills W. of Camp Creek by troops of the 15th & 16th Corps (F), Polk's A.C. (C) was aligned on the E. side of the creek, its center & left posted on a chain of hills S. of this road & overlooking the creek – its extreme left on the Oostanaula River.

5:30 P.M., the Federals crossed the creek & carried Polk's line, forcing it

E. to a position near U.S. Highway 41. Polk's repeated & unavailing attempts to recover his line prolonged the battle into the night.

(Located on GA 136 just west of junction with I–75/Exit 133. GHM 064-14-2, 1953.)

BATTLE OF RESACA

May 16, 1864. Johnston's forces (C) withdrew from Resaca via pontoon, R.R. & trestle bridges over the Oostanaula River.

The 4th & two divs. of the 14th Corps (F) rebuilt two bridges which had been burned & followed the retreating Confederates S., along R.R. and highway. Davis' (2d) Div., 14th A.C. (F) moved W. of R. to Rome.

The 20th & two divs. of 23d A.C. (F) moved E. to Fites Ferry, Conasauga R., enroute to Coosawattee R. crossings – McClure's Ferry & the one at Fields Mill. Army of the Tenn. (F) crossed Oostanaula R. at Lay's Ferry near Snake Cr., 6 mi. S.W.

(Located on US 41 at GA 136. GHM 064-11, 1953.)

BATTLE OF RESACA
MAY 14, 1864

Judah's (2d) Div., 23d A.C., & part of the 14th A.C. (F) moved from high bluff W. of Camp Creek to valley floor & attempted to carry Confederate works E. of the stream. Met by blazing musketry & artillery fire from Hindman's and Bate's Divs. (C), posted on the ridge E., the Federals sought refuge in stream-bed & made no further progress.

This tragic & futile episode is unique in the annals of the Atlanta Campaign.

(Located on US 41/GA 3 at Confederate Cemetery Road. GHM 064-7, 1953.) ♦ ★

ATLANTA CAMPAIGN
RESACA
MAY 13–15, 1864

In this vicinity the Confederate lines North and West of Resaca held firm against Federal attack. Sherman then executed a successful flank movement to the West and South around Johnston's position thus making the Confederate line untenable and compelling the troops of the Confederacy to move deeper into Georgia.

(Located on US 41 at Confederate Cemetery Road. NPS 064-98.)

CONFEDERATE CEMETERY RESACA

Established shortly after the war by Miss Mary J. Green & Associates for burial of Confederate soldiers who fell at the Battle of Resaca.

May 14, 1864, Maj. Gen. A.P. Stewart's Div., Hood's A.C. (rt. of Johnston's line) (C), posted 600 yds. N.E., attacked Stanley's Div. 4th A.C. (F) near Nance's Spring and drove it N.W. to Old Union Ch. above the County Line.

May 15. Stewart again attacked the Federals posted 1/4 mi. S. of the County Line (near Scale's house) but failed to dislodge Williams' Div. 20th Corps(F).

(Located off US 41, 0.4 mile down Confederate Cemetery Road in the Confederate Cemetery. GHM 064-15, 1953.)

BATTLE OF RESACA

Hood's line (C), beginning E. at State R.R., ran W. to point atop ridge (S) where Hardee's rt. joined it & together with Polk's Corps (C), the line was prolonged 3 miles S. to the Oostanaula River.

May 13, 1864, Sherman's forces (F) reached the old Dalton–Calhoun rd., W. of here (via Snake Cr. Gap). On 14th, from ridges W. of Camp Creek, 2 assaults were made on Johnston's line (C) – one, 2.5 mi. southward – the other in this vicinity.

In both attacks, the Federals moved across the creek toward ridges on this, the E. side of the valley.

(From US 41 and Confederate Cemetery Road take Rooker Road west 0.4 mile to marker. GHM 064-5, 1952.)

BATTLE OF RESACA
May 14, 1864.

A portion of Hood's A.C. (C), thrust forward to hold ridge in fork of cr., was driven back to hills this side of the valley & N. of the road.

Cox's (3d) Div., 23d A.C. (F) having taken the ridge in creek-fork, was relieved by 4th A.C., which, with 20th A.C. troops (F), moved E seizing the area between the creek & the State R.R. near the Conasauga River.

This movement completed the Federal alignment parallel to the Confederate line N & W of Resaca.

(Located on US 41/GA 3 at Chitwood Road near the Whitfield County Line. GHM 064-6, 1952.)

BATTLE OF RESACA
May 14–15, 1864

0.5 mi. W. is Camp Creek Valley, scene of the 23d Corps (F) assaults on Hood's left & Hardee's right (C), May 14.

On ridge 0.2 mi. W. was the position of Wood's (3d) Div., 4th A.C. & Capt. Wm. Wheeler's 13th New York Battery (F), May 14, 15.

225 yds. E., on wooded ridge is the emplacement of Capt. Max Van Den Corput's Cherokee Battery (C) – 4 twelve-pounders – captured & removed by 2d & 3d Divs. of the 20th A.C. (F) May 15.

(Located at US 41/GA 3 and Chitwood Road near the Whitfield County line. GHM 064-3, 1986.)

BATTLE OF RESACA
May 14–15, 1864

At this point the intrenched line of Gen. John B. Hood's Corps (C) crossed the road – this corps being 1 of

the 3 composing Lt. Gen. J. E. Johnston's Army of the Tennessee.

Line faced N. Hindman's Div. (C) on left extended W. to Camp Creek Valley; Stevenson's Div. (C) was astride the road & the right of Stewart's Div. was E. at State R. R. near Conasauga River.

Hardee's & Polk's Corps (C) were aligned parallel to Camp Creek 0.5 mile W. left of army being on Oostanaula River.

(Located on US 41 near the Whitfield County Line. GHM 064-4, 1953.) ♦ ★

BATTLE OF RESACA
May 14–15, 1864

May 13, 1864. Gen. J. E. Johnston's forces (C) withdrew from Dalton to Resaca, having been outflanked by Federal forces moving via Snake Creek Gap 7 mi. N.W.

Aligned upon hills, N. & W. of here, the Confederates withstood repeated Fed. assaults for two days, May 14 & 15.

Federal forces, having secured a river crossing at Lay's Ferry (near mouth of Snake Creek) 6 mi. S.W., Johnston withdrew S. to Calhoun, May 16. This was the 1st major battle of the campaign which ended with the capture of Atlanta.

(Located on I-75 in the southbound rest area. GHM 064-10, 1953.)

SONORAVILLE

OLD SONORA P.O.
NOW SONORAVILLE

May 18, 1864 Maj. Gen. J.D. Cox's (3d) Div., 23d A.C. (F) marching S. from Field's Mill, Coosawattee River, via Cash, took the direct rd. to Sonora. Moving S. 4 mi., the div. turned W. on the Fairmount–Adairsville rd. to Mosteller's Mills (near Folsom) where it camped that night.

Hovey's & Judah's divisions marched from the Philip's farm (Dew's Lake, near Cash) on the direct road to Mosteller's, where they were joined by Cox's division.

Schofield's 23d Corps (F) was the left flank of Sherman's army moving S. from Resaca, on a wide front, toward Cassville and Kingston.

(Located at GA 53 and Cash Road. GHM 064-26, 1959.)

GREENE COUNTY

Named in honor of Nathanael Greene (1742–1786), a hero of the Revolution. County Seat: Greensboro.

GREENSBORO

GREENE COUNTY

This County, created by Act of the Legislature Feb. 3, 1786, is named for Maj. Gen. Nathanael Greene, the strategist, who ranked second only to Gen. Washington. Born in Rhode Island in 1742, he died at his Georgia plantation in 1786. Seven miles north of Greensboro lies Penfield named for Josiah Penfield of Savannah who started the Fund to establish Mercer Institute there in 1833. The Institute was named for Jesse Mercer, leading Baptist divine of Georgia at that time. It received a Legislative Charter as Mercer University in 1837 and was moved to Macon after the War.

(Located on North Main Street between Greene and Court Streets on the courthouse lawn. GHM 066-1, 1954.)

FIRST COMMISSIONER
OF AGRICULTURE

In 1874, the Georgia Department of Agriculture was established by Act of the Legislature with Thomas P. Janes serving as its first Commissioner, 1874–79.

COURTESY, GEORGIA DEPARTMENT OF ARCHIVES AND HISTORY

NATHANAEL GREEN (1742–1786)

Commissioner Janes, born 1823 in present Taliaferro County, (formerly the eastern part of Greene County), moved to Penfield. There he attended Mercer Institute. In 1842 he entered Columbian College (George Washington Univ.), Washington, D. C., where he received his A. B. degree. Columbian College, Mercer University, and the College of New Jersey (Princeton University) awarded him A.M. degrees. In 1847 he was granted his M.D. degree from the University of the City of New York. A successful farmer and physician he was commis-

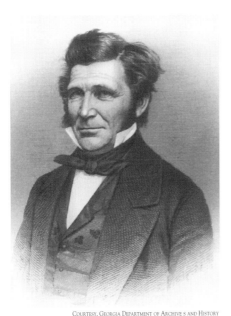

COURTESY, GEORGIA DEPARTMENT OF ARCHIVES AND HISTORY
WILLIAM C. DAWSON (1798–1856)

WILLIAM C. DAWSON
1798 – 1856
STATESMAN – SOLDIER
JURIST – FREEMASON

A native of Greene County, then on Georgia's Indian Frontier, he was educated in the Law and admitted to the Bar in 1818. The remainder of his exemplary life was spent in the public service as Legislator, Captain of Volunteers in the Indian War of 1836 in Florida, Judge of the Ocmulgee Judicial Circuit, Congressman and U.S. Senator from Georgia from 1849–1855.

A member and officer of historic San Marino Lodge No. 34 F.&A.M. Greensboro, GA., first chartered in 1821 and which lodge has had its quarters atop the Greene County Court House here since 1849, Brother Dawson served as a Grand Master of Masons in Georgia from 1843 until his death in Greensboro on 6 May, 1856. Two cities and one county in Georgia are named for him. Also named in his honor are two Masonic Lodges: Dawson No. 68 F.&A.M., Social Circle, GA., and Dawson No. 16, F&AM, at Washington, DC.

One of the most beloved, respected and distinguished Grand Masters in Georgia's long Masonic history his honored remains lie in the city cemetery near this spot. His entire life was a testimonial to his devotion to his fellowman, his country and to the sublime precepts of Freemasonry. His name will always be revered by the Freemasons of Georgia.

Marker placed by the Educational & Historical Commission, Grand Lodge of Georgia. F. & A. M., 1971.

(Located on North Main Street between Greene and Court Streets on the courthouse lawn. GLG 066-98, 1971.)

sioned in 1861 as Assistant Surgeon, 16th Regiment, Georgia Militia.

He died at his home, "Redcliff Farm," near this site, in 1885, and is buried in the family cemetery four miles northeast of this marker.

This marker was erected by the Georgia Department of Agriculture and the Georgia Historical Commission as directed in a resolution passed by the 1961 session of the Georgia General Assembly.

(Located on North Main Street between Greene and Court Streets on the courthouse lawn. GHR 066-99, 1961.)

CARROLL PROCTOR SCRUGGS

GREENE COUNTY "GAOL"

OLD
GREENE COUNTY "GAOL"

The old rock jail in the rear of the Court House is patterned after the bastilles where prisoners were housed and punished a hundred or more years ago. Built of granite about two feet thick, it is two stories in height and has a trap door in the floor of the upper story where condemned prisoners were hanged. An iron bar supported the trap door. When the signal was given the hangman pulled the lever that controlled the bar and the culprit was launched into eternity.

This prison was built about 1807, after the General Presentments of the Greene County Superior Court recommended that a substantial jail be built.

The cells are veritable dungeons without light or ventilation, except for the grated door downstairs and the small, grated windows above. The dungeons in Fort Marion are no more horrible. It was used as a jail until about 1895.

(Located on Greene Street between North Main Street and East Street behind the courthouse. GHM 066-5, 1957.)

BISHOP
GEORGE FOSTER PIERCE
(1811–1884)

Born February 3 in 1811 near Greensboro, George Foster Pierce was converted while at the University in Athens; in 1830 he followed his father, Dr. Lovick Pierce, into the Methodist ministry. He was first assigned twenty-two preaching stations on the Oconee Circuit, later he served pastorates in Augusta, Savannah, Charleston, and Columbus. He may have preached ten thousand times. His life with his family on his farm "Sunshine" near Sparta was idyllic.

He was in 1834 the first president of Wesleyan College, also editor of the "Southern Ladies' Book," then president of Emory (1848–1854). In 1844

COURTESY, SPECIAL COLLECTIONS DEPT., ROBERT W. WOODRUFF LIBRARY, EMORY UNIV.

GEORGE FOSTER PIERCE (1811–1884)

at the New York Conference he defended Bishop Andrew as a slaveholder, and in 1845 at Louisville, Kentucky, he helped organize the Methodist Episcopal Church, South. Elected Bishop in Columbus, Georgia, 1854.

He was without a peer as an orator. As a Methodist Bishop, he suffered with his people the hardships of the Civil War. He died in 1884 in Sparta and is buried there.

(Located at Broad and West Streets in front of the First United Methodist Church. UMC 066-97.)

UNKNOWN CONFEDERATE DEAD

Forty-five unknown Confederate soldiers, "known but to God," are buried in this cemetery. These men died of wounds or disease in the Confederate hospitals in Greensboro, 1863–1865. These hospitals were the Dawson, Bell, Polk, Court House, College and Factory. Federal troops who occupied this town for several hours on Sunday, November 20, 1864, did not molest the hospitals though they foraged the countryside and burned a number of homes, mills and business establishments.

(Located out East Street on Memorial Drive at the cemetery. GHM 066-4, 1955.)

"OLD MERCER"

Actuated by a legacy from Josiah Penfield, Mercer University was founded here in 1833 as Mercer Institute. After

PENFIELD CHAPEL, BUILT IN 1846

considering several locations, the Trustees moved the institution to Macon in 1871 and, in 1880, transferred all holdings in Penfield to the Georgia Baptist Association, except the venerable Penfield Cemetery where Jesse Mercer, Billington M. Sanders, Mrs. Sanders, and other notable Mercerians are buried. The chapel was given to the Penfield Baptist Church, founded in 1839 with Rev. Adiel Sherwood as pastor. The academy building became the Penfield public school building.

(From US 278, follow East Street 7.6 miles to Old Mercer site. Marker is 0.1 mile off road near the chapel. GHM 066-13, 1959.)

THE BURNING OF GREENSBOROUGH

During the early years of its settlement, Greensborough and Greene County suffered greatly from depredations committed by Indians who occupied the West bank of the Oconee River about eight miles from here. Most tragic of these was the destruction of Greensborough and the murder of its inhabitants in 1787.

At the time the town consisted of 20 cabins, a log court house and a fort for protection against hostile Indians. The Treaty of Shoulderbone Creek, entered into in November, 1786, by the State of Georgia and the Creek Indians, caused great dissatisfaction among the Indians. Hostilities increased, and in the summer of 1787 Indians crossed the Oconee River, swooped down upon Greensborough, murdered many of its citizens and burned every house. Later, some of the guilty Indians were captured and turned over to the authorities, who placed them in jail. There is no further record of the results of the capture.

(Located on Main Street just off Broad Street in front of the post office. GHM 066-12, 1958.)

STAGECOACH ROAD

About three miles from here ran the old stagecoach road from Augusta, Petersburg, Washington and Greensboro to Park's Mill, where a toll bridge crossed the Oconee. After crossing the river the highway diverged – the left fork going to Eatonton, Milledgeville, Macon, Knoxville, Talbotton and Columbus. The right fork led to Madison, Monticello, Indian Springs, Jackson, Griffin, Greenville, LaGrange, West Point. This was known as the "Seven Islands Road" because it passed the seven islands in the Ocmulgee River. Park's Mill was an important point from the earliest settlement of Greene County. Many prominent pioneer settlers lived nearby.

(Located on GA 44 near the junction with I–20. GHM 066-8, 1957.) ♦ ★

LIBERTY CHAPEL

LIBERTY CHAPEL

About 1786, John Bush built a brush arbor as a community center for camp meetings at what was then called "Crackers Neck." From this grew Liberty Chapel, "Cradle of Methodism" for this section. In 1797, Rev. James Jenkins, leader in the early days of Methodism and, at that time, on the Washington Circuit including Greene, Taliaferro, Wilkes, Lincoln, Elbert, Hart, Franklin, Madison, and Oglethorpe Counties, preached here and reported in his "Journal" that, after a "fiery exhortation," a man in uniform came down the aisle and fell at his feet, crying for pardon. Others followed and, according to Rev. Jenkins, then, at Liberty Chapel, began the Methodist custom of "going to the altar." The meeting became so noisy, he continued, that it was a wonder the horses did not take fright.

Most of the great men of early Methodism were identified with this church. Bishop Francis Asbury preached here several times and, in 1808 when the South Carolina Conference met here, he and Bishop William McKendree attended. At Liberty Chapel, Rev. Lovick Pierce was ordained an elder and Bishop William Capers was admitted as a preacher on trial.

(From East Broad Street, follow South Walnut Street/Verzey Road 6.9 miles. Turn right on Liberty Church Road and follow 4 miles to marker and church. GHM 066-11, 1958.)

FORT MATHEWS

About two miles South, in the fork of the Appalachee and Oconee Rivers, stood Fort Mathews, built in 1793. From this Fort, Thomas Houghton observed the activities of General Elijah Clark and his land hungry followers as they built forts and fortifications for the protection of Clark's "TRANS-OCONEE REPUBLIC." From here Houghton wrote to Governor George Mathews the report that led to the arrest of General Clark and the downfall of his dream of an independent republic established on land not yet ceded by the Creek Indians.

(Located on US 278, 10.8 miles west of junction with GA 15, at the Apalachee River. GHM 066-7, 1957.)

WATSON SPRINGS

Douglas Watson, credited with being the first white man to discover Indian Springs and a scout for the United States government, purchased this property from Jesse Sanders in 1786. The water of this spring was thought to have the same curative power as that at Indian Springs. On the property were several log houses, probably clustered together for protection from the Indians, and nearby was a ferry

COURTESY, SPECIAL COLLECTIONS DEPT., ROBERT W. WOODRUFF LIBRARY, EMORY UNIV.

REVEREND LOVICK PIERCE (1785–1879)

over the Oconee River. The Watson property was donated by Colonel James Dala Watson, U.S.A. retired, for the study of forestry in Georgia.

(Located on GA 15, 11.1 miles north of junction with US 278. GHM 066-3, 1955.)

GOVERNOR PETER EARLY

Near here, on a bluff overlooking the river, stood the home of Governor Peter Early, one of Georgia's great men. Born in Virginia, June 30, 1773, a graduate of Princeton, he was a lawyer, judge, State Senator, Congressman, Governor during the difficult years 1813–1815, and trustee of the University of Georgia. He died August 15, 1817 and was buried here. In December, 1914, his remains were reinterred in Greensboro with fitting ceremonies. Early County is named for him.

Near here, also, stood Fort Clarke, erected for the protection of the early settlers against Indian raids.

(Located on GA 15, 12.5 miles north of junction with US 278. GHM 066-6, 1986.)

UNION POINT

SITE OF WAYSIDE HOME

Here in 1862–1864 was located the Wayside Home, operated by 14 gallant Confederate women of this city. More than one million meals were served to Confederate soldiers, sailors and marines, passing through this town. More than ten thousand Confederates registered in a roster kept here. Weary, sick and wounded men of the South were made to feel at home here, to rest and receive aid. General James Longstreet and part of the First Corps, Army of Northern Virginia passed through here in September of 1863, (en route) to bloody Chickamauga.

(Located on US 278/GA 77 near the junction with GA 44. GHM 066-2, 1955.)

BETHANY PRESBYTERIAN CHUCH

BETHANY PRESBYTERIAN CHURCH

Organized in 1786, Bethany Presbyterian Church was the first church in Greene County. Dr. Francis Cummins, Dr. Francis Goulding, and other great ministers preached here. In 1886, Dr. James Woodrow was tried for heresy here in the first "monkey trial" of record. Around this church grew the first white settlement, while this was Washington County. Here was Dr. Moses Waddell's first school, and the homes of William Greer, William Daniel, the Baldwins, Loves, Kings, and other pioneer families. It was the inspiration for Thomas E. Watson's "Bethany," and around it William H. Sparks' "Memories of Fifty Years" begins.

(From US 278/GA 77, follow GA 77 south 2.2 miles, turn left and follow road for 3.9 miles to marker and church. GHM 066-10, 1957.)

BETHESDA BAPTIST CHURCH

When Bethesda Baptist Church was organized in 1785, it was known as Whatley's Mill Church, and was in Wilkes County before it was added to Greene in 1802. When the present building was erected in 1818, the name was changed to Bethesda. Jesse Mercer was pastor for a number of years and here he ordained Adiel Sherwood as minister of the Gospel. This splendid brick structure indicates that this section was populous and wealthy. In the early days of the church, worshippers, fearful of attack

BETHESDA BAPTIST CHURCH

by the Indians, carried their guns to services.

(From GA 44 and GA 77, follow GA 44 east 4.7 miles. Turn left on Bethesda Church Road and travel 1 mile to marker and church. GHM 066-9, 1957.)

HABERSHAM COUNTY

Named in honor of Major Joseph Habersham (1724–1790) of Savannah, who was a patriot of the Revolution, served as a Postmaster General and was speaker of the General Assembly of Georgia in 1785. County Seat: Clarkesville.

CLARKESVILLE

HABERSHAM COUNTY

Habersham County was created by Acts of the Legislature, Dec. 15, 1818, and named for Joseph Habersham (1751–1815), of Savannah, who had a summer home near Clarkesville. He served in the Revolution as a Lieut. Col. in the Ga. Continental line; was twice Speaker of the General Assembly; Mayor of Savannah, 1792–93; and Postmaster General of the United States, 1795–1801.

The first Habersham County officers sworn in after the County was created were Miles Davis, Clerk of the Superior Court; Wm. B. Wofford, Sheriff; Joseph Dobson, Clerk of the Inferior Court; Wm. Steedly, Coroner; William Wofford, Sr., Surveyor. Benjamin Cleveland, Absalom Holcombe and James R. Wyly were sworn in as Members of the Inferior Court, Feb. 25, 1819, and Holcombe was succeeded by Arthur Alexander on April 20, 1819.

James Allen, Benjamin Chastain, Absalom Holcombe, John Kiser, Thomas Brock, James O'Neal, Joseph

Whitehead and John Bryan were sworn in as Justices of the Peace in 1821.

Cicero H. Sutton was the first Ordinary of Habersham County.

Habersham County is noted for its healthful climate and beautiful scenery, its peaches and apples, and its fine schools.

(Located on US 441/GA 115 on the courthouse lawn. GHM 068-6, 1955.)

GRACE PROTESTANT EPISCOPAL CHURCH

GRACE PROTESTANT EPISCOPAL CHURCH

The first Episcopal service in Clarkesville was held Oct. 28, 1838, by the Rev. Mr. Ezra B. Kellogg, sent from N.Y. to the Diocese of Georgia as a missionary to this section. On Dec. 12, 1838, at his home, Grace Church was organized for three local Episcopal families and the many coastal families of the denomination who spent their summers here. On April 15, 1839, this, the sixth, Episcopal Church in the State, was admitted to the Diocese. On June 7, 1839, this square acre lot was purchased from James Brannon for $100. For the first year services were held in the Methodist Church and Clarkesville Academy.

In 1841, the Rev. J. B. Gallagher succeeded as Rector. Under his guidance, this building, begun in 1839, was completed in 1842. It was consecrated Oct. 6, 1842 by the Rt. Rev. Stephen Elliott, Jr., (first) Bishop of Georgia, who reported it as "a very neat wooden building, with tower and bell, pret-

tily located, and an ornament to the village."

Among prominent early members were: Richard W. Habersham, Sr., John R. Mathews, Wardens; Alexander Erwin, Benjamin F. Patton, George D. Phillips, John R. Stanford, Samuel A. Wales, John S. Dobbins, Dr. Phineas M. Kollock, Jacob Waldberg, Vestrymen; Richard W. Habersham, Jr., George R. Jessup, lay delegates to the convention that admitted this Church to the Diocese.

(Located at Green and Wilson Streets at the church. GHM 068-8, 1957.)

TOOMBS–BLECKLEY HOUSE

On this site Colonel S. A. Wales built a house in 1835. Robert A. Toombs (1810–1885), United States Congressman, Senator, and Secretary of State, of the Confederate States, purchased it in 1879 for a summer home. General Toombs sold the property to Judge Logan E. Bleckley (1827–1907) in 1884. The original house was destroyed by fire in 1897 and the present structure was built on the same site immediately thereafter.

Judge Bleckley was Associate Justice of the Supreme Court of Georgia 1875–1880, and was Chief Justice 1887–1894. Occasionally the other members of the Court met with Judge Bleckley at this place for conferences on its work. Judge Bleckley was a unique figure in Georgia's judicial history and was one of the most outstanding Chief Justices of the Supreme Court. He died at his residence here on March 7, 1907.

(Located at Jefferson and Marion Streets. GHM 068-9, 1958.)

BLAIR LINE

The historic Blair line between the State of Georgia and the Cherokee Nation crossed this highway at this point. This line was surveyed by James Blair in the early 1800's. It ran from the forks of the Soque and Chattahoochee rivers in a direct northerly line to the Tallulah river. It was the boundary line established in 1817 for the purchase of all the lands east of the Chattahoochee river by the State of Georgia from the Cherokee Nation by the Treaty of 1818.

(Located on GA 115, 0.2 mile west of junction with GA 105, 5.9 miles west of Clarkesville. GHM 068-1, 1953.)

Habersham Iron Works & Mfg. Co.

On the site of the Habersham Cotton Mills stood the Habersham Iron Works and Manufacturing Co., incorporated in late 1837 when this section of the state was Indian country. Jarvis Van Buren, a cousin of President Martin Van Buren, and a pioneer eastern railroad man, arrived in 1838 to operate the plant for its stockholders who included John C. Calhoun. In a region far from railroads necessary machines and supplies must have come by mule or ox wagon from Augusta. The iron mill operated for a few years, closed and reopened during the War Between the States when guns and cannon were urgently needed for the Confederacy.

(Located at the Habersham Mills Plant. From US Bus 441/GA 385 south of Clarkesville, take Habersham Mill Road 2.1 miles, turn left on paved road and follow 0.2 mile to marker. **Or**, from GA 115 follow Habersham Mill Road 1.3 miles, turn right on paved road and follow 0.2 mile to marker. GHM 068-5, 1955.)

SUMMER HOME OF JOSEPH HABERSHAM

This was the summer home of Joseph Habersham of Savannah (1751–1815), Georgia patriot, Revolutionary War

SUMMER HOME OF JOSEPH HABERSHAM

hero, and political leader. He was a Colonel in the Continental Army, a member of Continental Congress, and of the Georgia Convention that ratified the Constitution in 1788. Educated at Princeton, he returned to Georgia to aid in organizing the "Liberty Boys" as the Revolution approached. With other patriots, he organized the Council of Safety at Tondee's Tavern, June 22, 1775. On January 17, 1776, leading a small group, he captured and placed under guard Sir James Wright, British Colonial Governor. With Captain Bowen, he commanded the first commissioned vessel of the Revolution. Twice Speaker of the General Assembly, in Georgia's first legislative body, in 1785, Joseph Habersham signed the first charter granted to a state university in America – that of the University of Georgia. He served as Postmaster General under Presidents Washington, Adams and Jefferson. From 1802 until his death he was president of the Georgia branch of the Bank of the United States. Habersham County, created December 19, 1818, was named for Joseph Habersham.

(Located on US 23/441/GA 17, 2.4 miles north of Clarkesville. GHM 068-7, 1956.

RICHMOND WALTON McCURRY

Memorial Forest Park established 1940 in memory of honorary state regent and vice president general by the Georgia Society Daughters of the American Revolution and the United States Department of Agriculture, Forest Service.

COURTESY, GEORGIA DEPARTMENT OF ARCHIVES AND HISTORY

AN AFTERNOON ON THE TALLULAH RIVER AT THE FOOT OF THE GORGE BEFORE THE DAM WAS BUILT C.1895

(Located on US 23/441 at junction with Tugaloo Short Cut Road, 10.4 miles north of Clarkesville or 2.9 miles south of Tallulah Gorge. DAR 069-98.)

TALLULAH GORGE

This Gorge, 3 miles long and 600 feet deep has been cut in hard quartzite by the Tallulah River. The river once drained southwestward at this level to the Chattahoochee River and the Gulf. It was captured by the shorter, swifter Tugaloo–Savannah Rivers and now drains to the Atlantic. The falls, once at the point of capture, have worked back upstream forming the mighty gorge. The river above the falls was diverted in 1913 into a mile-long tunnel for hydro-electric power.

(Located on US 23/441 at Tallulah Gorge north of Clarkesville. WPA 069-99, 1941.) ♦ ★ – not standing.

CORNELIA

INDIAN WAR TRAIL

This highway runs along the divide between the Atlantic Ocean and the Gulf of Mexico. On the south the waters run into the Broad and Savannah rivers to the Atlantic Ocean. Waters on the north run into Chattahoochee and Apalachicola rivers and the Gulf of Mexico.

This divide was formerly the boundary line between the Cherokee and Creek Nations and along this ridge ran the Indian War Trail from Cherokee settlements on the Upper Tugalo to what is now Atlanta. A branch went southeast into the Creek Nation.

This trail was the route to "Chopped Oak" where the Indians once cut a gash in an oak tree for each scalp.

(Located on US 23/441. GHM 068-2, 1953.) ♦ ★

THE UNICOI TURNPIKE

The Unicoi Turnpike, first vehicular route to connect North Georgia and Tennessee with the head of navigation on the Savannah river system, passed here. Beginning on the Tugalo River to the east of Toccoa, the road led this way, thence across Nacoochee Valley, over the Blue Ridge through Unicoi Gap and past Murphy, N.C., to Nine Mile Creek near Maryville, Tenn.

Permission to open the route as a toll road was given by the Cherokees in 1813 to a Company of white men and

Indians. Tennessee and Georgia granted charters to the concern. Prior to its opening as a road, the way was part of a trading path from Augusta to the Cherokees of Tennessee.

(Located on US 23/441. GHM 068-4, 1953.) ♦ ★

HALL COUNTY

Named in honor of Dr. Lyman Hall (1724–1790), who was a patriot of the Revolution, a delegate from Georgia at the Continental Congress, and was one of the three Georgians who signed the Declaration of Independence. County Seat: Gainesville.

FLOWERY BRANCH

OLD FEDERAL ROAD

The route leading west from this point is the Old Federal Road, an early thoroughfare which linked Georgia and Tennessee across the Cherokee Nation. Rights to open the passage were granted informally by the Indians in 1803 and confirmed by treaty in 1805. Beginning 10 miles to the east, on the former Cherokee boundary, now the Hall–Jackson county line, the road crossed the Chattahoochee 4 miles to the west at Vann's Ferry and bore northwestward.

This highway was the first vehicular and emigrant route of northwest Georgia.

COURTESY, GEORGIA HISTORICAL SOCIETY

LYMAN HALL (1724–1790)
SIGNER OF THE DECLARATION OF INDEPENDENCE

Andrew Jackson passed here in 1818 enroute to the Seminole Campaign.

(Located at GA 13/Atlanta Highway and Radford Road, 0.8 mile north of Flowery Branch post office. GHM 069-3, 1954.)

JACKSON AT YOUNG'S TAVERN

At Young's Tavern, 12-room log home of Robert Young where travelers frequently stopped for lodging, Andrew Jackson, his staff and two companies of militia, spent a night on their way to the Seminole Campaign in 1818. General Jackson followed the road through Monticello and Hawkinsville, while the main body of troops went to south Georgia by way of Alabama. This was on the Federal Road, first vehicular way in northwest Georgia, opened in 1805. Robert Young, born in North Carolina in 1760, son of a Revolutionary soldier, had a 1,600 acre farm here and was a leading pioneer citizen of this section.

(Located on GA 13/Atlanta Highway, 2.0 miles north of the post office. GHM 069-5, 1957.)

GAINESVILLE

LYMAN HALL

Lyman Hall (1725–90), one of three Georgia signers of the Declaration of Independence, was born in Connecticut but moved to Georgia when young. Member of the Savannah Conventions 1774–75, and very influential in Georgia's joining in American Revolution; served in Colonial Congress from Parish of St. John, 1775–80.

When British seized Georgia and confiscated his property, he and his family refugeed in the north until 1782, when he returned to Georgia and served one term as Governor of the State.

He is buried under the Signers Monument in Augusta. Hall County (1818) was named for him.

(Located at Spring and Green Streets, in the park between the Hall County Courthouse and the Gainesville City Hall. GHM 069-2, 1953.)

LT.–GEN. JAMES LONGSTREET

This was the post-war home of General Longstreet, whom General Lee called his "Old War Horse."

Born in South Carolina January 8, 1821, Longstreet grew up at Augusta.

JAMES LONGSTEET (1821–1904)

The family moved to Alabama, and he entered West Point from that state, graduating in 1842. He played a gallant role in the Mexican War, and in 1861 resigned from the United States Army to serve the Southern Confederacy.

Under Lee his capable performance of duty caused Longstreet's rapid promotion to Lieutenant General.

After the war President Ulysses S. Grant, who had married Longstreet's cousin, Julia Dent, made him Surveyor of Customs at New Orleans. He also served as Supervisor of Internal Revenue, Postmaster at Gainesville, Minister to Turkey, United States Marshal and United States Railway Commissioner.

He married first Maria Louise Garland of Virginia on March 8, 1848; Second

Helen Dortch of Atlanta, September 8, 1897. He died January 2, 1904.

(Located at Spring and Green Streets, in the park between the Hall County Courthouse and the Gainesville City Hall. GHM 069-1, 1953.)

FIRST PRIVATE MINT
TEMPLETON REID MINT
1830-1831

Two hundred yards west, on the north side of Washington Street is the site of the first private mint in the United States to manufacture gold coins in dollar values. During the Georgia gold rush, trade suffered due to a shortage of sound money. There were few coins in circulation and most business was by barter. Templeton Reid (ca. 1787–1851), Milledgeville silversmith and expert machinist, saw an answer to the problem. He decided to buy raw gold, refine it and stamp coins of proven value, acceptable in any transaction. In 1830 he came to Gainesville, Georgia and opened an assay office. With machines and dies of his design and make he began to strike coins of $2.50, $5.00, and $10.00 denominations. Although questioned by many, this was legal under the U.S. Constitution. The business was not profitable and closed in 1831. The Reid gold coins minted in Gainesville are extremely rare and are eagerly sought by collectors.

(Located on Washington Street between Bradford and Main Streets, in the square. HCHS 069-2, 1979.)

HALL COUNTY SESQUICENTENNIAL

In memory of the pioneer citizens who gave a great heritage to this area, this plaque was presented December 19, 1968 to commemorate the 150th anniversary of the creation of Hall County, 44th county of Georgia. Named for Lyman Hall, one of the three signers of the Declaration of Independence from Georgia, Hall County was created from territory originally a part of the Cherokee Nation and from land in Franklin and Jackson counties by Act of the General Assembly of Georgia dated December 19, 1818. Neighboring counties Habersham, Gwinnett, and Walton were created by the same Act.

(Located on Green Street/GA 60 /US 129 in front of the Gainesville Civic Center. HCHS 069-1, 1968.)

TWO GEORGIA GOVERNORS

In Alta Vista Cemetery, two Georgia Governors, both officers in the Confederate Army are buried.

JAMES MILTON SMITH (1823-1890). A lawyer, he entered the Civil War as Captain of the 13th. Ga. Inf. and rose to the rank of Colonel. Resigning from the Army in Dec. 1863, he became a Georgia delegate to the Confederate Congress, 1864-65. In 1871 he served as Speaker of the Ga. House of Representatives. Elected Governor in 1872 to fulfill Gov. Bullock's unexpired term, he was reelected and served until 1877. He was later Judge of the Superior Court, Chattahoochee Circuit.

ALLEN DANIEL CANDLER (1834-1910). A graduate of Mercer University, he taught school until he entered the war as a Private, rising to the rank of Lt. Colonel, 4th Ga. Reserves. He served in both houses of the Ga. Legislature, in the U.S. Congress, as Ga. Secretary of State, and as Governor of Ga., 1898-1902. Later, by authority of the Legislature, he compiled the Colonial, Revolutionary, and Confederate Records of Ga.

(Located at Jesse Jewell Parkway/Broad Street and Auburn Avenue in front of Alta Vista Cemetery. GHM 069-6, 1962.)

HISTORIC REDWINE

Co. D. 27th Ga. Inf., Colquitt's Brig., CSA, organized here in early 1861, fought at Williamsburg, Seven Pines, Seven Days Battles. At South Mtn., Md., Sept. 14, 1862, against great odds, men of this Co. withstood four attacks by a heavy force of Federals, in a great display of bravery. Later, they fought at Antietam, Fredericksburg, Chancellorsville, Charleston. At Olustee, Fla., Feb. 20, 1864, they helped drive the Federals from Fla. Until Lee's arrival, they helped hold in check Grant's army at Petersburg, Va. They fought last at Bentonville, N. C., and surrendered at Durham, N.C., Apr. 26, 1865.

(Located on GA 332/Poplar Springs Road, 0.3 mile east of junction with GA 13, south of Gainesville. GHM 069-4, 1956.)

HARALSON COUNTY

Named in honor of General Hugh Anderson Haralson (1805–1854), U.S. congressman and officer in the state militia. County Seat: Buchanan.

BUCHANAN

HARALSON COUNTY

This County, created by Act of the Legislature Jan. 26, 1856, is named for Gen. Hugh A. Haralson, Member of Congress and Chairman of the Committee on Military Affairs during the Mexican War. The County Site is named for James Buchanan, last Democratic President before the War. Among the first County Officers were: Sheriff John K. Holcombe, Clerk of Superior Court Van A. Brewster, Clerk of Inferior Court Jesse M. Jeams, Tax Receiver Hiram Ray, Tax Collector Alfred H. Green, Ordinary George H. Hamilton, Surveyor William D. F. Mann and Coroner John McClung.

(Located on US 27 and GA 120 on the old courthouse lawn. GHM 071-1, 1954.)

TALLAPOOSA

HISTORIC TALLAPOOSA

Tallapoosa was a place of great ceremonial importance to the Indians. Here in 1826 settlers discovered "Charles Town," an Indian Village

named for one of their great warriors. Several Indian trails intersected here and the Choctaw, Creek, and Cherokee tribes frequently assembled here in a grove of "Seven Chestnuts" to trade or make war. A local farmer, William Owens, found gold here in 1842, and some 100,000 pennyweights were mined. Tallapoosa achieved international renown in 1890 when Gen. Benjamin F. Butler of Masachusetts and other notables including two United States Treasurers – A. U. Wyman and James W. Hyatt – organized the Georgia-Alabama Investment and Development Co., to build a new city along the tracks of the Georgia Pacific Railroad, which had been built in 1882. The new city of Tallapoosa attracted some 15,000 investors, 3,000 new inhabitants and a billion dollars in capitalization. It was a city "built as if by magic," Henry W. Grady said, "one which challenged the attention and admiration of the world."

(Located on US 78, at Freeman Street. GHM 071-3, 1980.)

SEVEN CHESTNUTS

On this site under seven chestnut trees the Creek Indians held their council meetings.

(Located at Chestnut and Bowdon Streets. UDC 071-98, 1970.)

SANDTOWN TRAIL

This road was originally the Sandtown Trail traveled by several tribes of Creek Indians.

BUDAPEST CEMETERY

It connected Sandtown on the Chattahoochee River near Atlanta, Ga. with another Sandtown in Tallapoosa Co., Ala. Later became Old Ala. Road over which early white settlers traveled. It was at one time a stage coach route through this section.

(Located at GA 100/Bowdon Street and GA 120/Broad Street. UDC 071-99, 1970.)

WACO

HUNGARIAN COLONY

In 1888, three wine-making communities were founded here on some 2000 acres. A local land developer, Ralph L. Spencer, invited some 200 Hungarian wine-making families to settle this region. They named their largest community BUDAPEST, in honor of the capital of Hungary. The village of TOKAJ recalled the famous wine-making region of Hungary, and NYITRA was named after an ancient fort in the northern region of their homeland. Homes, streets, shops, a school, a Catholic Church, a cemetery and other municipal facilities were built. The wine industry flourished in this climate. In 1908 the passage of the Prohibition Act in Georgia spelled their doom. The residents were forced back to the Pennsylvania mines. The rectory still stands on a hill, a fine tribute to the master masons who erected it. The pioneer Hungarians who became a part of the Georgia soil lie in the little fenced cemetery over the hill, many of the graves still marked with names which sound foreign to these parts. By ancient tradition the inhabitants lie with their heads toward the East and their beloved homeland.

(Located on US 78, 2.3 miles west of junction with Atlantic Avenue. GHM 071-2, 1988.) **Note:** To find the cemetery, follow the gravel road by the marker 0.3 mile until dead end. Turn left and follow road for 0.7 mile. Cemetery is hidden on the left.

HART COUNTY

Named in honor of Nancy Hart (c.1753 – c.1830), heroine of the Revolutionary War who served as a spy and captured a group of Tories. County Seat: Hartwell.

HARTWELL

HART COUNTY

Hart County was created by the Legislature on Dec. 7, 1853 out of portions of Franklin and Elbert Counties. It is the only county in Georgia named for a woman – Nancy Hart.

Nancy Hart and her husband, Benjamin Hart, obtained a 400-acre grant 25 miles SE from Hartwell in Colonial days and erected a log cabin home. During the Revolutionary War six Tories forced their way into the Hart home and demanded that Nancy cook a meal for them. She started cooking an old turkey, meanwhile sending her daughter to the spring to

blow a conch shell for help. Detected slipping the third Tory rifle through a crack in the wall, Nancy killed one of the Tories and wounded another. Hart and several neighbors, coming to her rescue, wanted to shoot the five surviving Tories but Nancy insisted that they be hanged, and they were. Tradition has it that Nancy Hart served as a spy for Gen. Elijah Clarke, sometimes disguised as a man. The Indians respectfully called Nancy Hart "War Woman," giving that name to a creek adjacent to her cabin, which is memorialized in a State Park on State Highway Route 17.

Hart County's first officers elected in Feb. 1854 were Inferior Court Justices Henry F. Chandler, Micajah Carter, Clayton S. Webb, Daniel M. Johnson, James V. Richardson; Inferior Court Clerk Frederic C. Stephenson, Ordinary James T. Jones, Superior Court Clerk Burrell Mitchell, Sheriff William Myers, Tax Receiver W. C. Davis, Tax Collector Richard Shirley, Surveyor John A. Cameron, Coroner Richmond Skelton and Treasurer Samuel White.

(Located at Howell Street and North Forest Avenue on the courthouse lawn. GHM 073-4, 1955.)

"CENTER OF THE WORLD"

This was Ah-Yeh-Li A-Lo-Hee, the Center of the World, to the Cherokee Indians. To this assembly ground, from which trails radiate in many directions, they came to hold their councils, to dance and worship which were to them related functions, and to barter their hides, furs and blankets for the trade goods of the white men from Augusta and other settlements. At one time there was a move to establish here the Hart County seat. This site was also a noted roost in the days when the now extinct passenger pigeons migrated here in the autumn in such numbers that "their weight broke the tree limbs."

(Located on US 29, 2.9 miles south of Hartwell. GHM 073-3, 1954.)

REDWINE CHURCH

Redwine Church was apparently founded prior to 1800 & named after Jacob R. Redwine, Revolutionary soldier born in Pa. who moved here from N.C. This is the 4th church, built in 1906. The first was a log cabin several hundred yards west near the old cemetery in which lies Maj. Nathaniel Durkee, hero of the Revolutionary Battle of Kettle Creek. Lorenzo Dow, noted Methodist preacher, once spoke here. Laid in & about this Church are many scenes in "The Circuit Rider's Wife" by Corra Harris, wife of Rev. Lundy Harris who was preacher here in 1887 when he married.

(Located off US 29, 8.7 miles south of Hartwell, north on Airline–Goldmine Rd for 0.8 mile, left on Redwine Church Rd for 0.9 mile. GHM 073-2, 1954.)

PARKERTOWN – 1832

Parkertown was founded in 1832 in what was then Franklin County, now Hart County, by Joseph A. Parker who was born in Virginia in 1774 and moved to Elbert County, Ga. in 1796. He later moved to Big Shoal Creek

where Jacob Parker & Co. founded by his sons built what is said to have been the first woolen mill in Georgia on the upper shoal. At the lower shoal they constructed a dam and a flour and grist mill together with a cotton gin and a thresher.

(From GA 366 and GA 59, follow GA 59 north 0.7 mile, then follow the road to Shoal Creek Baptist Church 0.9 mile to marker. GHM 073-1, 1954.)

JACKSON COUNTY

Named in honor of General James Jackson (1757–1806) of Revolutionary fame, who was the hero of the Yazoo affair when he left the United States Senate to come home and fight the Yazooists. County Seat: Jefferson.

COMMERCE

BLUE STAR MEMORIAL HIGHWAY

A tribute to the Armed Forces that have defended the United States of America. Sponsored by The Garden Club of Georgia, Inc. In cooperation with Department of Transportation, State of Georgia and The Four Seasons Garden Club of Commerce Honoring Major Leon F. Ellis, Jr. USAF.

(Located on US 441 at Pittman Creek Roadside Park, 2.3 miles east of I-85. GCG 078-99, 1975.) ♦ ★

Dr. Crawford W. Long (1815–1878)
Staging a Demonstration of an Amputation Using Ether Anesthesia, c.1855

JEFFERSON

JACKSON COUNTY

This County, created by Act of the Legislature, February 11, 1796, is named for James Jackson who later became Governor in 1798–1801. A soldier of the Revolution he served in Congress 1789–1791 and in the Senate 1793–95 and 1801–06. He strongly opposed the Yazoo fraud, and died in 1806. Here in Jefferson ether was first used as an anaesthetic in surgery by Dr. Crawford W. Long on March 30, 1842. Among the first County Officers were: Sheriff John Hart, Clerk of Superior Court George Taylor, Clerk of Inferior Court Daniel W. Easley, Coroner Isham Williams and Surveyor James Harper.

(Located at Washington Street and North Avenue on the courthouse lawn. GHM 078-1, 1954.)

BUILDER OF THE NATION

This steam locomotive was presented to the City of Jefferson in 1959 by the Seaboard Air Line Railroad Company as a permanent exhibit in memory of the important service engines of this type gave to the nation. It was one of the last steam-powered locomotives to operate in this section of the country. It was built in 1907 and was last operated on the Gainesville Midland Railroad.

(Located on US 129, 0.7 mile west of the courthouse. GHM 078-98.)

LINCOLN COUNTY

Named in honor of General Benjamin Lincoln (1733–1810) of the Revolutionary War. County Seat: Lincolnton.

LINCOLNTON

LINCOLN COUNTY

Lincoln County was created by Act of Feb. 20, 1796 from Wilkes County. It was named for Maj. Gen. Benjamin Lincoln (1733–1810) of Hingham Mass., who held the Chief Command of the Southern Department in the Continental Army. In 1781 he became Secty. of War. In 1789 he was appointed Collector of the Port of Boston. First County Officers, commissioned Sept. 15, 1796, were: James Hughes, Sheriff; Wm. Dowsing, Clerk Inf. Court; Abner Tatom, Clerk Sup. Court; Britain Lockhart, Coroner; Joel Lockhart, Surveyor; John Middleton, Reg. of Probate. In 1798 John Seale became Tax. Col. and Edward Smith, Tax Rec.

BUILDER OF THE NATION

(Located on Humphrey Street at Perryman Avenue on the courthouse lawn. GHM 090-2, 1956.)

GRAVES MOUNTAIN

Graves Mountain to the Southeast has long been known to mineral collectors for its excellent specimens of rutile (shiny black), lazulite (deep blue), and pyrophyllite (radiating needle like crystals.) The mountain was first described by Professor C. E. Shepard in 1859, for many years it was owned by the late Dr. Geo. F. Kurts, gem expert of Tiffany & Company of New York City.

(Located on US 378/GA 47, 0.4 mile from the Wilkes County Line. WPA 090-D2.) ♦ ★ – not standing.

PETERSBURG ROAD

North Georgia's oldest road, which crosses the Highway U.S. 378 at this point, was originally an Indian Trail which led to their Trading Post in Augusta, Georgia.

Later, this important trade route was used by pioneer white settlers in transporting cotton and tobacco from Petersburg, Georgia, on the Broad River to Augusta, Georgia. The present highway to Augusta traverses the original Petersburg Road at several points.

(Located on US 378/GA 47, 1.8 miles east of Lincolnton. GHM 090-6, 1957.)

TORY POND

Tory Pond, 100 yards south from this marker, is the spot where a band of Tories were hanged for the murder of Colonel John Dooly, in 1780, while he slept in his home, located some ¾ mile to the east.

Previously, a number from this band had escaped across Broad River, were captured and executed at the cabin of Nancy Hart in Elbert County.

(Located on US 378/GA 47, 5.7 miles east of Lincolnton. GHM 090-5, 1957.)

DOOLY SPRING

The spring, to the left of this marker, was used by the John Dooly family.

The simple log cabin, in which Colonel John Dooly and his family resided, was situated across the road opposite the spring. It was here that Colonel Dooly was murdered by a band of Tories.

Colonel Dooly fought with General Elijah Clark during the Revolutionary War.

Dooly County was named for Colonel Dooly.

(Located off US 378 on the grounds of Elijah Clark State Park. GHM 090-4, 1957.)

GENERAL ELIJAH CLARK

General Elijah Clark, "Hero of The Hornet's Nest," and members of his family are buried in the enclosed cemetery. Their graves were first moved from their original burial places near Graball (10 miles North) to a site on the Community House Grounds in Lincolnton in 1952 to prevent inundation by the Clark Hill Lake. Following the establishment of Elijah Clark Memorial State Park by Legislative enactment, the graves were removed to the present site in 1955 by special dispensation of the Army Corps of Engineers.

General Clark was born in Edgecombe County, N.C., in 1733 and moved to what was then a part of Wilkes County, Georgia, (now an area of Lincoln) in 1774. When the Revolutionary War broke out he became a colonel of militia. His activities against the Tories gave him his nickname. He led American forces against the British in battles at Alligator Creek, Kettle Creek, Musgrove's Mill, Fish Dam, Blackstock's, Long Cane, Beatties Mill and two sieges at Augusta, the last one successful. He became a Brigadier General.

(Located off US 378 at the cemetery, on the grounds of Elijah Clark State Park. GHM 090-3, 1957.)

A RECONSTRUCTION OF ELIJAH CLARK'S
SECOND HOME

ELIJAH CLARK (1733–1795)

GEN. ELIJAH CLARK

Gen. Elijah Clark, "Hero of the Hornet's Nest," and members of his family are buried here. Their graves were removed from near Graball (10 mi. N.) to prevent inundation by the Clark Hill Lake in 1952.

Gen. Clark was born in Edgefield Co., S. C., in 1733 and moved to Wilkes Co., Ga., in 1774.

When the Revolutionary War broke out he became a colonel of militia. His activities against the Wilkes Co. Tories gave him his nickname. He led American forces against the British in battles at Alligator Creek, Kettle Creek, Musgrove's Mill, Fish Dam, Blackstock's, Long Cane, Beattie's Mill and two sieges of Augusta, the last one successful, becoming a Brigadier-General.

(Located off US 378 on the grounds of Elijah Clark State Park. GHM 090-1, 1956.) ♦ ★ – not standing.

COURTESY, GEORGIA DEPARTMENT OF ARCHIVES AND HISTORY

WILLIAM LUMPKIN (1783–1870)

LUMPKIN COUNTY

Named in honor of William Lumpkin (1783–1870), governor of Georgia and US congressman and senator. County Seat: Dahlonega.

AURARIA

AURARIA

Auraria, (Gold), in 1832 the scene of Georgia's first gold rush, was named by John C. Calhoun, owner of a near-by mine worked by Calhoun slaves. Auraria and Dahlonega were the two real gold towns in the U. S. before 1849. Between 1829 and 1839 about $20,000,000 in gold was mined in Georgia's Cherokee country.

From Auraria in 1858 the "Russell boys," led by Green Russell, went west and established another Auraria near the mouth of Cherry Creek that later became Denver, Colo. Green Russell uncovered a fabulous lode called Russell Gulch near which was built Central City, Colo., "richest square mile on earth."

(Located at old GA 9E and Castleberry Bridge Road. GHM 093-5, 1954.)

THE STATION

This is the site of one of the forts or stations used by the United States Government in Cherokee country in 1838 to round up the Cherokee Indians for their removal to western reservations. General Winfield Scott, commander of the troops used to assemble and protect the Indians in that period, had his headquarters here at one time.

It is believed that Federal troops also used this station as early as 1830 to guard the gold mines from intruders – Indians or Whites – until the question of ownership of the territory was established.

(Located on GA 9E near Auraria. GHM 093-6, 1954.) ♦ ★

AURARIA

The town of Auraria, first known as, Nuckollsville, 4 miles south, sprang up in 1832 during the North Georgia gold rush and its name, meaning "gold," was selected by Senator John C. Calhoun. In ten months it had a population of 1000 and one of the first newspapers in Cherokee section, but lost the county seat to the then smaller Dahlonega. Today only a few houses remain, but gold is still mined in the vicinity.

(Located on GA 9 west of Dahlonega. WPA 093-B11.) ♦ ★ – not standing.

DAHLONEGA

LUMPKIN COURT HOUSE

This court house, built in 1836, replaced the small log structure used, since the establishment of Lumpkin County in 1832. The town was named Dahlonega in October 1833, for the Cherokee word "Tahlonega" meaning "golden."

From its steps in 1849, Dr. M. F. Stephenson, assayor at the Mint, attempted to dissuade Georgia miners from leaving to join the California gold rush. His oration gave rise to the saying, "There's millions in it" and "Thar's gold in them thar hills."

(Located on the square opposite the gold museum. WPA 093-B7.)

GOLD DAHLONEGA

Gold in the original gold veins was first discovered in Georgia in 1828 by Benjamin Parks 3 miles south in what was then Cherokee Indian territory. The resulting gold rush hastened the exodus of the Indians and settled the region. The discovery mine, known as the Calhoun, was later owned and operated by Senator John C. Calhoun of South Carolina. Others operated it at intervals and periodically have made discoveries of ore.

(Located on the south side of the Dahlonega Gold Museum. WPA 093-B8, 1941.) ♦ ★ – not standing.

PRICE MEMORIAL BUILDING

Erected here in 1837 was a U. S. Branch Mint which operated until seized by the Confederates in 1861. It produced gold coins estimated to exceed $6,000,000.00 in value. In 1871 the mint building and ten acres of land were transferred to the state for use as an agricultural college, largely through the efforts in Congress of Representative William Pierce Price, founder of North Georgia College and President of its Board of Trustees until his death in 1908. The mint building was destroyed by fire in 1878 and in the following year a second building was constructed on the old foundation walls. The new structure came to serve as the college administration building and in 1934 by action of the state Board of Regents was named the Price Memorial Building to honor the founder.

Leafing of the steeple with gold from the surrounding hills was sponsored by the Dahlonega Club to commemorate in 1973 the 100th anniversary of the college.

(Located on West Main Street/GA 9 at the entrance to North Georgia College. GHM 093-9, 1973.)

DAHLONEGA MINT

The building, with the tower, is built on the foundations of the U.S. Branch Mint, established in 1837 and operated until 1861, minting gold coins to the amount of $6,115,596. The Mint building was transferred to the State of Georgia for educational purposes in 1871 and burned in 1878. The present building, erected in 1878, is now the Administration Building of the North Georgia College.

(Located on West Main Street/GA 9 at the entrance to North Georgia College. WPA 093-B9, 1939.) ♦ ★ – not standing.

FINDLEY RIDGE

Many famous gold mines of the Dahlonega era were along this ridge on both sides of this highway. The saprolite and vein gold mining operations along here contributed much to the $35,000,000 in gold taken from this district.

Surface and underground mining began here with the discovery of rich gold shoots. This occurred near the close of the placer mining period during which much gold was recovered

by working rich gravels along the streams with so-called "Dahlonega method." Water was conducted by canals from the headwaters of Yahoola Creek. The many huge cuts observable along this ridge were made by this method of mining.

(Located on GA 60 on the south edge of Dahlonega. GHM 093-2, 1953.) ♦ ★

CALHOUN GOLD MINE

Famous Calhoun gold mine where it is said vein gold was first discovered in Georgia by white men.

In 1828 while deer hunting, Benjamin Parks, of Dahlonega, accidentally found quartz gold in pockets or lodes. His find was so rich in gold that it was yellow like yolk of eggs.

Shortly after discovery this mine was sold to U.S. Senator John C. Calhoun, of South Carolina. It was operated by Thomas G. Clemson, son-in-law of Calhoun, and some of the gold was used to found Clemson College, S. C. Specimens from this mine are exhibited at the State Capitol in Atlanta.

(Located on US 19/GA 60, 3.7 miles east of Dahlonega. 093-1, 1953.)

CONSOLIDATED GOLD MINES

One mile southeast of here, from 1900 to 1906, the Dahlonega Consolidated Mining Company operated what is considered the largest gold plant ever constructed east of the Mississippi River.

Capitalized at $5,000,000, the plant included a 120-stamp mill, a large chlorinator, a 550 foot tunnel and numerous small buildings.

The Consolidated Mining Company furnished much of the setting for one of the earliest moving picture westerns, "The Plunderer," starring William Farnum. The film was made in Dahlonega and its environs before the first World War.

(Located at GA 52 and Consolidated Gold Mine Road. GHM 093-4, 1954.)

DAHLONEGA MUSTERING GROUNDS

During the War Between the States nine companies were organized on this site; five were mustered here in 1861, two in 1862 and two in 1864. Men from other north Georgia counties came to Dahlonega to be mustered here in the companies of Lumpkin County. Most of these were from White, Dawson and Floyd Counties.

The old mustering grounds were the rallying point for troops in other periods of national and state crises. Lumpkin County men met here to join Texans fighting for independence in 1836, to aid U.S. troops in removing the Cherokees in 1838, and to wage war against Mexico in 1846–1848.

(Located at North Grove and North Hawkins Streets. GHM 093-8, 1960.)

COURTESY, GEORGIA DEPARTMENT OF ARCHIVES AND HISTORY

A GOLD MINING OPERATION ABOUT 1910

COURTESY, GEORGIA DEPARTMENT OF ARCHIVES AND HISTORY

GOLD MINING

"GOLD DIGGERS' ROAD"

This section of highway was once a part of the "Gold Diggers' Road," one of the earliest ways used in reaching this area during the Gold Rush days.

Beginning on the Chestatee River to the east, where it connected with a route coming from South Carolina via Toccoa, Clarkesville and Cleveland, the Gold Diggers' Road led here; thence southward, along U.S. 19 to Dahlonega, and from there to Auraria.

Much of its original course is now abandoned.

(Located on US 19/GA 60/9, at Cavenders Creek Road, 4 miles north of Dahlonega. GHM 093-7, 1954.)

TRAHLYTA'S GRAVE

This pile of stones marks the grave of a Cherokee princess, Trahlyta. According to legend her tribe, living on Cedar Mountain north of here, knew the secret of the magic springs of eternal youth from the Witch of Cedar Mountain.

Trahlyta, kidnapped by a rejected suitor, Wahsega, was taken far away and lost her beauty. As she was dying, Wahsega promised to bury her here near her home and the magic springs.

Custom arose among the Indians and later the Whites to drop stones, one for each passerby, on her grave for good fortune.

The magic springs, now known as Porter Springs, lie ¾ mile northeast of here.

(Located at GA 60 and US 19/GA 9, 9 miles north of Dahlonega. GHM 093-3, 1953.)

TRAHLYTA'S GRAVE

MADISON COUNTY

Names in honor of James Madison (1751–1836), the fourth president of the United States and who was the chief drafter of the U.S. Constitution. County Seat: Danielsville.

DANIELSVILLE

MADISON COUNTY

This County, created by Act of the Legislature December 5, 1811, is named for James Madison, Virginia Democrat, fourth President of the United States, 1809–17. The site for Danielsville was given by Gen. Allen Daniel of Revolutionary fame. In this town was born Dr. Crawford W. Long who first used ether in a surgical operation (1842). Among the first County Officers were: Sheriff Nathan Williford, Clerk of Superior Court James Long, Clerk of Inferior Court Samuel Williford, Tax Receiver Britton Sanders Jr., Tax Collector James Ware Jr., Coroner William Hodge and Surveyor Edward Ware Jr.

(Located on US 29 on the courthouse lawn. GHM 097-1, 1954.)

CRAWFORD LONG BIRTHSITE

Dr. Crawford W. Long who first used ether as an anesthetic, in a surgical operation at Jefferson, Ga, March 30, 1842, was born in a house that stands about 1 block from here. Dr. Long, born Nov 1, 1815, was barely 27 when he performed the famous operation on

James Venable to remove a neck tumor. He attended Franklin College (U. of Ga.) obtaining his M.A. at 19. He roomed with "Little Alec" Stephens, future Vice President of the Confederacy. He received his M.D. at University of Pennsylvania in 1839 and moved to Jefferson in 1841. He died June 16, 1878 and is buried in Athens.

(Located on US 29 on the courthouse lawn. GHM 097-2, 1955.)

MORGAN COUNTY

Named in honor of Major General Daniel Morgan (1736–1802), a distinguished hero of the Revolution and U.S. Congressman. County Seat: Madison.

BUCKHEAD

FEDERAL RAID

On Saturday, November 19, 1864, Federal troops under Gen. Geary, Sherman's 20th Army Corps, drove a small detachment of Confederate soldiers out of Buckhead, ate dinner and then destroyed the water tank, all railroad buildings and a large supply of cordwood. Moving out of Buckhead, the Federals destroyed the railroad to the Oconee River, there burning the bridge and railroad supplies. They destroyed gins and mills, 330 bales of cotton and 50,000 bushels of corn.

That night they camped at Blue Springs (now Swords) on the plantation of Col. Lee Jordan.

(Located in the village, at the railroad crossing. GHM 104-5, 1955.)

THE MARCH TO THE SEA

On Nov. 15, 1864, after destroying Atlanta and cutting his communications with the North, Maj. Gen. W. T. Sherman, USA, began his destructive campaign for Savannah – the March to the Sea. He divided his army (F) into two wings. The Right Wing marched south from Atlanta, to feint at Macon but to cross the Ocmulgee River above the city and concentrate at Gordon.

The Left Wing (14th and 20th Corps), Maj. Gen. H. W. Slocum, USA, marched east to Decatur where the 20th Corps, Brig. Gen. A. S. Williams, USA, took the road to Social Circle, striking the Georgia Railroad there and destroying through Madison.

On the 19th, at Madison, the 2nd Div., Brig. Gen. John W. Geary, USA (formerly Mayor of San Francisco), was detached to burn the RR bridge 13 miles E. of Madison. At Buckhead, after his advance "exchanged a few shots with the enemy's scouts," Geary burned the depot and large stocks of cord wood, ties and cut timbers.

At Blue Spring (Swords), he camped on Col. Lee Jordan's plantation where he "found 280 bales of cotton and 50,000 bushels of corn stored for the rebel Government." That day, about five miles of track, the RR bridge over the Oconee River, ferry boats on the Apalachee River, several mills, gins and presses, and about 250 more bales of cotton were destroyed.

On the 20th, Geary marched to Park's Mill, which he burned, destroyed the ferry boat there, and turned south into Putnam County to rejoin the 20th Corps south of Eatonton.

(From Buckhead, travel Park Mill Road 3.1 miles, turn left onto Blue Springs Roadand follow 0.7 mile to marker. GHM 104-9, 1957.)

PARK HOME AND SITE OF PARK'S MILL

This house, built in early 1800 and used as a stagecoach stop, was located on Seven Islands Road which ran from Philadelphia to New Orleans. On Nov. 20, 1864, Federal raiders under Gen. Geary destroyed the nearby mill and ferry. At the request of Mrs. Park, the house and contents were not molested though everything was taken from the yard and smokehouse. A Negro servant, Cyrus Park, by using wet blankets on the roof, saved the house from flying embers from the mill. Pres. Jefferson Davis is said to have spent the night of May 4, 1865 in this house, barely escaping capture by the Federals.

(From Buckhead travel Park Mill Road 4.9 miles, turn right onto Reids Ferry Road for 3.2 miles, take left on Woods Road for 0.1 mile, turn left 1.1 miles to marker and house. GHM 104-4, 1955.) **Note:** The house was moved in 1981 to its present site about 1.5 miles south of its original location. House is privately owned.

MADISON

MORGAN COUNTY

Morgan County was created by Act of Dec. 10, 1807 from Baldwin County. It was named for Gen. Daniel Morgan (1736–1802), a native of N. J. "Exactly fitted for the toils and pomp of war," he served with distinction on Benedict Arnold's expedition to Quebec in 1775–6, commanded the riflemen at Saratoga in 1777 and defeated Tarleton at Cowpens in 1781. After the War he served two terms in Congress. First county officers of Morgan County, commissioned January 14, 1808, were: Joseph White, Sheriff; John Nesbitt, Clk. Sup. Ct.; Isham S. Fannen, Clk. Inf. Ct.; Daniel Sessions, Surveyor; Miles Gibbs Coroner.

(Located at Hancock and East Jefferson Streets, in front of the courthouse. GHM 104-6, 1956.)

WILLIAM TAPPAN THOMPSON

William Tappan Thompson, famous Georgia journalist and author, was born in Ohio in 1812. Moving to Augusta in 1835, he became associated with Augustus Baldwin Longstreet in the publication of the *State Rights Sentinel*. In 1838 he founded a literary journal, the *Mirror*, which in 1842 was merged with a Macon periodical, the *Family Companion*, to become the *Family Companion and Ladies' Mirror*. The first Major Jones letter appeared in one of the last issues of this journal.

In 1843 Thompson took over the editorial direction of the *Southern Miscellany*, a Madison publication. In the

COURTESY, GEORGIA DEPARTMENT OF ARCHIVES AND HISTORY

WILLIAM TAPPAN THOMPSON (1812–1882)

pages of the *Miscellany* he printed more of the Major Jones letters, using the people and incidents of Madison as a basis for many of his sketches. These letters met with such success that Thompson published them in book in 1843 as *Major Jones's Courtship*.

Thompson left the *Miscellany* in 1845 and continued his career as journalist and author. In 1850 he founded the *Savannah Morning News*, which he edited until his death in 1882, building it into one of the state's most powerful newspapers.

(Located at Hancock and East Jefferson Streets, in front of the *Madisonian* office. GHM 104-11, 1963.)

THE STONEMAN RAID

Closing in on Atlanta in July, 1864, Maj. Gen. W. T. Sherman, USA, found its vast fortifications "too strong to assault and too extensive to invest."

To force an evacuation, he sent Maj. Gen. George Stoneman's cavalry (F) (2112 men and 2 guns) to cut the Central of Georgia R R by which the city's defenders (C) were supplied. Retreating from an attempt on Macon, Stoneman was intercepted on the 31st at Sunshine Church (19 miles NE of Macon) by Brig. Gen. Alfred Iverson, Jr., who, with only 1300 cavalry (C), deluded him into believing that he was being surrounded. Stoneman covered the escape of Adams' and Capron's brigades, then he surrendered, with about 600 men and his artillery and train, to what Iverson had convinced him was a superior force.

Clear of the field, both brigades marched toward Eatonton (22 miles S). At Murder Creek (8 miles SW of Eatonton), Capron turned toward Rutledge (9 miles W), through which he passed next day and joined Adams north of Madison. Adams continued to Eatonton and camped about five miles north of town on the Madison road.

Reaching Madison about 2 P.M. on August 1st, Adams "destroyed a large amount of commissary and quartermaster stores" and other property. Marching on, he met Capron and camped about midnight "twelve miles from the bridge crossing the Oconee River, near Athens." Separated again next day, Adams reached the Union lines safely; but Capron, resting for two hours near Winder, was surprised before dawn on August 3rd and lost his entire command.

(Located at 434 South Main Street/ US 441/129/278 in front of the Madison–Morgan Cultural Center. GHM 104-2, 1957.)

THE MARCH TO THE SEA

On Nov. 15, 1864, after destroying Atlanta and cutting his communications with the North, Maj. Gen. W. T. Sherman, USA, began his destructive campaign for Savannah – the March to the Sea. He divided his army (F) into two wings. The Right Wing marched south from Atlanta, to feint at Macon but to cross the Ocmulgee River above the city and concentrate at Gordon.

The Left Wing (14th and 20th Corps,) Maj. Gen. H. W. Slocum, USA, marched east to Decatur where the 20th Corps, Brig. A. S. Williams, USA, took the road to Social Circle (16 miles NW), striking the Georgia Railroad there and destroying it to Madison. At Rutledge, all railway facilities were destroyed, those at Social Circle having been destroyed late in July by Garrard's cavalry (F).That night, the 20th Corps camped two miles west of Madison on the old Covington road.

On the 19th, Geary's division was detached to destroy the RR bridge over the Oconee River (13 miles E) and other bridges down-river toward Milledgeville. Jackson's division marched through town and camped four miles south on the Eatonton road. Ward's division destroyed the depot, water tank, warehouses, switching tracks, side-tracked cars and other railway facilities here in Madison, and quantities of cotton and army supplies.

This was Madison's second ordeal by fire, large stocks of army supplies and valuable industrial property having been

JOSHUA HILL HOME

burned by Adams' brigade (of Stoneman's cavalry) (F) on August 1st.

(Located at 434 South Main Street/ US 441/129/278 in front of the Madison–Morgan Cultural Center. GHM 104-8, 1957.)

JOSHUA HILL HOME

Joshua Hill, noted Georgian of the Civil War and Reconstruction eras, was born in 1812 in the Abbeville District, S. C. He studied law and came to Ga. to practice, settling in Madison after living in Monticello for a time. Having strong Whig and Unionist principles, he was drawn into the American or Know-Nothing party when the Whig party in Ga. collapsed and was elected to Congress in 1856, defeating Linton Stephens. An outspoken opponent of secession, Hill resigned his seat in 1861 rather than withdraw with the other members of the Ga. delegation. In 1863 he made an unsuccessful bid for the governorship.

After the war, Hill participated actively in the work of Reconstruction as a member of the constitutional convention of 1865 and as a U.S. Senator.

UNKNOWN CONFEDERATE DEAD

Elected to the Senate in 1868, he qualified in 1871 and served until 1873. Although he entered Republican party and supported Radical Reconstruction, he never lost the respect and admiration of the people of Ga.

When his term ended in 1873, Hill retired from politics, coming out of retirement only to take part in the constitutional convention in 1877. He died in 1891 and is buried in Madison.

(Located at South Main/US 441/129/ 278 and Hill Streets. GHM 104-1, 1963.)

CONFEDERATE DEAD

Here are buried 51 unknown and one known Confederate soldier and one Negro hospital attendant. These men died of wounds or disease in the Confederate hospitals located nearby, the Stout, Blackie, Asylum, Turnbull, and some temporary ones. These hospitals operated from late 1862 to early 1865. Gallant Confederate women of this vicinity helped care for the sick and wounded men. The Federal raid here on November 18, 1864 did not molest the hospitals.

(From South Main Street, turn by the First Methodist Church onto Central Avenue and Travel 0.3 mile, passing two cemeteries and crossing the railroad tracks to the city cemetery. GHM 104-7, 1956.)

BLUE STAR MEMORIAL HIGHWAY

A tribute to the Armed Forces that have defended the United States of America. Sponsored by The Garden Club of Georgia, Inc. in cooperation with The Department of Transportation of Georgia and the Boxwood Garden Club, Madison, Georgia.

(Located at US 441/129 and US 78/ GA 12/83 in a small park at the south edge of Madison. GCG 104-99, 1976.)

ANTIOCH BAPTIST CHURCH

Three miles from here in a grove of oaks Antioch Baptist Church was established in a primitive log cabin, Sept. 18, 1809. Soon a building 40 x 60 was erected on 4 ½ acres of land including the original site.

In Sept. 1827, 4,000 people including many ministers attended a session of the Ocmulgee Association in the churchyard. A sermon by Antioch's minister, Dr. Adiel Sherwood, started a revival that swept through about 22 counties bringing 16,000 converts in two years. Dr. Sherwood preached 333 sermons in 30 counties in that period. In 1845 Antioch Church moved to its present location.

(Located at GA 83 and Godfrey Road, 4.9 miles south of I-20. GHM 104-3, 1961.)

SEVEN ISLANDS ROAD

The Seven Islands – Alabama Road – was an important emigrant route to

ADIEL SHERWOOD (1791–1879)

the west. Travellers from northeast Georgia and the upper Carolinas followed this trace to the Mississippi Territory, Louisiana, and later Texas.

Originally an important link in the Oakfuskee or Upper Creek Trading Path, the Seven Islands Road became a wagon road long before the Creeks were expelled from Georgia. As an Indian trail, the Seven Islands path crossed both the Oconee and Apalachee rivers at what is now Swords, Ga. When Park's bridge was opened about 1807 some eight miles from here, however, the trace began there on the west bank of the Oconee and ran to the Seven Islands of the Ocmulgee.

Beyond the Seven Islands, the road travel led westward via Indian Springs, where it became the Alabama Road. The Alabama Road ran past Marshall's Ferry on the Flint to what is now Columbus and crossed the Chattahoochee at Kennard's Ferry to join the Federal Road a few miles west of Fort Mitchell, Ala.

(Located at US 441/129 and Seven Islands Road, south of Madison. GHM 104-12.) ♦ ★ – not standing.

RUTLEDGE

THE MARCH TO THE SEA

On Nov. 15, 1864, after destroying Atlanta and cutting his communications with the North, Maj. Gen. W. T. Sherman, USA, began his destructive campaign for Savannah – the March to the Sea. He divided his army (F) into two wings. The Right Wing marched south from Atlanta, to feint at Macon but to cross the Ocmulgee River above the city and concentrate at Gordon.

The Left Wing (14th and 20th Corps), Maj. Gen. H. W. Slocum, USA, marched east through Decatur, the 20th Corps, Brig. Gen. A. S. Williams, USA, taking the road to Social Circle (7 miles NW) to strike the Georgia Railroad there and destroy it through Madison. On the night of the 17th, the 20th Corps camped NW of Social Circle near the Ulcofauhachee (Alcovy) River.

On the 18th, the railroad was destroyed from Social Circle to Madison (16 miles). Here at Rutledge, the depot, water tank, warehouses and other R R facilities were destroyed by the 28th Pennsylvania Veteran Volunteer Infantry, those at Social Circle having been destroyed in July by Garrard's cavalry (F). That night, the 20th Corps camped with its leading division (Geary's) two miles west of Madison, on the railroad, from which point it marched next day to destroy the bridges over the Oconee River.

Between Atlanta and Milledgeville, the movements of the Left Wing were almost unopposed, the few Confederate troops available being employed against the Right Wing to protect Macon, a principal arsenal center, and the Central of Georgia Railway.

(Located on US 278 in the village. GHM 104-10, 1957.)

MURRAY COUNTY

Named in honor of attorney Thomas Walton Murray (1790–1832) who was a state legislator. County Seat: Chatsworth.

CHATSWORTH

MURRAY COUNTY

Murray County, created by Act of Dec. 3, 1832 from Cherokee, originally contained Whitfield, Walker, Catoosa, Dade and part of Chattooga Counties. Settled by people from Tenn., N.C., and Ga., it was named for Thomas Walton Murray (1790–1832). A native of Lincoln County, a lawyer, legislator, and speaker of the house, he acquired distinction for his independence and honesty. A candidate for Congress, he died before the election. First officers of Murray County, commissioned March 20, 1833, were: Nelson Dickerson, Clk. Sup. Ct.; John Sloan, Clk. Inf. Ct.; James C. Barnett, Sheriff; Thomas Gann, Surveyor; Adam Gann, Coroner.

(Located at Market Street and Third Avenue on the courthouse lawn. GHM 105-11, 1956.)

FORKS OF THE OLD FEDERAL ROAD

The Old Federal Road, leading across the Indian Country from the Cherokee boundary, in the direction of Athens, branched at this point toward Knoxville and Nashville. The right turn led northward into Tennessee via Chatsworth and Tennga, while the left fork bore northwestward via Spring Place and Rossville.

Formal permission for the white people to use this way was granted by the Cherokees in the 1805 Treaty of Tellico, Tenn.

This thoroughfare, following the course of an early trading path to Augusta, became northwest Georgia's first vehicular and postal route.

(Located south of Chatsworth on US 76 and GA 282 at junction with Mountain Road, 0.1 mile east of junction with US 411. GHM 105-9, 1954.)

FORT GILMER

One hundred yards east is the site of Fort Gilmer, built in 1838 to garrison US troops ordered to enforce the removal from this region of the last Cherokee Indians under terms of the New Echota treaty of 1835.

One of seven such forts erected in the Cherokee Territory, Gilmer was the temporary headquarters of Gen. Winfield Scott, under whose command the removal was effected. The reluctant Indians were brought here and guarded until the westward march began.

(Located south of Chatsworth on Old US 411, 0.7 miles south of junction with US 76 & GA 282 or 5.5 miles north of junction with US 411. The junction of Old US 411 & US 411 is near Carters Lake dam. GHM 105-2, 1953.)

OLD FEDERAL ROAD

The route veering southeastward is a remnant of the Old Federal Road, northwest Georgia's earliest vehicular way and the first thoroughfare linking Tennessee and Georgia across the Cherokee Nation. Permission to open the highway was granted by the Indians in 1803 and confirmed by treaty in 1805.

The trace, which followed the course of an early Indian trading path to Augusta, became a noted route down which Kentucky and Tennessee cattlemen drove stock to markets in Georgia and South Carolina.

The site, called "Bloodtown" was a resting point for the stock drovers.

(Located south of Chatsworth on Old US 441, 2.8 miles south of junction with US 76 and GA 282 or 3.4 miles north of junction with US 441. The junction of Old US 441 and US 411 is near Carters Lake dam. GHM 105-7, 1954.)

DE SOTO IN GEORGIA

In May, 1539 Hernando de Soto landed in Florida with over 600 people, 220 horses and mules, and a herd of swine reserved for famine. Fired by his success in Pizarro's conquest of Peru, De Soto had been granted the rights, by the King of Spain, to explore, then govern, southeastern North America.

After wintering in Tallahassee, the De Soto expedition set out on a quest for gold which eventually spanned four years and crossed portions of nine states. This was the first recorded European exploration of the interior of the Southeast. Over 300 members died on the expedition, including De Soto in 1542. This tremendous effort forever changed the lives of the Indians who were infected with old world diseases, killed in battle, enslaved, made destitute and sometimes befriended.

Many scholars believe that the De Soto expedition entered Georgia north of here and reached the central town of the Chiefdom of Coosa, July 16, 1540. The Spanish spent over a month at a rich fortified town between two streams. Spanish accounts from the De Soto and Tristan de Luna expe-

ditions, and 16th century Spanish artifacts indicate this was the location of Coosa.

(Located in the park near the visitor's center at Carter's Lake, 2.3 miles off GA 136 south of Chatsworth. GHM 105-12, 1990.)

ETON

OLD FEDERAL ROAD

This highway follows closely the course of the Old Federal Road, the first vehicular and postal route to link Georgia and Tennessee across the Cherokee Nation. Informal permission to use the thoroughfare was granted by the Indians in 1803 and confirmed by a treaty in 1805. Beginning on the southeast boundary of the Cherokees in the direction of Athens, the road led this way via Tate and Talking Rock. At Ramhurst, another branch ran by Spring Place and Rossville toward Nashville.

The noted Vann family of the Cherokees maintained a stage stop and stand near this spot.

(Located on US 411 near the south edge of town. GHM 105-6, 1954.)

SPRING PLACE

CHIEF VANN HOUSE

Built of locally made brick in 1804, this house, the finest in the Cherokee Nation, was the home of a Town Chief, James Vann, son of a Scotch trader, Clement Vann, and his wife, a Cherokee chieftain's daughter. Around his home were several of his business ventures and many acres of land tilled by his slaves. Sponsor of Spring Place Mission, shrewd, amiable but violent, James Vann shot his brother-in-law in 1808 and, in accordance with tribal law, was killed by relatives in 1809. His son, Joseph (Rich Joe) Vann (1798–1844), inherited this estate, increasing the wealth and influence of the Vanns. When expelled in early 1834, Joseph Vann fled to Tennessee and settled, finally, at Webbers Falls, Oklahoma. Racing his steamboat *The Lucy Walker* on the Ohio River, he died when the overheated boiler exploded near Louisville, Kentucky, in October, 1844.

A tempting prize to white men, the Vann house was the scene of a bloody battle between rival claimants in 1834. Deteriorating since, it was purchased in 1952 by a group of public-spirited citizens of Atlanta, Chatsworth and Dalton, and deeded to the Georgia Historical Commission. Restored to its original grandeur, it is a monument to the culture of the Cherokees.

(Located at GA 225 & 52A. GHM 105-4, 1958.)

OLD FEDERAL ROAD

The earliest vehicular and postal route across northwest Georgia was the Federal Road, which led from the southeast Cherokee boundary, in the direction of Athens to Tennessee; a Y-shaped thoroughfare, it forked at Ramhurst toward Knoxville and Nashville. The western prong passed Spring Place, running northwestward by Ringgold and Rossville.

Rights of the white people to use this way were formally granted by the Cherokees in the 1805 Treaty of Tellico. Prior to that time the trace had served as a trading path to Augusta.

James Vann of Spring Place was instrumental in opening the Federal Road. He established the ferry where the highway crossed the Chattahoochee in Forsyth County.

The second post office in northwest Georgia was opened on this route at Spring Place on November 15, 1819 with John Gambold as postmaster.

(Located at GA 225 & 52A. GHM 105-8, 1954.) ♦ ★

CARROLL PROCTOR SCRUGGS

THE CHIEF VANN HOUSE

SPRINGPLACE MISSION

Southward from this spot stood this famous mission, founded in 1801 by Moravian Brethren from Salem, N.C.

The first school among the Cherokees, this mission continued until 1833, and added much to their remarkable advancement.

Here were taught many leaders of the Cherokee Nation. One was Elias Boudinot, later editor of "The Cherokee Phoenix."

The work begun here was not abandoned with the forced removal of the Cherokees, but was transferred to New Springplace, in Oklahoma.

(Located on GA 52A, 0.4 mile east of junction with GA 225 **or** 2.7 miles west of junction with US 441 in Chatsworth. GHM 105-1A, 1953.)

OLD HOLLY CREEK P. O.

May 16, 1864. Brig. Gen. J. D. Cox's Div., 23d A.C. (F), having crossed the Conasauga River at Hogan's Ford, 2 mi. S. of Tilton, camped at or near Holly Creek P.O., in this vicinity.

May 17. Learning that 20th Corps troops (F) had usurped the Coosawattee River crossing at McClure's Ferry (at Pine Chapel), Cox moved his troops S. (via AUDUBON crossroads) to Field's Mill two miles above McClure's, where they were joined by the other 2 divisions.

The 23d A.C. was the left flank of Sherman's army, enroute S. in pursuit

COURTESY, NEW ECHOTA HISTORIC SITE

ELIAS BOUDINOT (1804–1839)

of the Confederate army retreating from the battlefield of Resaca after two days of battle.

(Located on GA 225, 7.1 miles south of junction with GA 52A. GHM 105-1B, 1954.)

TENNGA

OLD FEDERAL ROAD

For the next 25 miles southward this highway coincides closely with the course of the Old Federal Road, the first vehicular and postal way to join Tennessee and Georgia across the Cherokee Nation. Beginning on the southeast Indian boundary in the direction of Athens, the route led this way by Tate, Jasper and Talking Rock.

Rights to open the trace were granted informally by the Cherokees in 1803 and confirmed by the Treaty of Tellico,

Tenn. in 1805. Prior to that period the thoroughfare served as an Indian trading path to Augusta.

(Located on US 411, 0.5 mile south of the Georgia/Tennessee state line. GHM 105-10, 1954.)

OCONEE COUNTY

Named for the Oconee River which forms its eastern boundary. County Seat: Watkinsville.

WATKINSVILLE

OCONEE COUNTY

This County, created by Act of the Legislature February 25, 1875, is named for the Oconee River which forms its eastern boundary. In 1801 Watkinsville was made County Site of Clarke County but in 1875 the Clarke County Site was changed to Athens. As a result indignant local citizens brought about the formation of Oconee County with Watkinsville as County Site. Among the first County Officers were: Sheriff Weldon M. Price, Clerk of Superior Court Jas. M. A. Johnson, Ordinary James R. Lyle, Tax Receiver David M. White, Tax Collector Robert R. Murray, Treasurer Thomas Booth, Coroner James Maulden and Surveyor Wm. E. Elder.

(Located on US 129/441/Main Street, on the courthouse lawn. GHM 108-1, 1954.)

EAGLE TAVERN

Eagle Tavern, or Hotel, was the center of social and political life in Watkinsville for more than a hundred years. It was saved from destruction in 1934 by Lanier Richardson Billups of Decatur, Georgia, who deeded it to the State in 1956.

The oldest section of the building, which is of the "Plain Style," has been restored. It has two rooms upstairs and two rooms downstairs. Separate doors lead into the two rooms on the first floor. One door enters the tavern, the other a store or trading area. This part of the Tavern was built in the first decades of the 1800's when Watkinsville was a growing frontier town, the County Seat of original Clarke County, and the crossroads of travel northward from Madison and Greensboro.

In 1836 Richard C. Richardson bought and, over a period of years, made additions to the original tavern, stage-stop, and store. Having removed these additions, restored the earliest section, and installed appropriate furnishings and exhibits, the Georgia Historical Commission presents Eagle Tavern as a museum devoted to the pre-Civil War, pre-railroad era when wagon and stage travel was at its height.

(Located on US 129/441/Main Street in front of the Eagle Tavern. GHM 108-5, 1966.)

EAGLE TAVERN

THE STONEMAN RAID

Closing in on Atlanta in July, 1864, Maj. Gen. W. T. Sherman found it "too strong to assault and too extensive to invest." To force its evacuation, he sent Maj. Gen. Geo. Stoneman's cavalry (F) to cut the railway to Macon by which its defenders (C) were supplied. Repulsed at Macon, Stoneman's retreat was stopped at Sunshine Church (19 miles NE of Macon) on the 31st by Brig. Gen. Alfred Iverson, Jr., with a smaller force (C). Deluded as to Iverson's actual strength, Stoneman covered the escape of Adams' and Capron's brigades, then surrendered the rest of his command.

Both brigades marched toward Eaton-ton (42 miles S). Separating, they rejoined next day north of Madison (20 miles S), Adams having marched via Eatonton and Madison (where he destroyed valuable property and sup-plies) and Capron via Rutledge (9 miles W of Madison). Late on August 1st, they camped "twelve miles from the bridge crossing the Oconee River, near Athens."

Next morning they entered Watkins-ville. Hoping to resupply his command at Athens, and to "destroy the armory and other government works" there, Adams advanced to the river bridge (4 miles N). Unable to cross in the face of artillery fire, he turned up the west bank toward Jefferson (26 miles NW). Capron, who had waited near Watkinsville, attempted to follow but took the road to Jug Tavern (Winder) instead. Adams reached the Union lines with few losses; but Capron, rest-ing for two hours N W of Winder, was surprised before dawn on August 3rd and lost his entire command.

(Located on US 129/441/Main Street in front of the Eagle Tavern. GHM 108-4, 1957.)

Birthplace of Bishop A. G. Haygood and Miss Laura A. Haygood

This house, about 150 years old, was the birthplace of Bishop Atticus Green Hay-good in 1839 and his sister, Laura Askew Haygood, in 1845. Bishop Haygood was chaplain and missionary to the Army, 1861–65; President of Emory College, 1876–84; editor Wesleyan Christian Advocate, 1878–82; administrator Slater Fund, 1882–91; Bishop from 1890 until his death in 1896. Miss Haygood was principal of an early school for girls in Atlanta and was one of the first mis-sionaries to China. She died in Shanghai in 1900. A brother and sister are buried in the yard of this house, now the Methodist parsonage.

(Located on US 129/441, 0.4 mile south of the Eagle Tavern. GHM 108-2, 1955.)

COURTESY, SPECIAL COLLECTIONS DEPT., ROBERT W. WOODRUFF LIBRARY, EMORY UNIV.

BISHOP ATTICUS GREEN HAYGOOD (1839–1896)

OGLETHORPE COUNTY

Named in honor of General James Edward Oglethorpe (1696–1785), founder of Georgia, member of Parliament, general in the British Army. County Seat: Lexington.

CRAWFORD

WILLIAM HARRIS CRAWFORD

William Harris Crawford, teacher, lawyer, duelist & statesman, was born in Va. Feb. 24, 1772, son of a poor farmer. Moving to Ga. at 14 he studied, taught & was admitted to the bar in 1799. He killed P. L. Van Alen, was severely wounded by Gov. Clark in duels. Elected legislator in 1803, U.S. Senator in 1807, he was the youngest Pres. pro-tem of the Senate 1812–13. He was made Minister to France, 1813, U. S. Sec. of War 1815, & U. S. Sec. of Treas. 1816–25. Democratic nominee for Pres. 1824, he lost to John Q. Adams after a paralytic stroke. He was later elected Circuit Judge and died in Elberton Sept. 15, 1834. Arrow points toward his homesite and grave (150 yds).

(Located on US 78, 0.6 mile west of Crawford. GHM 109-1, 1954.)

WILLIAM BARTRAM TRAIL
TRACED 1773–1777

On this site in 1773, William Bartram with the Indians and Traders concluded the western boundary of "Treaty of Augusta."

(Located on US 78 near the Oglethorpe and Clarke County boundary. GCG 109-99, 1989.)

LEXINGTON

OGLETHORPE COUNTY

This County created by Act of the Legislature Dec. 19, 1793, is named for Gen. James E. Oglethorpe, founder of Georgia. Born in London, England, Dec. 22, 1696. Oglethorpe left England in Nov. 1732 with 116 settlers and arrived at Yamacraw in Jan. 1733, where he established the settlement which is now the city of Savannah. He later brought over 150 Scotch Highlanders & some German Protestants from Salzburg. He returned finally to England in 1743 and resigned his Georgia Charter to the British Government in 1752. Always a friend of America, he died July 1, 1785.

(Located at US 78/Boggs Street on the courthouse lawn. GHM 109-4, 1954.)

GOVERNOR GILMER'S HOME

George Rockingham Gilmer, of Scotch descent, was born in 1790 in that part of Wilkes Co. that is now Oglethorpe Co. Soon after admittance to the bar in 1813 he was appointed 1st Lt. in the regular army and served with distinction in the Creek Indian War. He was elected to the State Legislature in 1818, to Congress in 1821 and Governor in 1828, re-elected to Congress in 1833 and Governor in 1837. He was a Presidential Elector for Harrison in 1840 and President of the Electoral College. A Trustee of the Univ. of Ga. for 30 years he died here Nov. 15, 1859 and is buried in the Presbyterian Cemetery. The arrow points to his home.

(Located at US 78/ Boggs Street on the courthouse lawn. GHM 109-3, 1954.)

BETH–SALEM
PRESBYTERIAN CHURCH

Beth–Salem Presbyterian Church was organized on December 20, 1785, in the wilderness about three miles west of this site, under the leadership of Mr.

John Newton, then a licentiate. It was the first of a chain of Presbyterian churches established in North Georgia in the latter part of the 18th century, by the Presbytery of South Carolina. The Rev. John Newton was the first minister, serving Beth–Salem until his death in 1797. Ezekiel Gilham, James Parks and James Espey were elders.

Later, Beth–Salem was moved to the present site, and on December 20, 1827, was chartered by the Legislature. Charter members were: William Campbell, David McLaughlin, William Lesley, Samuel McCauley, John Pharr, John F. Wallace, Joseph Espey, Mrs. Marion Greer, Mrs. Jane Jewell, Mrs. Jane Campbell, Sam McLaughlin, Mrs. Lesley, Mary Espey, Ann Gaulding, Damary Baldwin, Hannah Upson, Sarah Walley, Martha Gilham, Sarah Moore, Mrs. Mary Kennedy, Miss Maria Harrison, The Rev. Thomas Goulding.

(Located at Meson and Church Streets. GHM 109-6, 1958.)

MESON ACADEMY

Francis Meson (1761–1806), an Irishman and "wandering schoolteacher," became a rich merchant in Lexington. He bequeathed $8,000.00 for an academy building and valuable property for an endowment, "the income to be used forever for the benefit of the teachers." His executors erected a building, excelled among Georgia educational structures only by Franklin College, the sole building at the University of Georgia at that time.

In 1825 a Female Department was added under the direction of The Rev.

Thomas Goulding. The income from the endowment was liquidated when a new building was constructed in 1896. In 1917, Lexington voted a school tax and Meson Academy became a free school. In 1920 it became the Oglethorpe County High School.

The first rector or principal of the academy was the Rev. Francis Cummins. Of the outstanding educators who followed him, Thomas Britton Moss served from 1849 through the difficult War and Reconstruction periods until 1889. Some of Georgia's most eminent men were on the Meson Academy Board of Trustees: William H. Crawford, George R. Gilmer, Joseph Henry Lumpkin, Thomas W. Cobb.

(Located at the intersection of US 78/ Main and Academy Streets. GHM 109-7, 1959.)

GOVERNOR MATHEWS' HOMESITE

George Mathews born in Va. in 1739, of Irish descent, lived in this area then known as "Goose Pond" from 1785. His home since burned. He won distinction fighting Indians in the N. W. Ter. and in 1775 became a Col. serving under Washington at Brandywine & Germantown. He came to Oglethorpe Co. in 1785 and after but one years residence was elected both Governor and Congressman. Re-elected in 1793 he signed the "Yazoo Act." In 1811 he was appointed by Pres. Madison U. S. Commissioner to negotiate the annexation of Florida. He died in Augusta Aug. 30, 1812 and is buried there.

(Located on GA 77, 16 miles north of Lexington or 1.1 miles south of the bridge over the Broad River. GHM 109-2, 1954.)

WATSON MILL BRIDGE

Built by W. W. King in 1885, Watson Mill Bridge is Georgia's longest existing covered bridge. Of the Town lattice type it has four spans and is 236 feet long.

Covered primarily to protect the structural timbers, the bridge served local traffic, the workers of the now missing grist mill and saw mill and even for picnics and square dances.

The bridge was restored in 1973, by the Georgia Department of Transportation to serve as a nucleus for the surrounding state park.

(Located in Watson Mill State Park, follow GA 22 from Lexington. GHM 109-8, 1974.)

WATSON MILL COVERED BRIDGE

PHILOMATH

LIBERTY – SALEM
WOODSTOCK – PHILOMATH

This ancient Church has served under four names and in four counties. Liberty Presbyterian Church was organized by the Rev. Daniel Thatcher, about 1788. The original place of worship, a log house, was erected near War Hill, about seven miles from the present site. The church was called "Liberty," because, though built by Presbyterians, all orthodox denominations were allowed to use it. The Presbytery of Hopewell, formed Nov. 3, 1796, held its first session in Liberty Church on March 16, 1798. Soon after 1800, the log house was abandoned, and a new structure erected at the top of Starr's Hill on the old Greensboro Post Road. The name of the church was then changed to Salem. The Rev. Francis Cummins was the first minister to preach there. This building was used until 1834, when the location of the Greensboro road was changed, and a new church edifice was erected at the site of the present Phillips Mills Baptist Church. The Rev. S. J. Cassels was the first pastor, followed by the Rev. Francis R. Goulding. In 1848, the Salem church building was sold to the Baptists, and the entire Presbyterian membership moved to Woodstock, now Philomath, where a new church edifice had been built. The Rev. John W. Reid was pastor at the time of the removal.

(Located on GA 22 in the town. GHM 109-5, 1958.)

PAULDING COUNTY

Named in honor of John Paulding (1759–1818), one of the captors of Major André, accomplice of Benedict Arnold. County Seat: Dallas.

DALLAS

PAULDING COUNTY

Created December 3, 1832, and named for John Paulding, one of the captors of Major André, accomplice of Benedict Arnold. Van Wert, the first county seat, was named for another of the captors.

When Polk County was created in 1851, Dallas became the Paulding County seat.

Construction of the Seaboard and Southern Railroads through the county, and introduction of the textile industry, were of much importance to county growth.

In 1864 major battles were fought at New Hope and Dallas.

(Located at Main Street and Court House Square at the courthouse. GHM 110-05, 1953.)

FEDERAL LINE

Here, the intrenched line held by Maj. Gen. J. B. McPherson's Army of the Tenn. (F) crossed the road; erected & occupied May 26 & abandoned June 1, 1864.

These troops were the right of Federal forces on the Dallas–New Hope Ch. front which had been halted in a flanking move around the Allatoona Mtns. by Gen. J. E. Johnston's forces, deployed to oppose the Federal move back to the State R.R.

From lines 4 mi. E., Hardee's A.C., of Johnston's Army (C), faced McPherson. Repeated attempts by Hardee to crush the Federals, failed to dislodge them.

(Located on Hardee Street, between GA 61 and GA 6B, 0.2 mile from the junction with each highway. GHM 110-12, 1953.)

RT. OF FEDERAL LINE
MAY 26–JUNE 1, 1864

May 26. Maj. Gen. John A. Logan's 15th A.C. (F) was posted on the hills N. & W. of this, the salient angle of the intrenched line.

The Federals fought defensively during the 6 days of fighting, climaxed by a concerted assault on the salient by Lt. Gen. Wm. J. Hardee's A.C. (C), in columns of regiments, along the Villa Rica Rd. – an attack that extended N. 2 mi. along the 15th & 16th corps fronts – May 28.

McPherson's forces (F) were shifted N. from the Dallas front, June 1, pursuant to the Federal move E. toward the state R. R.

(From the courthouse, follow GA 61 south for 2.2 miles, turn right on Vernoy Aiken Road and follow 0.1 mile to marker. GHM 110-9, 1953.)

LEFT OF THE
CONFEDERATE LINE

Hardee's A.C. was on the left of General J. E. Johnston's line (C) – Dallas–New Hope front, May 26–June 4, 1864. Dallas was the southern-most objective of Federal forces in their flanking march around Allatoona.

During the Federal occupation of the Dallas–New Hope line, the Confederate forces maintained parallel lines of defense from Dallas to & beyond New Hope Church, which checked Sherman's (F) shift back to the State R.R. Daily conflict marked the period which ended when Federal thrusts N.E. forced Johnston to retire Eastward.

(Located on GA 61, 2.9 miles south of the courthouse. GHM 110-10, 1953.)

ARMY OF THE TENN.
AT DALLAS

May 25,1864. McPherson's Army of the Tenn. (F), marching from Wooley's Bridge (Etowah River), via Van Wert, reached Pumpkin Vine Cr. Logan's 15th A.C. (F) camped near Pumpkin Vine Church, 2 mi. S.

May 26, Dodge's 16th A.C. (F), reached Pumpkin Vine Cr. (via State Highway 6) before dawn & by 10 o'clock was across.

Both corps entered Dallas 2 p.m., Logan marching from Pumpkin Vine Church (via State Highway 120). Opposed by Confederate Cavalry, the Federals advanced E, to the Marietta & Villa Rica roads.

(From the courthouse follow GA 6 west 0.7 mile, continue straight, which later joins US 278/GA 6, and follow 2.4 miles to marker. GHM 110-7, 1989.)

ARMY OF THE TENN. TO DALLAS

May 24, 1864. McPherson's 15th & 16th A.C. (F) left Euharlee Cr. (at Aragon, Polk County) & passed through Van Wert, his route being present State Highways 101 & 6. Turning E. (toward Yorkville, Paulding Co.), camp was made at Raccoon Creek near here.

At this stage of the Federal march to outflank Johnston's forces (C) at Allatoona, McPherson was on extreme right. Next on left was Davis (2d) div., 14th A.C. (F), which turned E., May 25, at Van Wert to reach Dallas via Bishop's Mill.

(From the courthouse follow GA 6 west 0.7 mile, continue straight, which later joins US 278/GA 6, and follow 9.2 miles to marker. GHM 110-6, 1953.)

DALLAS – NEW HOPE LINE

Four to six mi. N.E., on State Highway 92 at & near New Hope Church, are the battlefields of New Hope Church & Pickett's Mill – two of the notable engagements of the Atlanta Campaign, May 25 & 27, 1864.

From a point 2 mi. S. of Dallas, the embattled Confederate & Federal forces, extending N.E. on a 10 mi.

front, maintained daily conflict for 10 days, May 25–June 4.

This Paulding County phase of the Atlanta Campaign was incident to Sherman's flanking operations (F) W. & S.W. of the Allatoona Mtns. Johnston's forces (C) held the Federals in this sector until they moved E, to the State R.R.

(Located on GA 6B at the junction with the Dallas–Acworth Road, 0.4 mile east of the courthouse. GHM 110-29, 1953.)

THE ORPHAN BRIGADE AT DALLAS

May 28, 1864. On ridge W., were the intrenched lines of the 1st div., 15th A.C. & the 2d div., 16th A.C. (F); beyond ravine E., the lines of Bate's div. of Hardee's corps (C).

Late afternoon, Lewis' Ky. (Orphan) & Finley's Florida brigades, (C) made a desperate assault across the ravine & scaled the high ground W. – the Orphans in the advance – their losses, 51 per cent because of failure to receive orders to withdraw.

This futile attempt by the Ky. Orphans is one of the notable instances of heroism & disaster in the Atlanta campaign.

(Located on GA 6B, 0.9 mile east of junction with GA 61. GHM 110-13, 1953.)

CONFEDERATE LINE

Here, the intrenched line held by Gen. J. E. Johnston's forces (C) during the fighting on the Dallas–New Hope Church front, crossed the road; line erected and occupied May 26 and abandoned June 4, 1864.

Three of the 10 miles of this line were on the summit of Ellsberry Mountain, NE.

In the 10 days of constant fighting between Confederate and Federal forces, no advantage was gained – a stalemate that was broken by Sherman's (F) flanking movement around the Confederate right at Old Allatoona Church 11 miles NE in Cobb County.

(Located on GA 6B, 1.7 miles east of the courthouse. GHM 110-11, 1983.)

DAVIS' DIV. AT DALLAS

May 26, 1864. Brig. Gen. J.C. Davis' (2d) div. 14th A.C. (F), reached Dallas on this rd. from Bishop's Bridge (Pumpkin Vine Cr.).

These troops left Resaca, Gordon County, May 16, & marched to Rome via a route W. of the Oostanaula River. Leaving Rome May 24, the command moved by Peek's Spring (at Aragon), to Van Wert, where a road E. led via Bishop's Bridge to Dallas.

Entering the town, Davis' div. marched E. to the New Hope Church Rd. (State Highway 92) & established an intrenched line on the left of McPherson's Army of the Tenn (F).

(Located at North Confederate Avenue/GA 61 and Polk Avenue, 0.4 mile north of the courthouse. GHM 110-8, 1953.)

20TH CORPS DETOURS TO NEW HOPE CHURCH

One-half mile E. the old road from Burnt Hickory to Dallas joined one leading E. via Pumpkin Vine Bridge, near Owen's Mill, to New Hope Church.

May 25, 1864: Geary's (2d), followed by Williams' (1st) divs., 20th A.C. (F), turned E. when assailed by outposts of Hood's A.C. (C) which had reached New Hope from Allatoona.

Pressing forward and reinforced by the 4th & 23d A.C. (F), Geary's div. assaulted the intrenched line of Hood's A.C. posted in and near the cemetery at New Hope Church – a battle fought in rain and thunderstorm.

(Located on GA 61 at High Shoals Road, 3.8 miles north of the courthouse. GHM 110-4, 1985.)

OLD BURNT HICKORY P. O.

May 24, 1864: The 4th, 20th & a div. of the 14th A.C. – Army of the Cumberland (F), enroute from Stilesboro, camped in this vicinity, & on the 25th, marched to New Hope Church.

The 23rd Corps (F), at Sligh's Mill, 3 mi. N.E., night of the 24th, moved by Burnt Hickory late afternoon of the 25th & followed the 20th A.C. to the battlefield of New Hope Church.

COUTESY, LIBRARY OF CONGRESS

LT. GENERAL JOHN B. HOOD (1831–1879)

These troops were center & left of Sherman's flanking march around the Allatoona Mtns. which was checkmated by Johnston's Confederate Army at New Hope & Dallas.

(Located on GA 61, 7.7 miles north of the courthouse. GHM 110-3, 1953.)

SLIGH'S MILL POTTERY & TANYARD

Noted crossroads settlement of the 1860's.

Schofield's 23rd corps (F), marching from Milam's Bridge (Etowah River) camped here May 24–25, 1864.

This corps was the rear & left guard of Sherman's flanking march to by-pass the Allatoona Mtns. & it was sta-

tioned here 24 hrs. as a pivot, while McPherson's Army of Tennessee (F) moved in a left wheel from Van Wert to the Dallas front.

May 25, 5 P.M. The corps moved to Burnt Hickory P. O. (Huntsville), enroute to New Hope Church.

(Located on GA 61 at Harmony Grove Church Road, 11 miles north of the courthouse. GHM 110-2, 1953.)

HIRAM

POLK'S CORPS AT DALLAS AND NEW HOPE CHURCH

Lt. Gen. Leonidas Polk's corps which had moved from Allatoona as left flank of Johnston's army (C) – via Lost Mtn. & Mt. Tabor Ch. – reached this vicinity May 24, 1864.

After return of Hardee's A.C. (C) from Powder Springs (May 25), Polk's troops formed the center of Johnston's line facing the Federal lines to the West.

When deployed, Polk's left was at Wigley's Mill in gap of Ellsberry Mtn., his center & rt. at & above New Hope Ch. – a position he held in the 10 days of conflict mostly fought on the left & right of the army.

(Located on GA 120/360/Marietta Road at GA 6 Spur. GHM 110-20, 1953.)

SITE: ROBERTSON HOUSE

May 24, 25, 1864. Lt. Gen. Wm. J. Hardee (C) maintained h'dq'rs here during operations of his command in this sector, incident to finding the position of McPherson's Army of the Tenn. (rt. wing, Sherman's forces) (F).

On the 24th, uncertain of where McPherson would place his troops, Hardee extended Johnston's (C) left S.E. to Powder Springs, only to be recalled on the 25th when McPherson's seizure & occupation of Dallas became known. Cleburne's div. of the corps (C), passed the house enroute to Powder Springs & the return march N. to New Hope Ch. & battlefield of Pickett's Mill.

(Located on GA 120/360/Marietta Road at Bobo Road near the junction with GA 6 Spur. GHM 110-19, 1953.)

GEORGE DARBY HOUSE
CLEBURNE'S HEADQUARTERS

May 25, 1864. Maj. Gen. P. R. Cleburne's div. marched with Hardee's A.C. (C) from New Hope Church May 24 to Powder Springs.

These troops, the left flank of Johnston's army, marched S.E. to find the position of the Federals known to be near Dallas. Recalled from Powder Springs, the corps counter-marched at 3 a.m., May 25.

Enroute back toward Dallas, Cleburne's div. detoured N. from the Henry Lester house & camped at Darby's until dark, when it was ordered to New Hope Ch. where Hood's A.C.

(C) had been fighting the 20th A. C. (F) that P. M.

(Located on GA 92, 0.2 miles south of the junction with GA 360/ Macland Road. GHM 110-22, 1953.)

SITE: COLLEY HOUSE
HOOD'S H'DQ'RS

Oct. 3-6, 1864, Lt. Gen. John B. Hood (C) had h'dq'rs at the Colley house which stood 500 ft. N. of this marker.

Hood, enroute with his army to Tennessee, after the fall of Atlanta, marked time in this vicinity while Stewart's A.C. wrecked the State R.R. between Marietta & the Etowah River – a noted episode being French's (C) attempt to capture the Federal garrison at Allatoona – Oct. 5.

Oct. 6, Hood's forces resumed march to Dallas, Van Wert, Cedartown, Cave Spring, – to battle and defeat at Nashville.

(Located on Macland Road/GA 360, 1.6 miles east of junction with GA 120 and 0.4 miles east of junction with GA 92. GHM 110-23, 1953.)

HENRY LESTER HOUSE

May 24, 25, 1864. Hardee's corps. of Gen. J. E. Johnston's army (C), having marched on the 23d from Stegall's Station (Emerson), passed this way to Powder Springs, where it camped until 3 a.m. of the 25th, when it counter-marched toward Dallas because of McPherson's (F) approach to that place.

At this time, Hardee's troops formed the left flank of Johnston's army.

Enroute back to Dallas, Cleburne's div. of the corps detoured N. from here to the George Darby house (near Macland Rd.) where it halted until ordered forward to New Hope Church that night.

(Located at US 278 and GA 92. GHM 110-21, 1953.)

NEW HOPE

BATTLE OF NEW HOPE CHURCH

Lt. Gen. J. B. Hood's A. C. (C), having marched from the Etowah River, reached New Hope Ch., May 25, 1864, in time to halt Gen. J.W. Geary's (2d) div., 20th A.C. (F), which had detoured near Owens' Mill enroute to Dallas by New Hope.

Checked by Hood's outposts near the mill, the Federals advanced & struck Stewart's div. (C) astride the road at this point – the left brigade (Stovall's) in the cemetery, with no intrenchments.

Followed then several hours of bitter conflict – late afternoon & night – in rain & thunderstorm. Battle renewed next day.

(Located off GA 381/Dallas–Acworth Road at New Hope Church. GHM 110-28B, 1953.)

ATLANTA CAMPAIGN
NEW HOPE CHURCH
MAY 25–JUNE 4, 1864

Here, at New Hope Church Confederate and Federal Armies engaged in a desperate battle as the former blocked the way to Atlanta, key industrial center of the Confederacy, Sherman again outflanked the Confederates and the two armies moved to renew the struggle at Kennesaw Mountain.

(Located off GA 381/Dallas–Acworth Road at New Hope Church. NPS 110-99.)

POLK'S MARCH TO LOST MOUNTAIN

June 4, 1864. The embattled forces of Gen. J. E. Johnston's army (C), having confronted Sherman's army (F) on the Dallas–New Hope Church front, since May 25, abandoned the position & shifted eastward because of Sherman's movement back to the State R.R.

Lt. Gen. Leonidas Polk's corps (C) held the center of Johnston's line, at New Hope Church, & in the withdrawal E. from this sector, marched by this road toward Lost Mountain, the imposing peak of which is visible from this marker.

(Located off GA 381/Dallas–Acworth Road at New Hope Church. GHM 110-18, 1953.)

THE MARCH OF HARDEE'S CORPS, MAY 23–25, 1864

Lt. Gen. Hardee's A.C. (C), having marched from Stegall's Station (Emerson) near the Etowah River & camped at the Dr. Smith house, May 23d, passed New Hope Church on the 24th, enroute to the Dallas front.

This moving left flank of Gen. J. E. Johnston's army (C) sought to checkmate the right of Sherman's army (F) marching from Kingston in a wide circuit via Van Wert to Dallas.

Hood's corps (C), following Hardee's from the Etowah, reached New Hope Church, May 25, in time to intercept Hooker's troops (F) in their move toward this position.

(Located off GA 381/Dallas–Acworth Road at New Hope Church. GHM 110-16, 1953.)

THE FEDERAL ATTACK ON HOOD'S CORPS

May 25, 1864. Brig. Gen. J.W. Geary's (2d) div. 20th A.C. (F), deployed in dense woods, N.W., advanced toward this ridge at New Hope Ch. – (5 p.m.) – supported on his right by Williams' (1st) & on his left by Butterfield's (3d) divs. – the corps front astride this road.

Repeated assaults on Hood's corps (C), posted on this ridge (Stovall's brigade on left; Clayton's, center; Baker's, right) failed to dislodge it after several hrs. of fighting.

Reinforced 20th corps assaults, May 26, were likewise devoid of results.

(Located off GA 381/Dallas–Acworth Road on Old Cartesville Road next to the New Hope Cemetery. GHM 110-24, 1953.)

JOHNSTON'S HEADQUARTERS

During the fighting at Dallas, New Hope Church, Pickett's Mill & elsewhere along the opposing Confederate & Federal lines, General J. E. Johnston (C) had h'dq'rs at the Wm. Wigley house (which stood near here) May 25–June 1, 1864.

Posey Wigley (10 yr. old son of Wm. & Fanny), later recalled seeing Gen. Johnston at his widowed mother's house & removal of family & household goods to a place of safety – hence, Lt. T. B. Mackall's reference to "Widow Wigley's deserted house" as Johnston's headquarters. (O. R. 38, III, 987).

(Located on Bobo Road, 0.7 mile from the junction with GA 381 at New Hope Church. GHM 110-17, 1953.)

BATTLE OF PICKETT'S MILL

After the successful defense at New Hope Church by Hood's Corps (C), May 25, 1864, Johnston (C) extended his right N E to keep pace with the Federal leftward shift to outflank him.

Elements of the 4th, 14th and 23rd Corps under Maj. Gen. Oliver O. Howard (F) with over 18,000 men passed this point seeking the extreme right of the Confederate army. The Federal forces attacked a point where the Army of Tennessee's line bent back to the south. The brigades of Hazen, Gibson and Scribner blundered into a deep ravine one-half mile east of here to attack the Confederates under Maj. Gen. Patrick Cleburne. The brigades were defeated one after another in the heavily-wooded ravine where fired upon from three directions.

The Confederates were the clear victors of the five-hour battle. The result of the victory was a few days delay in Sherman's (F) Atlanta Campaign.

(Located on Mt. Tabor Church Road 0.9 mile from junction with Dallas–Acworth Road north of New Hope. GHM 110-27, 1983.)

BROWN'S MILL

One-half mi. S.W., on Pumpkin Vine Cr., was the site of Brown's saw-mill, a landmark during military operations May 25–June 5, 1864.

The 23d Corps, moving from Sligh's Mill, Burnt Hickory P.O. & Owens' Mill, occupied lines on this ridge facing S.E., from May 26–June 2, in active support of & in line with the 4th, 14th & 20th (F) corps (Army of the Cumberland (F).

These troops faced Hood's, Polk's & Hardee's A.C. (Johnston's Army of Tennessee) (C). Two of the notable battles of the Atlanta Campaign were fought near here – at New Hope Church (2 mi. S.), May 25, & at Pickett's Mill (1 mi. S. E.) May 27.

(Located on the Dallas–Acworth Road, 2.9 miles south from the junction with GA 92 and Old Burnt Hickory Road or 1.4 miles north of New Hope Church. GHM 110-28A, 1953.)

CROSS ROADS CHURCH

One tenth mi. W. at the intersection of the old Dallas–Acworth & Burnt Hickory rds. – a key point of Federal operations at New Hope Church and Dallas. May 25–June 5,1864.

Hardee's & Hood's A.C. (C) moved this way, S. – from the Etowah River, to New Hope Church, May 24, 25. June 2: the 23d A.C. (F) marched N.E. from Brown's Mill to this point – turning S.E., 1.5 mi. to the Foster house. Ensuing operations outflanked the Confederate forces & caused their retreat toward Kennesaw Mt., June 4.

June 5: McPherson's 15th & 16th A.C. (F) leaving the Dallas front June 1, marched by this Church to Acworth, on their way to Kennesaw Mtn.

(Located at GA 92/Dallas–Acworth Road and Old Burnt Hickory Road, 2.1 miles from the Paulding/Cobb County line or 4.3 miles from New Hope. GHM 110-26, 1953.)

HARDEE'S, HOOD'S & FRENCH'S H'DQ'RS.

Site of Dr. Augustus Smith house, 1864. May 23: Gen. Wm. J. Hardee's (C) headquarters during the march of his Corps from Stegall's Station (Emerson) to points south.

May 24: Gen. John B. Hood (C) spend night here enroute with his corps from Etowah River to New Hope Church.

Oct. 5: Gen. S. G. French, (C), withdrawing from an abortive attempt on the Federal garrison at Allatoona, stopped here enroute to rejoin Hood's forces at New Hope Church.

(Located on GA 92/Dallas–Acworth Road, 0.3 miles from the Paulding/Cobb County line near Acworth **or** 6.1 miles from New Hope. GHM 110-1, 1953.)

PICKENS COUNTY

Named in honor of General Andrew Pickens (1739–1817) of South Carolina, Revolutionary hero who defeated the British at Kettle Creek. County Seat: Jasper.

JASPER

PICKENS COUNTY

Created December 5, 1853, and named for General Andrew Pickens of Revolutionary fame. The first settlements sprang up along the Old Federal Road which followed in general the route of the highway through Tate, Jasper and Talking Rock.

Mount Oglethorpe, (formerly called Grassy Knob), Burrell Top of Burnt Mountain and Sharp Top Mountain dominate the skyline in the northeastern part of the county; to the southwest is Sharp Mountain.

Coming of the railroad in 1883 made possible development of a large and important marble industry.

(Located at Main and Depot Streets on the courthouse lawn. GHM 112-1, 1953.)

OLD FEDERAL ROAD

From Tate through Jasper to Talking Rock, this highway coincides closely with the course of the Old Federal Road, northwest Georgia's first vehicular way which linked Tennessee and Georgia across the Cherokee Country. Permission to open the route was granted informally by the Indians in 1803 and confirmed in a treaty of 1805.

Emigrants from the lower Southeast followed this course into Tennessee and Alabama. It became the first postal route of this section and was used by travellers in reaching the gold fields of North Georgia.

(Located at Main and Court Streets on the courthouse lawn. GHM 112-4, 1954.)

OLD PICKENS COUNTY JAIL

This 1906 jail was built to replace the old rock jail that stood behind the courthouse. The rock jail had replaced the first county jail, a two-story log building. Dr. William B. Tate urged

OLD PICKENS COUNTY JAIL

the construction of the jail as a grand juror and on two Citizens Committees. The architects were J. W. Coluke and Co.; contractors were William L. Landrum and Son. The steel work was installed by the Pauly Jail Co. of St. Louis, Mo., specifically by Luthor Cartwright, who while here married and, eventually settled in Jasper. He later supervised construction of the pink marble mansion in Tate. The work on the front of the jail was done by Lee W. Prather, a local stone worker, using marble from the Delaware Quarry at nearby Marble Hill. The Delaware Quarry was opened c. 1840 by pioneer marble entrepreneur Henry Fitzsimmons.

The jail still has a gallows (non-functioning) although no one was ever executed on this device. The most regular residents of the jail were the sheriffs and their families, who lived here rent free. The jail was ordered closed by a federal court order in 1980. The well in the rear, now filled in, provided water for the hundreds of people who came to Jasper for singing conventions.

(Located at Main and College Streets. GHM 112-6, 1986.)

TALKING ROCK

OLD FEDERAL ROAD

The highway leading right is the Old Federal Road, northwest Georgia's earliest vehicular route. It began on the Cherokee boundary, in the direction of Athens, Georgia and led this way to Tennessee. Permission to open the trace was granted informally by the Indians in 1803 and formally by the 1805 Treaty of Tellico, Tennessee.

This location on the old thoroughfare was a Cherokee settlement known as Sanderstown. It was an early post office and the site of Carmel or Talona Station, a missionary establishment founded here among the Cherokees in 1821.

(Located at GA 5 and GA 136, 1.4 miles north of Talking Rock. GHM 112-3A, 1954.)

SITE OF CARMEL (TALONEY) MISSION STATION

Just west of here in 1819 the American Board of Commissioners for Foreign Missions established a mission station to the Cherokee Indians. Moody Hall and Henry Parker were the first missionaries sent to Carmel (originally known as Taloney). March 12, 1831, Rev. Isaac Proctor, then residing here, was arrested by the Georgia Guard for not complying with the new state law requiring all white men residing on Cherokee land, now claimed by Georgia, to apply for licenses to remain and take an oath of allegiance to the State. Many of the missionaries abstained, feeling that Georgia had no power to enforce her laws over land rightfully belonging to the Cherokees. Rev. Daniel S. Butrick, also a missionary at Carmel, away at the time, escaped arrest. Rev. Proctor and the other missionaries which were arrested were released very shortly on grounds that they were agents of the U. S. Government in the educating of the Cherokees. Soon afterwards the issue again became critical and, rather than take the oath of allegiance, Butrick and Proctor left Georgia. Rev. Proctor remained in that portion of the Cherokee Nation now Tennessee and started a new mission. Carmel continued in existence until 1839.

(Located at GA 5 & GA 136, 1.4 miles north of Talking Rock. GHM 112-5, 1962.)

FEDERAL ROAD CISCA ST. AUGUSTINE TRAIL

The road turning west of here down Talking Rock Creek to the site of Coosawatee Old Town is a portion of the Old Federal Road opened through the Cherokee Nation, in 1805, by Georgia and Tennessee. It follows the course of a trail shown on a map of 1864 as connecting the ancient Indian town of Cisca in the Tennessee Valley with St. Augustine in Spanish Florida.

It became the principal mail and stage coach road along which pioneers settled in the Cherokee Territory.

(Located on GA 136 near Talking Rock Creek. WPA 112-C5.) ♦ ★ – not standing.

TATE

GEORGIA MARBLE

Georgia marble, known the world over for its beauty and enduring qualities, was first systematically quarried in 1836 by Henry Fitzsimmons four miles east of here. The present extensive use as an exterior and interior building stone and for statuary, mausoleums, and monuments is due largely to the vision and energy of Colonel Sam Tate.

(Located on GA 53 near the rail station. WPA 112-C7.) ♦ ★ – not standing.

OLD FEDERAL ROAD

The highway coming from the right is the Old Federal Road, northwest Georgia's first vehicular way and the earliest postal route of this area. It began on the southeastern boundary of the Cherokees in the direction of Athens, linking Georgia and Tennessee across the Indian Country.

Rights to open the thoroughfare were granted informally by the Cherokees in 1803 and confirmed in the 1805 Treaty of Tellico, Tennessee.

"Daniels," an early stand and stage stop on the old trace stood here.

(Located on GA 53 at Long Creek Swamp, 1.7 miles east of junction with GA 108. GHM 112-2, 1954.)

OLD FEDERAL ROAD

This highway from Tate to Talking Rock follows substantially the course of the Old Federal Road, the earliest thoroughfare to link Georgia and Tennessee across the Cherokee Nation. Permission to use the way was granted informally by the Indians in 1803 and formally by the 1805 Treaty of Tellico, Tenn. The Federal Road was the first vehicular thoroughfare west of the Chattahoochee, the earliest postal route of this section of the State, and a leading emigrant trace to Tennessee and North Alabama. Kentucky and Tennessee stockmen drove animals down this artery to Southeastern markets.

(Located on GA 53 in a small park, 3.2 miles north of Tate. GHM 112-3B, 1954.)

POLK COUNTY

Named in honor of James K. Polk (1795–1849) of North Carolina who was the eleventh president of the United States. County Seat: Cedartown.

ARAGON

DODGE & DAVIS AT PEEK'S SPRING

The spring 175 yds. E. was the camping place of Maj. Gen. Grenville M. Dodge's 16th A.C. of McPherson's

Army of the Tennessee (F), May 23, 1864, enroute from the Etowah River to Dallas, Paulding County.

May 24. Brig. Gen. J. C. Davis' (2d) div., 14th Corps, Army of the Cumberland (F), camped at the spring, enroute from Rome to Dallas.

These troops were part of the right wing of Sherman's forces, moving to outflank Johnston's army (C) at Allatoona. This resulted in 10 days of battle at New Hope Church & Dallas, in Paulding County.

(Located on GA 101. GHM 115-2, 1992.)

LOGAN'S 15TH CORPS AT SWAINTOWN

May 23, 1864. Maj. Gen. John A. Logan's 15th A.C. (F), camped here at Euharlee Cr., on the site of old Swaintown, while Maj. Gen. G.M. Dodge's 16th A.C. (F) camped at Peek's Spring one mile Northwest.

These two A.C., comprising McPherson's Army of the Tennessee, had moved from Woolley's Bridge, Etowah River, to this vicinity. The next day they marched by Van Wert toward Dallas, Paulding County.

May 25. Brig. Gen. J. C. Davis' (2nd) div., 14th, A.C. (F), crossed Euharlee Creek here also enroute to Dallas.

(Located on GA 101. GHM 115-3, 1990.) ♦

CEDARTOWN

POLK COUNTY

Created December 20, 1851 and named for President James Knox Polk. Cedartown is fittingly named for the trees which flourish in this beautiful valley. The city is a railroad center, has a thriving textile industry, and a large paper mill.

Rockmart, thirteen miles to the east, has textile mills that give the area much employment and a large payroll and as well is the center of portland cement production.

(Located on Prior Street on the courthouse lawn. GHM 115-1, 1953.)

IVY LEDBETTER LEE
FOUNDER OF
MODERN PUBLIC RELATIONS
1877–1934

Ivy Ledbetter Lee, public relations expert, author, lecturer, and philanthropist, was born July 16, 1877, near Cedartown. He attended Emory College for two years and then went to Princeton, where he earned his A. B. in 1898, paying his way by working on university and New York newspapers. In January, 1899, he arrived in New York "with a raincoat, a diploma, and five dollars," and found work as a reporter.

In 1904 pursuing his idea that Big Business needed better public relations, he opened a counseling office in New York. By 1915 he had begun a lifetime association as John D. Rockefeller's publicity counsel, especially in Rockefeller's widespread benevo-

lences. Among Lee's other clients were the Pennsylvania Railroad and Bethlehem Steel, as well as numerous charities and churches to which he donated his services.

The founder of the profession of Public Relations, Ivy Lee, a Georgia gentleman who described himself as a "physician to corporate bodies," believed that corporations should not conceal the truth from the press and that business leaders should not shun publicity. His principles helped to make American business more public-spirited and humanitarian.

He died of a brain tumor in New York City, Nov. 8, 1934.

(Located on Prior Street on the courthouse lawn. GHM 115-7, 1965.)

BIG SPRING PARK

Asa Prior, born in Virginia about 1785, pioneered into this valley and purchased a large tract of land including this spring and Cedar Creek in 1834. In 1852 he deeded the spring and 10 adjacent acres to the City of Cedartown. Another pioneer, Mr. Walthall, established the Walthall Indian Trading Post near the spring. Peace-loving Cherokees gathered here. Indian young people danced their corn dance under the cedar trees. The Cedar Valley Garden Club beautified this park. A shrine was dedicated to the memory of Sen. William Julius Harris, whose funeral was held in the park, April 21, 1932.

(Located at Essex Street and Wissahickon Avenue in the park. GHM 115-6, 1956.)

ROCKMART

OLD VAN WERT
POLK COUNTY

County Seat of Paulding when that county was created in 1832; inc. 1838. Named for Isaac Van Wert and John Paulding, two of the captors of Major André.

Polk County was organized in 1851 from parts of Floyd and Paulding; this placed Van Wert in Polk Co.; Dallas became the county seat of Paulding – Cedartown, that of Polk.

May 25, 1864. Davis' (2d) div., 14th A. C. (F), having camped the night before at Peek's Spring, 4.5 mi. N., turned E. here and marched to Dallas in Paulding County.

(Located at Springdale Road and GA 6/101, 0.4 mile south of junction with US 278. GHM 115-5, 1978.)

TAYLORSVILLE

McPHERSON'S MARCH
TO DALLAS

May 23, 1864. The Army of the Tennessee (F), consisting of Logan's 15th & Dodge's 16th A.C., crossed the Etowah River at Woolley's Bridge & by Old Macedonia Church & roads not now existing, reached this, the intersection with the Old Alabama Rd., 7.5 mi. W. of Stilesboro.

Keeping W. of Euharlee Creek, the troops continued S.W. to a creek cross-

ing at (the present) Aragon, in Polk County.

These troops (right wing of Sherman's Army) (F), were moving to Dallas, in Paulding County to out-flank Johnston's army (C) at Allatoona.

(Located on the Aragon–Taylorsville Road which is parallel to the railroad track, west 3.1 miles. GHM 115-1, 1953.)

RABUN COUNTY

Named in honor of William Rabun (1771–1891), a native of North Carolina who served as governor of Georgia. County Seat: Clayton.

CLAYTON

RABUN COUNTY

This County created by Act of the Legislature Dec. 21, 1819, is named for William Rabun, 11th Governor of Georgia who was elected in 1817 and died in 1819. Self-educated by reading he served as a member of the Legislature and as President of the Senate.

Here now is located the famous Rabun Gap–Nacoochee School for the education of entire families. Among the first County Officers were: Justices of the Inferior Court Edward Coffee, John McClure, Samuel Farris, William Kelly, William Gillespie, Andrew

Miller, James Dillard, and Clerk Thomas Kelly.

(Located on US 76 West/Savannah Street on the courthouse lawn. GHM 119-1, 1954.)

MEMORIAL LANDS
AND COTTAGES
GEORGIA DIVISION UDC

The Georgia Division UDC has contributed 115 acres of land and four cottages to the farm family program of the Rabun Gap-Nacoochee School. The plan was first proposed by Miss Mildred Rutherford in 1905. FRANCIS S. BARTOW COTTAGE built in 1938, was named for Francis S. Bartow, the first Confederate General to be killed in the War Between the States. WORLD WAR I MEMORIAL COTTAGE was built in 1939. ALICE BAXTER COTTAGE, built in 1951, was named for Miss Baxter for her outstanding service as sixth president of the Georgia Division UDC. WORLD WAR II MEMORIAL COTTAGE was erected in 1954.

(Located on US 441/23, 5.4 miles north of Clayton. GHM 119-2, 1956.)

COURTESY, RABUN GAP-NACOOCHEE SCHOOL

A FARM FAMILY IN FRONT OF THIER HOME

RABUN GAP
NACOOCHEE SCHOOL
ANDREW JACKSON RITCHIE, 1868–1948, FOUNDER

One of Rabun County's first college graduates, Andrew Jackson Ritchie received his B.A. and M.A. degrees from Harvard University before returning to his native county to devote his life to the education of the mountain people.

In 1903 he founded the Rabun Gap Industrial School and in 1917 originated the "Farm Family Plan," by which entire families work their way through school. The school operated independently until 1926 when it merged with the Nacoochee Institute, a school owned and supported by the Presbyterian Synod of Georgia. Under Dr. Ritchie's presidency, the new school, chartered in 1927 and named Rabun Gap–Nacoochee, acquired more land, larger dormitories and classrooms, and began new educational programs.

Dr. Ritchie, whose unique approach to education has attracted strong financial support, served as President of the school until his retirement in 1939. In 1948, the year of his death, his *Sketches of Rabun County History* was published.

Dr. Ritchie, educator, scholar, and historian, is buried on the hill overlooking this school which his complete devotion created.

(Located on US 441/23, 6.1 miles north of Clayton. GHM 119-3, 1967.)

DR. ANDREW JACKSON RITCHIE (1868–1948)

RABUN GAP
ELEVATION 2,160 FT.

Here in Rabun Gap the divide of the Blue Ridge has been cut across by stream action, forming one of the lowest passes in the southern Appalachians. Water flows north through the Tennessee and Mississippi to the Gulf, and south through the Savannah to the Atlantic. Through this gap ran an old Cherokee Indian trail; pioneer traders and settlers crossed here, later the railroad, finally this scenic highway through the mountains.

(Located on US 441/23 several miles north of Clayton. WPA 119-A4, 1941.) ♦ ★ – not standing.

WILLIAM BARTRAM TRAIL
TRACED 1773–1777

In 1775, William Bartram wrote in "Travels" of the flora and fauna of this area as he gathered specimens to ship to London.

(Located on War Woman Road, 2.7 miles east of junction with US 441/23 where the Bartram Trail crosses the road just before War Woman Dell. BTC/GCG 119-99.)

ELLICOTT'S ROCK

Ellicott's Rock, 5 miles east on the east bank of the Chattooga River, marks the northeast corner of Georgia at its junction with South Carolina and North Carolina. Andrew Ellicott, a noted surveyor of Pennsylvania, established the rock in May 1812 to mark the 35th parallel which was to be the northern boundary of Georgia. Recent surveys show the rock to be 500 feet north of the true 35th parallel, which is remarkably accurate for the instruments of those days.

(Located on GA 28 near the Georgia/North Carolina state line. WPA 119-A2.) ♦ ★ – not standing.

COMMISSIONER'S ROCK

Commissioner's Rock, 6 miles west, on the road to Rabun Bald, is one of the few surviving original markers on the Georgia North Carolina line. Timothy Terrell, surveyor for Georgia, and Robert Love, surveyed this portion of the line in 1819. Recent surveys show that Commissioner's Rock is 1,390 feet south of the true 35th parallel, which was to have been the northern boundary of Georgia.

(Located on GA 28 near the Georgia/North Carolina state line. WPA 119-A3.) ♦ ★ – not standing.

STEPHENS COUNTY

Named in honor of Alexander H. Stephens (1812–1883) who was vice president of the Confederacy and elected governor of Georgia. County Seat: Toccoa.

MARTIN

RED HOLLOW ROAD

Winding along a ridge from the mouth of Broad River to the head of Tugalo, RED HOLLOW ROAD evolved from the noted trace, UPPER CHEROKEE PATH, and became part of a complex pioneer road system.

In 1736–1737, Oglethorpe had River Road laid out to Augusta from Savannah; it was Georgia's first long road built by white men. At Augusta, River Road joined UPPER CHEROKEE PATH whose origins are lost in antiquity. From Augusta northward to Petersburg, the PATH became Petersburg Road. The PATH crossed not a single stream for approximately 70 miles between Petersburg and Toccoa. Continuing north through Amandaville, Eagle Grove,

and Aquilla to a point near Martin, the PATH became RED HOLLOW ROAD. The ROAD intersected at Toccoa with Unicoi Turnpike which ran into East Tennessee. The ROAD at Toccoa also had a spur, Locust Stake Road, which ran to the Ga.–N.C. line.

The track of Southern R.R., completed in 1878, cut RED HOLLOW ROAD 13 times between Toccoa and Martin including the station intersection at Hayes Crossing, Eastanollee, and Avalon.

(Located on GA 17 in Martin. SCHS 127-99, 1986.)

TOCCOA

STEPHENS COUNTY

This County, created by Act of the Legislature August 18, 1905, is named for Alexander Hamilton Stephens, Vice President of the Confederacy. A state legislator and Senator, he was elected to Congress at 31, serving from 1843 to 1859. Elected to the Senate in 1866 he was refused his seat but again served in Congress from 1873 to '82 when he became Governor. He died March 4, 1883. Among the first County Officers were: Sheriff W. A. Stowe, Clerk of Superior Court W. A. Bailey, Ordinary B. P. Brown, Jr., Tax Receiver M. C. Jarrett, Tax Collector C. L. Mize, Treasurer C. H. Dance, Coroner Sidney Williams and Surveyor M. B. Collier.

(Located on West Doyle Street between North Sage and North Alexander Streets, on the courthouse lawn. GHM 127-1, 1954.)

GEORGE WASHINGTON HITT
1913–1958
Artist, Humanitarian, Philosopher

"An unforgettable personality whose courage shone with such crystal brilliance as to brighten the world about him and uplift the spirits of those even more fortunate, but not fashioned of such heroic fibre. His is a name to remember when the going gets tough and the seductive voices of defeat sing their siren song." – Rogers, The Atlanta Journal. Born March 31, 1913, his life was spent in Toccoa. Despite crippling rheumatoid arthritis, he led and active, creative life as an internationally know silhouette artist, reporter and technical writer. His philosophy was, "No person is handicapped unless he perceives himself to be." He received the Army–Navy E Award in 1945, the same year the U.S. Department of State distributed the story of his life abroad. In 1954 he received

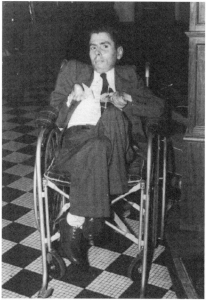

COURTESY, BETTY SWORDS

GEORGE HITT (1913–1958)

the National Who's Crippled Award. His delicate silhouettes depicted people and events, but his most beautiful were of nature. His feeling for composition and sensitivity in artistic portrayal ranked him among the foremost silhouette artists of his day.

(Located in Henderson Falls Park. SCHS 127-98, 1984.)

THE OLD TOCCOA FALLS POWER PLANT

The Old Toccoa Falls Power Plant is an outstanding example of the early hydroelectric generating facilities that served America's rural communities. Built in 1899 by E. Palmer Simpson of Toccoa, the plant was franchised in that year by the Toccoa City Council to supply the city and area with electricity. A log dam to provide headwa-

COURTESY, BETTY SWORDS

ONE OF GEORGE HITT'S SILHOUETTES

ter for the penstock at the rear of the building formed a small lake on the mountain above the plant. The bricks were handmade – swirls of the paddle can be clearly seen – and then brought to the site in wagon loads that took two days each round trip. Water from the penstock spun the 200 kilowatt (266 horsepower) generator, and the electricity was distributed through the old switchboard. The plant was acquired by the Georgia Power Company in 1927; then in 1933 it was given to the Toccoa Falls Institute, which used the power exclusively to furnish all its electrical needs until 1957. At that time, the school returned to Company lines and the plant fell into disrepair. In 1972, the Georgia Power Company and the Institute cooperated in renovating the old plant in order that it can be maintained as a historical site.

Acknowledgement is given to the vision and progressive contributions of Mr. P. S. Arkwright, president and founder of the Georgia Power Company and to Dr. R. A. Forrest, founder of the Toccoa Falls Institute.

(Located off GA17/Falls Road on the Campus of Toccoa Falls College near

the entrance to the falls. GPC 127-97, 1972.)

HISTORIC TRAVELER'S REST

Historic Traveler's Rest was built upon land granted to Major Jesse Walton in 1785. Walton, a Revolutionary soldier and political leader, was killed by Indians near here in 1789. The Walton family sold the land to James Rutherford Wyly who built the main part of the house between 1816 and 1825. Devereaux Jarrett bought the house on August 21, 1838. Jarrett added to the original structure and opened it to the public. Due to the growing population and increased through traffic, the structure served as an inn, trading post, and post office. While the ten room house was open to the public it entertained many illustrious travelers. The Jarrett account books, that doubled as hotel registers, contain the name of the English scientist and author, G. W. Featherstonehaugh, who stayed the night and ate breakfast for "a quarter of a dollar." While the Jarrett family owned the house that they called Jarrett Manor, Mrs. Mary Jarrett White, the last family owner, made history. She was the first woman in Georgia to vote. Historic Traveler's Rest is on the National Register of Historic Places and is a Georgia Historical Commission Site.

(From US 123 and GA 63/106/184 in Toccoa, follow US 123 north 6.5 miles, turn left on Riverdale Road and follow for 0.4 mile to marker. GHM 127-4, 1970.)

TRAVELER'S REST

OLD TUGALOO TOWN

North of this marker, in the center of the lake, once stood an important Indian town. The area now marked by a small island was settled around 500 A.D. and occupied by Cherokee Indians around 1450. Traders were coming to the town by 1690.

In 1716, while Col. Maurice Moore treated with Charity Hague, Cherokee Conjuror, a group of Creek ambassadors arrived. The Creek Indians, supported by Spain and France, wished to drive the British from the Carolinas in the Yamassee War. The Cherokees killed the Creek ambassadors and joined the British. By 1717, Col. Theophilus Hastings operated a trading center at Tugaloo where gunsmith, John Milbourne cared for Cherokee firearms. Indian agent, Col. George Chicken visited Tugaloo in 1725 and described it as "the most ancient town in these parts."

Tugaloo remained a principal Cherokee town until destroyed by American patriots fighting these allies of the British in 1776.

(From US 123 and GA 63/106/184 in Toccoa, follow US 123 north 6.9 miles to marker near the GA/SC state line. GHM 127-5, 1985.)

TUGALO BAPTIST CHURCH AND CEMETERY

Tugalo Baptist Church, established before 1789, was first known as the Tugalo River Church. Founded by the Rev. John Cleveland, a Revolutionary Soldier, Tugalo is the oldest church in what was then Franklin County. The county covered and area in Ga. and S. C. about the size of Rhode Island.

The church has been called "The Mother Church" of Baptist churches in this area. Cleveland was to become known as "The Father of Baptist Principles." He and the Rev. Thomas Gilbert represented Tugalo River Church when the Tugalo Baptist Association was formed in 1818.

The land upon which the church stands was deeded to the church by Robert and Sarah (Wheeler) Craig July 28, 1895, and both the church and the cemetery have remained on their original site since its founding.

In the cemetery is the grave of Henry Fricks who lived his life during three centuries. He was born in 1799 and died in 1901.

This marker was erected by the Tugalo Baptist Church and Stephens County Historical Society in 1984. Romans 8:31-39.

(From GA 17 and US 123, travel GA 17 1.6 miles. Bear left on Brookhaven Circle/Rock Creek Road for 6.0 miles, continue on East Silver Shoals Road 2.7 miles to marker. SCHS 127-95, 1984.)

EASTANOLLEE BAPTIST CHURCH

One of the oldest churches in the Tugalo Baptist Assoc., this church was established in 1801 as Leatherwood Baptist Church on John Stonecypher property.

Later, members moving to Habersham County established Leatherwood Baptist Church there. The members here continued meeting until Sept. 8, 1810 when it was constituted as Eastanollee Baptist Church with a membership of 118. Nancy Meeks was first pastor. Others were Francis Calloway, Lewis Ballard, Matthew Vandiver, John A. Davis, Barwick Chambers, Davis Simmons, John G. York, Marion Sewell, William Kelly, William Morton, T. G. Underwood, H. M. Barton, E. L. Sisk, Thomas Burgess, Jesse Brown, J. F. Goode, L. B. Norton, T. J. Stonecypher, J. Fullbright, W. W. Stowe, J. P. Dendy and S. E. Macomson. The present building was dedicated in 1946 under the leadership of Ben F. Turner who was pastor from 1934 till 1959.

(Located at GA 17 and Scott Road, 5.9 miles east of GA 17 and US 123. SCHS 127-96.)

TALIAFERRO COUNTY

Named in honor of Colonel Benjamin Taliaferro (1750–1821), a Revolutionary War hero, state senator and a judge. County Seat: Crawfordville.

CRAWFORDVILLE

TALIAFERRO COUNTY

This County, created by an Act of the Legislature Dec. 24, 1825, is named for Colonel Benjamin Taliaferro, Revolutionary soldier in Lee's Legion and a member of Congress from 1799 to 1802.

In this city stands Liberty Hall, now a State Shrine, beloved home in life and the last resting place of Alexander H. Stephens, affectionately known as "Little Alec" and "The Great Commoner."

Born in a log cabin in this county in 1812 and graduating from the University of Georgia in 1832, Mr. Stephens began his public career by serving six consecutive terms in the Georgia Legislature with distinction. He was elected to Congress in 1843 and served through 1859. He voted against secession in the Georgia Convention of 1861 but accepted his State's decision and was a delegate to the Montgomery convention at which the Confederacy was born. Elected Vice President of the Confederacy he served throughout the war, opposing many of the policies of President Jefferson Davis.

Mr. Stephens was elected to the United States Senate in 1866 but a seat was refused him. He was again elected to Congress in 1873 and served until 1882, when he was elected Governor of Georgia, dying in office on March 4, 1883.

Among Taliaferro County's first officers were Sheriff Asa C. Alexander, Superior Court Clerk Marcus Andrews, Inferior Court Clerk Henry Perkins, Coroner Solomon Harper and Surveyor Henry Stewart.

(Located on Broad Street between Alexander and Monument Streets on

LIBERTY HALL
HOME OF ALEXANDER H. STEPHENS

the courthouse lawn. GHM 131-1, 1954.)

THE COMMON ROAD OF THE ENGLISH FOLLOWING OLD INDIAN TRAIL

The colonial road from Charleston to Vicksburg followed the highway at this point. The route, used by Col. Langdon Welch on his expedition to the Mississippi in 1698, was thereafter followed by British traders. Through Taliaferro Co., it followed the present route, Raytown to Crawfordville to Union Point, then Ogeechee River Old Town. Wm. Bartram, celebrated traveler, crossed here in 1773 with the party, headed by Col. Barnett, which surveyed 2,000,000 acres of land ceded by the Creeks and Cherokees to the Colony of Georgia. Lafayette followed this road on his American tour in 1825.

(Located at Broad and Alexander Streets on the courthouse lawn. GHM 131-9, 1956.)

ALEXANDER H. STEPHENS 1812–1883

On the hill to the north stands Liberty Hall, home of the Vice-President of the Confederacy. Born in a Log cabin two miles north, Stephens came here to live in 1834 and begun his career as a lawyer in the first court house built on this block.

Liberty Hall is today preserved as a part of the Alexander H. Stephens Memorial State Park.

(Located at Broad and Monument Streets on the courthouse lawn. WPA 131-C5.) ♦ ★ – not standing.

ROSELLE MERCIER MONTGOMERY

The renowned Georgia poetess, Roselle Mercier Montgomery, daughter of Col. William Nathaniel and Emma Smith Mercier, was born on this site in 1874. Educated at Washington Female Seminary and Mary Baldwin Seminary, she married distinguished N. Y. lawyer, J. Seymour Montgomery and lived in Conn. Her early death in 1933 cut short an outstanding career. Her famous poem, "Evening on a Village Street," was written about this corner in Crawfordville. Considered Georgia's best and one of America's finest poetesses, she is best known for her "Ulysses Returns" and "To Helen, Middle-Aged."

(Located at Alexander and Commerce Streets across from the courthouse. GHM 131-17, 1956.)

Evening on a Village Street

The sun flings lengthening shadows through the trees
That green the village street. They come to life,
The houses that have seemed to sleep all day.

The evening meal is over, dishes done,
And prim, trim women sit and rock and knit
Upon the porches, read the village news
Recorded in the paper, out today,
Or move about the yards to give their plants
Their evening watering, or chat across the hedge
With friendly neighbors on the other side,
Or swap rose-cuttings and geranium slips.

The men, shirt-sleeved, walk leisurely behind
Their lawn-mowers, or rake and sweep their paths,
Or tie their vines up to their trellises--
Small, pleasant tasks, with which they rest themselves
At evening, when their day of work is done.

The children call and shout there in the street,
Or play hide-and-seek from yard to yard.
And arm in arm young lovers stroll in pairs,
Bound for the moving-pictures in the square.

The sun has dropped, now, low, behind the hill--
The high, blue hill that rises to the west.
The dark leaps on; high up, a sudden star
Blooms out like some pale flower; a thin, young moon
Hangs like a silver string caught in the trees,
And in the houses lights begin to glow.

Here on the street another day is done--
So like the last day and the coming one--
So like this street to other village streets!
And yet the total of such days is -- Life,
The sum of streets like this -- America!

— Roselle Mercier Montgomery

CRAWFORDVILLE METHODIST CHURCH

This church, originally known as "Bird's Chapel," was founded in 1826 as the first church in the newly formed town of Crawfordville. It was an outgrowth of the now defunct Powder Creek Meeting House near Sandy Cross, which came into existence about 1805. "Bird's Chapel" was ministered to by the Rev. Williamson Bird, Jr., who built and lived in the house now known as "Liberty Hall," the home of Alexander Hamilton Stephens. This chapel, originally located at the corner of what is now Jackson and Askin Streets, was later moved closer in to town for the convenience of its members. It was disbanded just before the War Between the States due to the moving away of many of its members, but was re-formed by the Rev. Allen Thomas, in 1876, on the southwest corner of the Liberty Hall lawn on land donated by Alexander H. Stephens. By 1911, this old church was outgrown and a new and larger building was built a half-block north of this present site; that building was destroyed by a cyclone in 1918. The present building, of Greek Colonial design, was erected in 1920.

(Located at Alexander and Moore Streets. GHM 131-20, 1956.)

OLD TAVERN SITE

On this site, Lot 17, provided for, in 1826, in the Town Plan by Hermon Mercer, who laid out the town of Crawfordville, a tavern, inn or hotel has stood continuously. The original tavern, built by Gilbert Rossignol, a refugee from the French Revolution, stood near Locust Grove. That building, a large, two-story house with broad veranda and columns, was bought in 1826 by Sylvester B. J. Cratin and reerected on this site. It was operated by Mr. and Mrs. Anderson Little. The old tavern stood until 1902 when the present brick hotel was built.

(Located at Broad and Askin Streets. GHM 131-7, 1956.)

SITE OF CHILDHOOD HOME OF RICHARD MALCOLM JOHNSTON

Richard Malcolm Johnston (1822–1898), educator and author, was born at Powelton. Later, his father moved to Crawfordville for better school facilities for his children. The Powelton home was torn down and reerected on this site. Johnston was educated at old Crawfordville Academy and Mercer University. Among his best known works are "Dukesborough Tales," "Old Mark Langston," and, with W. H. Browne, "Alexander H. Stephens." Stephens is said to have received his idea of keeping open house at "Liberty Hall" from the great hospitality of the Johnston family in their home across the street.

(Located at Memorial Drive and Sharon Street across from Liberty Hall. GHM 131-16, 1956.)

CRAWFORDVILLE ACADEMY ALEXANDER STEPHENS INSTITUTE

This school, one of the finest of the early Georgia Academies, was chartered by the Legislature, Dec. 26, 1826. First trustees were Archibald Gresham, R. Q. Dickinson, Wylie Womack, Hermon Mercer, Leonidas B. Mercer. Among the first masters were William D. Cowdrey and Simpson Fouche, outstanding classical scholars. The name was officially changed to Stephens High School in 1886 to honor Alexander Stephens and a new building was erected. That building burned in 1907 and was replaced by another. In 1920 it became Alexander Stephens Institute, a county high school. In 1955 the school moved to a new site.

(Located on Memorial Drive across from Liberty Hall. GHM 131-4, 1956.)

CRAWFORDVILLE BAPTIST CHURCH

This, the first Protestant Church in the Taliaferro area and originally called Bethel, was established in 1802 by Rev. Jesse Mercer and Rev. James Matthews on land given by William Janes, one of Georgia's largest planters. The first pastor was Rev. James Robertson; first deacons were John Walker and Etheldred Wilder. Known widely for its liberality, this church granted the use of its building to other denominations while their churches were being organized. Many fiery political speeches have been made in the church building. The present structure was erected in 1889.

(Located off Memorial Drive across from Liberty Hall. GHM 131-11, 1956.)

BIRTHSITE OF ALEXANDER HAMILTON STEPHENS

"Little Alec," Vice-President of the Confederacy was born nearby in a log cabin Feb. 11, 1812, son of Andrew B. & Margaret Grier Stephens, a poor farm family. At his parents' death he was educated by an uncle, Gen. A. W. Grier, at Washington, and Franklin College (U. of Ga.) and was admitted to the Bar in 1834. He served as state legislator & senator from '36 to '42, as Congressman from '43 to '49 and again in 1855. After the War he was elected U. S. Senator but was not allowed to take his seat. He served in Congress from '73 until '82 and was Gov. of Georgia at his death in 1883. "He was strong by his moral intrepidity."

(Follow US 278 east 0.4 mile, turn left on GA 47/Sharon Road. (1) turn left immediately beyond the railroad track and follow road 0.2 mile, turn right on Old Sandy Cross Road and follow 2.1 miles to marker. Or (2) follow GA 47 for 2.1 miles, turn left on Sandy Cross Road for 1.5 miles, turn left on A H. Stephens Road and travel 0.9 mile. GHM 131-3, 1955.)

SITE OF CHIVERS PLANTATION & STORE

At this crossroads stood the store and drug shop of Col. Robert Chivers, father of Georgia's "lost poet," Dr. Thomas Holley Chivers. Born at his father's plantation home nearby in

ALEXANDER H. STEPHENS (1812–1883) – VICE PRESIDENT OF THE CONFEDERACY

1809, Dr. Chivers graduated in medicine at Transylvania Univ. in 1830. He practiced for a short time at this store and, after an unhappy marriage, left this section. After wandering for some time, he settled in Decatur until his death in 1858. "The Lost Pleiad and Other Poems" (1842) is his most popular work. He is known for his influence on Swinburne, Rossetti and, especially, Edgar Allen Poe.

(Follow US 278 east 0.4 mile, turn left on GA 47/Sharon Road and follow for 2.1 miles. Turn left on Sandy Cross Road for 5.2 miles to marker at junction with Hillman Road. GHM 131-15, 1956.)

ROBINSON

CONFEDERATE GUN SHOP

Fifty yards from here, in a brick building, stood the gun shop of Henning Daniel Murden (1815–1903), who, during the War Between the States, made and supplied guns and molds to Confederate troops. Like virtually all rural gun shops in the South, it was a limited operation. "Stephens Home Guards," later Co. D., 15th Ga. Inf. Reg., first company organized in Taliaferro County, was equipped with guns made by Murden. Grandson of Rev. soldier, Richard Asbury, Sr. is buried in the cemetery slightly to the east of here.

(Located on US 278/GA 12. GHM 131-6, 1992.)

INDIAN MOUNDS

Near this highway are three Indian mounds, great cairns of white stone on the east-west ridge of a high hill rising from the headwaters of the Ogeechee River. Presumably burial or ceremonial mounds, they are surrounded by many small rock cairns. The last Indians to occupy this area were an alien tribe, "Yuchis" or "Children of the Sun." Supposedly Iroquois–Mohawk origin, they spoke the language of the Sioux. A warlike race, they constantly fought the Creeks and Cherokees and were driven west of the Chattahoochee River in the Yamassee War of 1715.

(Located on US 278/GA 12. GHM 131-10, 1956.) ♦ ★ - not standing.

SHARON

THE CHURCH OF THE PURIFICATION
LOCUST GROVE ACADEMY

In 1790 several Catholic families of English descent from Maryland settled near Locust Grove. They established the first Roman Catholic Church in Georgia and erected a log church in 1792. A priest, Father John LeMoin, was sent to it from Baltimore. French families, fleeing the French Revolution and, later, several Irish families joined the colony. After 1860 a church was erected in Sharon, as the Locust Grove location had become too remote. Locust Grove Academy, the first chartered Roman Catholic Academy in Georgia, was formed about 1818. Many prominent Georgians have come from these early Catholic families.

(Located on GA 47 at the church. GHM 131-5, 1956.)

SOUTH LIBERTY
PRESBYTERIAN CHURCH

In 1820, several members of Liberty Church, Wilkes County, petitioned to form a new church, South Liberty, because of "distance, bad roads, high water in winter." A log church was built in 1828 about 4 miles east of Sharon on land given by Joshua Morgan. Services began in May 1828 and were held continuously except during the War Between the States when the minister and members were on military duty. In 1855 the log church was replaced by a frame building and, in 1877, that was moved to the present

THE CHURCH OF THE PURIFICATION
LOCUST GROVE ACADEMY

location in Sharon. First elders were Moses Alexander, C. C. Mills and Joshua Morgan. Dr. Carlyle P. Beman was the first minister.

(Located on Barnett Road, 0.3 mile from junction with GA 47. GHM 131-12, 1956.)

ROBERT GRIER, ASTRONOMER

On this land, in the plantation home of his father, Aaron Grier, Sr., Revolutionary soldier, Robert Grier, founder of the nationally famous "Grier's Almanac," was born in 1782. The remarkable astronomical calculations which led to the publishing of the almanac were made on the large boulders in the fields near this road. First published in 1807 as "The Georgia and South Carolina Almanack," the almanac made Robert Grier's name a household word in the nation until his death in 1848. Published continuously since its founding, it became "Grier's Almanac" soon after Robert Grier died. Circulation is almost 2½ million copies annually.

(Located on the road to Raytown, 1.9 miles from Sharon. GHM 131-13, 1956.) Note: *Grier's Almanac* continues to be published and is generally distributed through local drugstores. You may also obtain a copy by writing Grier's Almanac, P O Box 888281, Atlanta, GA 30356.

GRAVE OF BRIG. GEN. AARON W. GRIER

About ¾ miles from here, in the Grier family cemetery, is the marked grave of Brig. Gen. Aaron Grier, born near here Dec. 2, 1794. When quite young, with Gen. Floyd, he fought the Creek Indians, distinguishing himself at the Battles of Autossee and Chalibbee in Alabama. Promoted rapidly for his military talent, he became a Brig. Gen. in the Indian and later the Mexican Wars. In 1826, his home became that of his orphan nephew, Alexander H. Stephens. He lived to see his nephew and ward become vice-president of the Confederacy but died during the war, January 14, 1864.

(Located on the road to Raytown, 1.9 miles from Sharon. GHM 131-14, 1956.) ♦ ★

RAY'S PLACE
NOW RAYTOWN

Ray's Place, oldest community in Tal-iaferro County, was, in the late 1790's and early 1800's, a recreation center on Little River for the "livelier social set" of Washington. It was named for a Ray family from New York who lived in Washington for several years. In later years the famed Wrightsboro Road came through Raytown and the stage road from Double Wells (Bar-nett) to Washington. The parents and grandparents of Jefferson Davis owned plantations near Raytown in the early 1800's. Mrs. Davis, fleeing Federal forces in 1865, spent a night in Ray-town.

(Located at Double Wells and Lower Mill Roads in Raytown, 2.6 miles east of Sharon. GHM 131-8, 1956.)

RAYTOWN METHODIST CHURCH

This church is located in that part of the original Wilkes Circuit of 1786, "the cradle of Georgia Methodism," from which Bishop Francis Asbury formed the Little River Circuit at the Camden, S. C. Conference in January 1802. The Raytown Methodists from Virginia, Maryland, North and South Carolina, were "formed into Society" in the early 1800's, held their first meetings in the homes of members, and, after 1828, worshiped for some years in the old South Liberty Meeting House. When rapid growth created a need for a separate church, this land, given by James Moore, Sr., and Mrs. Mary Shaw Pearson, was surveyed Nov. 25, 1845, deeded Dec. 17, 1845,

RAYTOWN METHODIST CHURCH

and the first building erected. Trustees named were Bedor Proctor, George W. Flynt, Nathaniel Parham, Aaron T. Kendrick, John Wright, William Cicero Wright, John C. Byrd and John Hartwell Phelts. Disrupted by absence of men and ministers during the War Between the States, services were resumed, April 2, 1865, on the reor-ganization of the Raytown Union Sab-bath School, John H. Beall, Superintendent, and William H. Brooks, Secretary. The present build-ing was erected in 1890. Among the ministers of the church in the 1800's were Josiah Lewis, Allen Thomas, Felix Persons Brown, Miles Wesley Arnold, and Andrew Jackson Hugh-es, all known for their outstanding work in building the great rural churches of Georgia Methodism.

(Located on Lower Mill Road in Ray-town, 3.1 miles east of Sharon. GHM 131-19, 1956.)

TOWNS COUNTY

Named in honor of George Washington Towns (1801–1854), state senator, congressman and governor of Georgia. County seat: Hiawassee.

HIAWASSEE

TOWNS COUNTY

Towns County was created by Act of March 6, 1856 from Rabun and Union Counties. It was named for George Washington Towns, Governor of Georgia from 1847–1851. Gov. Towns was born in Wilkes County, May 4, 1801, of a Virginia family. Self-educated, he was a merchant, lawyer, legislator, state senator, Congressman. He died in 1854. First officers of Towns County, commissioned April 21, 1856, were: Andrew I. Burch, Sheriff; Martin L. Burch, Clerk Superior Court; James H. Moore, Clerk Inferior Court; Milton Brown, Tax Receiver; George M. Denton, Tax Collector; Robert S. Patton, Coroner; James Alston, Surveyor; John W. Holmes, Ordinary.

(Located at West River and Berrong Streets on the courthouse lawn. GHM 139-2, 1956.)

THE UNICOI TURNPIKE

The Unicoi Turnpike, first vehicular thoroughfare in this part of Georgia, passed here leading from Nine Mile Creek near Maryville in East Tennessee to the head of poleboat navigation on the Tugalo River, to the east of Toccoa.

Permission to open the route as a toll road was given by the Cherokees in 1813 to a Company of Indians and white men. Georgia and Tennessee granted charters to the concern.

Prior to its opening as a wagon road, the trace was part of an important trading path from the Cherokees to Augusta.

Noted Unicoi Gap to the south derives its name from the road which used that pass to cross the Blue Ridge.

(Located at US 76 & GA 17/75 east of Hiawassee. GHM 139-1, 1956.) ♦ ★

BRASSTOWN BALD

The high, rounded peak, Brasstown Bald or Mt. Enotah, is the highest mountain in Georgia, 4,748 feet. Its Indian name, Itseyi, means "a place of fresh green," referring to its grassy, instead of timbered, summit. Early white settlers mistook the Indian name for a similar one meaning brass.

According to Cherokee legend, there was once a great flood and all men died except a few Cherokee families who landed on top of Brasstown Bald in a giant canoe. The Great Spirit killed all the trees on top of the mountain so the survivors could plant crops and live until the floods subsided.

(Located at GA 17/75 and GA 180, 6.3 miles south of GA 17/75 with US 76. GHM 139-4, 1956.) **Note:** The correct height for Brasstown Bald is 4,784 feet.

UNICOI GAP
ELEVATION 2,949 FT.

Unicoi Gap is the first pass in the Georgia Blue Ridge through which a public road was constructed. The Unicoi Turnpike built 1813-1816 by a company of Georgians, Tennesseeans, and Cherokees extended from the head of navigation of Tugaloo River through Nacoochee Valley, across this Gap, and down the Hiawassee River to Echota in Tennessee, then the capitol of the Cherokees. From 1819 to 1832 this gap marked the last boundary between Georgia and Cherokee Nation.

(Located on GA 75 near the Towns County/White County line. WPA 139-A5, 1941.) ♦ ★ – not standing.

BRASSTOWN BALD
The Highest Point in
Georgia – 4,784 Ft.

The name is derived from the Cherokee word Itse'yi (New Green Place) or (Place of Fresh Green), from Itse'hi (green or unripe vegetation), and yi, the locative. It occurs in several places in the old Cherokee country, variously spelled Echia, Echoe, Etchowee, and sometimes "Brasstown," from a confusion of Itse'yi with Uñtsaiyi' (brass). One settlement known to the whites as Brasstown was on Upper Brasstown Creek of Hiawassee River directly NW of this point. The area near the Spring to the SW was once an Indian camping ground.

(Located off GA 180 at the summit of Brasstown Bald. GHM 139-5, 1958.)

HIAWASSEE RIVER BASIN

Along this river, a principal tributary of the Tennessee River flowing through Georgia, North Carolina and Tennessee, TVA has 3 reservoirs for power and flood control purposes. By its source in Unicoi Gap ran the Unicoi Turnpike to Great Echota, the ancient capital and sacred "Peace Town" of the Cherokee Nation. The Cherokees called the river Ayuhwa'si, meaning a savannah or meadow and applied the name to two or more settlements. Great Hiawassee was at Savannah Ford in Polk County, Tenn.; another was at the junction of the river and Peachtree Creek, in Cherokee County, N.C.

(Located off GA 180 at the summit of Brasstown. GHM 139-3, 1956.) ♦ ★

MONTGOMERY CORNER

Montgomery Corner, 5 miles northeast, on the Georgia–North Carolina line, marks the southern end of a half mile of the State boundary line. It was established in 1818, by J. Camack and H. Montgomery, to mark the end of a survey run east from the corner of Georgia, Alabama, Tennessee, along what was thought to be the 35th parallel.

The line run west in 1819 from the northeast corner of Georgia ends one-half mile north of the Montgomery Corner stone marker.

(Located on US 76 about 8 miles east of Hiawassee. WPA 139-A5.) ♦ ★ – not standing.

UNION COUNTY

When the question as to the name of the new county was introduced in the state legislature, John Thomas, who was representing this region answered, "Union, for none but Union men reside in it." County Seat: Blairsville.

BLAIRSVILLE

UNION COUNTY

Union County was created by Act of Dec. 3, 1832, from Cherokee. Originally, it contained part of Fannin and Towns Counties. In 1832 there was much discussion over Union and States' rights. John Thomas, chosen by the people as a representative for the new County, when asked to suggest a name, is reported to have said, "Name it Union, for none but union-like men reside in it." First officers of Union County, commissioned March 20, 1833, were: James Crow, Sheriff; Arthur Gilbert, Clerk Superior Court; Joseph Jackson, Clerk Inferior Court; James Gaddis, Sr., Coroner; Joseph Chaffin, Surveyor.

(Located at Town Square and Cleveland Street on the courthouse lawn. GHM 144-5, 1956.)

DAVENPORT MOUNTAIN

Davenport Mountain in view to the east was named for John Davenport who came to this section in 1838. He built his 40 foot long log house ½ mi. to the east, over the peak of the mountain. It survived until removed in 1942 to make way for Nottely Lake.

William Poteet came to this section about the same time and settled near the junction of Camp Creek and Nottely River. William and Hosea Thomas took up homesteads at the west about 7 years later. George Loudermilk built his home on Camp Creek.

Thomas Lance, another pioneer, settled 4 mi. west at the foot of Lance Mountain.

(From US 76/GA 2 west of Blairsville follow GA 325/Nottely Dam Road 6.9 miles to marker or from US 76/GA 2 in Blairsville, follow US 19/129/GA 11 North 8.6 miles, turn left onto GA 325/Nottely Dam Road and follow 4.4 miles to the marker. GHM 144-1, 1954.)

BLOOD MOUNTAIN
ELEVATION 4458 FT.
CHATTAHOOCHEE NATIONAL FOREST

In Cherokee mythology the mountain was one of the homes of the Nunnehi or Immortals, the "People Who Live Anywhere," a race of Spirit People who lived in great townhouses in the highlands of the old Cherokee Country. One of these mythical townhouses stood near Lake Trahlyta. As a friendly people they often brought lost hunters and wanderers to their townhouses for rest and care before guiding them back to their homes. Before the coming of white settlers, the Creeks and Cherokees fought a disastrous and bloody battle in Slaughter Gap between Slaughter and Blood Mountains.

(Located off US 19/129, 13.1 miles south of Blairsville at the Walasi-Yi Center, a few hundred feet up the trail to Blood Mountain. GHM 144-3, 1958.)

WALASI–YI INN

This gap, according to the Cherokee myth is the abode of Walasi, "The Great Frog," leader of the ancient animal council. Until 1926, it was known as Frogtown Gap and was traversed only by the Frogtown Indian Trail.

Blood Mountain on the west is the home of the Nunnehi, friendly spirit folk of the Cherokee. Blood and Slaughter Mountains form a traditional battle site upon which the Cherokees defeated the Creeks. Neal Gap elevation 3,125 feet.

(Located on US 19/129, 13.1 miles south of Blairsville at the Walasi-Yi Center. WPA 144-A10, 1939.) ♦ ★ – not standing.

NOTTELY RIVER BASIN

One of the principal tributaries of the Hiwassee River, the Nottely River derives its name from the Cherokee word Na'du li', a former Cherokee settlement on the river, near the Georgia line, in Cherokee County, North Carolina. The upper slopes of this valley are in the Chattahoochee National Forest. Part of the first tract of land purchased by the United States under the Weeks law for flood control purposes can be seen on the horizon near Skeenah Gap. In 1912 Andrew and N. W. Gennett sold 32,000 acres – for

the sum of $220,626.22. With this purchase the National Forests of the eastern United States were begun.

(Located off GA 180 at the summit of Brasstown Bald. GHM 144-4, 1956.) ♦ ★

TRACKROCK GAP

The road leading south crosses Trackrock Gap, two miles from here. Soapstone boulders in the gap are covered with tracks, symbols, and patterns carved in the rocks by primitive man. The gap was called by the Cherokee Datsu nalasgun'yi, "where there are tracks."

One tradition calls it the landing place of a big canoe containing survivors of a worldwide flood, and the heavens are supposed to thunder when a stranger approaches.

(Located at US 76 east and Trackrock Road east of Blairsville but only 2.1 miles west of Young Harris. WPA 144-C1, 1941.) – not standing.

BRASSTOWN BALD

The high rounded peak to the south, with lookout tower, is Brasstown Bald or Mount Enotah, the highest mountain in Georgia, 4,748 feet above sea level. Its Indian name, Itseyi, means "place of fresh green" and refers to its grassy instead of timbered summit, as does the name "Bald." The first white settlers mistook this name for the similar one meaning "brass." A forest service road leads to a picnic area near the summit.

(Located at US 76 east and Track Rock Road east of Blairsville but only 2.1 miles west of Young Harris. WPA 144-C2, 1941.) **Note:** The correct height for Brasstown Bald is 4,784 feet.

TRACK ROCK GAP

The micaceous soapstone rocks bear ancient Indian petroglyphs from which the Gap gets its name. The Cherokees called this place Datsu nalas gun yi, (where there are tracks), or Degaye-lunha, (Printed Place). Of the many theories of the origin of the tracks held by the Cherokees, probably the most sensible is that they were made by the Indians for their own amusement. Another tradition is that they were made by a great army of birds and animals while the newly created earth's surface was still soft, to escape some pursuing danger from the west – some say a great "drive hunt" of the Indians.

(Located on Track Rock Road, 2.1 miles south of junction with US 76. Track Rock Road is 2.1 miles west of Young Harris. GHM 144-1, 1958.)

SUCHES

HOMESITE OF JOSEPH EMERSON BROWN

Joseph Emerson Brown (1821–1894), born in Pickens District, South Carolina, moved to Union County, Georgia, as a boy. The old Brown home was on the present site of the Woody Gap School, opened in 1941 for mountain students. Brown worked on his father's farm until he was nineteen, when he went to school in South Carolina. Returning to Georgia, he settled in Canton as head of the local academy. Admitted to the bar in 1845, Brown entered Yale Law School, practicing in Canton after graduating.

In 1849, Brown became a State Senator. He was elected Governor, 1857, as the Democratic compromise candidate and reelected 1859, 1861, 1863. During the Civil War, Brown's extreme states' rights views conflicted with President Davis' efforts to centralize the Confederate government. After the war, Brown, unpopular for affiliating with the Republican party and advocating submission to Reconstruction, was defeated in the U. S. Senate race of 1868. Appointed Chief Justice of the Georgia Supreme Court, 1868, he remained on the bench until in 1870 he became President of the Western & Atlantic Co. After Georgia regained home rule, Brown returned to the Democratic party and was appointed to the U. S. Senate in 1880. Reelected, he served until 1891.

(Located on GA 60, in front of Woody Gap School, 0.2 mile west of junction with GA 180. GHM 144-6, 1964.)

WALKER COUNTY

Named in honor of Major Freeman Walker (1780–1827) who served as U.S. senator from Georgia. County Seat: LaFayette.

CATLETT

CHESTNUT FLAT

May 7, 1864. McPherson's Army of the Tennessee (F) (15th & 16th A.C.), enroute E. to Snake Cr. Gap reached this point on Little Chickamauga Creek at evening and camped for the night.

This camp was in close proximity to two gaps in Taylor's Ridge, which barrier had to be passed by the Federal forces enroute to Villanow, Snake Cr. Gap and the road to Resaca. That night, Col. Sprague's (2d) brigade, Veatch's (4th) Div., 16th A.C., was sent 4 mi. S. to Ship's Gap, which was seized at 9 p.m. – a surprise move that insured an unopposed march of the 16th A.C. eastward, May 8. The 15th A.C. passed the ridge at Gordon Springs Gap on the same day.

(Located on GA 95, 0.4 miles southeast of Catlett. GHM 146-5, 1953.) ♦ ★

CHICKAMAUGA

LEE AND GORDON'S MILL

Lee and Gordon's Mill was built by James Gordon shortly after he came to this region from Gwinnett County in 1836. He rebuilt the grist mill in 1857, adding a saw mill and the first general store in this section.

At the outbreak of the War Between the States the mill was being operated by James Morgan Lee, who had married Gordon's daughter, Elizabeth Mahala. Union forces seized the mill in 1863, taking Lee prisoner and forcing him to operate the mill to supply Union troops. Later the mill served as headquarters for Bragg's Confederate troops from Sept. 7 to 10, 1863, then for Crittenden's Corps of the Union Army from Sept. 10 to 20. Both armies extended along Chickamauga Creek, the Confederates on the east bank and the Federals on the west bank, with this mill at the center. There was almost constant skirmishing around it.

In 1867 the mill burned but was rebuilt by James Lee, Gordon having retired shortly before his death in 1863. Lee died in 1889 but the mill continued to operate, being idle only a few years before its purchase in 1929 by the Wallace Brothers, of Pond Spring.

(Located on US 27 in a small park, GHM 146-15, 1955.)

LAFAYETTE

WALKER COUNTY

Created December 18, 1833, and named for Major Freeman Walker of Augusta, prominent attorney and United States Senator.

Here the fierce Chickamaugas preyed upon pioneers, and were in turn defeated and driven away; here Federals and Confederates locked in combat in 1863.

Lookout Mountain and its spur Pigeon Mountain on the West, Taylor's and Dick's Ridges on the east of the county provide spectacular scenery. Rich coal and iron deposits abound; between the mountains lie fertile valleys.

(Located at North Main and Margaret Streets in front of John B. Gordon Hall. GHM 146-3, 1953.)

JOHN B. GORDON HALL

This old academy, built in 1836, was in the line of fire during the Battle of LaFayette in the War Between the States. General Braxton Bragg (C) who had his headquarters in LaFayette, planned the Battle of Chickamauga under an old oak tree that stood in front of this building and was known as "Bragg's Oak." The tree was destroyed by lightning a few years ago. The LaFayette Chapters of the D.A.R. and U.D.C. purchased this historic building to preserve it. It was renamed John B. Gordon Hall for General Gordon (C), former pupil in the academy.

(Located at North Main and Margaret Streets in front of John B. Gordon Hall. GHM 146-2, 1953.)

GENERAL LAFAYETTE

Marie Jean Paul Roch Yves Gilbert Motier Marquis de LaFayette (1757–1834) was born in the Castle of Chavagnac, in Auvergne, France. He entered the French Army early in life and in 1777 came to America and volunteered for service in the Revolutionary Army. Congress made him a Major General. He became a close friend of General George Washington, was wounded at Brandywine, suffered a winter at Valley Forge and distinguished himself in the Yorktown campaign.

In 1824 he revisited America, including Georgia. Congress voted him $200,000 and a township of land. He died in Paris. This city is proudly named for him.

(Located at North Main and Margaret Streets in front of John B. Gordon Hall. GHM 146-11, 1953.)

THE ARMY OF TENNESSEE

Late in August, 1863, the Army of the Cumberland (F), Maj. Gen. Wm. B. Rosecrans, USA, crossed the Tennessee River near Bridgeport and threatened Chattanooga. On Sept. 7th, learning that Rosecrans was moving toward his rear in the direction of Rome (42 miles S), Gen. Braxton Bragg, CSA, withdrew his Army of Tennessee (C) from Chattanooga to this vicinity, with headquarters in LaFayette, to meet the Union advance when it crossed Lookout Mountain.

Deciding that Bragg was retreating via Ringgold (21 miles NE) and Summerville (18 miles S), Rosecrans divided his army to pursue both columns and to strike at Bragg's flanks. Thomas' 14th Corps moved through Stevens' Gap into McLemore's Cove, west of LaFayette; McCook's 20th Corps toward Summerville; Crittenden's 21st Corps toward Ringgold. By the 12th, when Rosecrans realized his error, his flanks were widely separated, leaving Thomas alone in front of Bragg's whole army. Although a hasty reconcentration was begun, it was not completed until the night of September 17th.

In the meantime, an effort by Bragg to crush Thomas and Crittenden in turn failed for want of strong leadership. This failure forced Bragg to fight Rosecrans' reassembled army near West Chickamauga Creek (15 miles N) on the 19th and 20th. Although Bragg won the Battle of Chickamauga, it required two days of desperate fighting, during which his losses almost nullified his victory.

(Located at North Main and Margaret Streets in front of John B. Gordon Hall. GHM 146-13, 1957.)

THE BATTLE OF LAFAYETTE

On June 18, 1864, during Gen. Sherman's campaign for Atlanta, Col. Louis D. Watkins, commanding the 3rd Brigade, 1st Cavalry Division (F), occupied LaFayette with about 450 men of the 4th, 6th and 7th Kentucky cavalry regiments (F) "to endeavor to rid the country of several guerrilla bands." His headquarters were in the Court House, then in the center of the square, and his men were quartered in adjacent buildings.

On June 24th, about 3 A.M. he was attacked by Brig. Gen. Gideon J. Pillow, CSA, who, with about 1600 cavalry (C) was moving to North Georgia to burn the railroad bridges over Chickamauga Creek and harass Gen. Sherman's communications.

Although surprised, Watkins' men barricaded their quarters and fought stubbornly; but without water, and with ammunition running low, their plight was becoming desperate when, about 8:30 A. M., relief arrived. Escaping the Confederate encirclement, one of the Union pickets had ridden for help and, at Rock Springs Church (8 miles N), he had found the 4th Kentucky Mounted Infantry (F), Col. John T. Croxton, encamped for the night.

Riding hard to LaFayette, Croxton surprised in turn Pillow's heavily engaged force and stampeded many of their horses. Uncertain of Croxton's strength, and with his own ammunition depleted, Pillow abandoned the attack and withdrew. Losses: (F) – 4 killed, 7 wounded, 53 captured: total 64. (C) – 24 killed, 53 wounded, 78 captured: total 155.

(Located at North Main and Margaret Streets in front of John B. Gordon Hall. GHM 146-16, 1957.)

FORT CUMMING

Here stood a Cherokee Indian Stockade with blockhouse on hill built by U. S. Government in 1836.

Capt. Samuel Fariss and a company of Georgia volunteers guarded Cherokee Indians here before their removal to the west.

This fort was presumably named for Rev. David B. Cumming, Methodist minister and missionary to the Cherokees.

(Follow Main Street/US 27 north, turn left on Indian Street and proceed 0.5 mile, cross railroad track, marker is on the right. GHM 146-1, 1952.)

NAOMI

SHIP'S GAP

May 7, 1864. Col. J. W .Sprague's (2d) brigade, Veatch's (4th) Div., 16th A.C., having camped with the corps on the little Chickamauga (near Catlett 4 mi. N.), pushed forward in a surprise move and seized this gap in Taylor's Ridge at 9 p.m.

This enabled Dodge & the 16th A.C. McPherson's Army of the Tenn. (F) to march E., unopposed, to Villanow & Snake Creek Gap, May 8.

The 15th Corps (same army) crossed at Gordon Springs Gap, 4 miles N.E. McPherson's move to Snake Creek Gap outflanked the Confederate forces under Gen. J. C. Johnston (C) at Dalton – resulting later in the evacuation of that place and the two days of battle at Resaca.

(Located on GA 136, 1 mile east of junction with GA 151. GHM 146-7, 1992.)

GORDON SPRINGS GAP

The old road to Gordon Springs in Whitfield County, began at this point (State Highway 151) & passed E. through a gap in Taylor's Ridge.

May, 1864, this gap road was traversed by Federal forces enroute toward Rocky Face, Dug Gap, & Snake Creek Gap.

May 7. Butterfield's (3d) Div. (with Gen. Hooker in person) crossed the ridge, followed by Geary's (2d) Div., 20th A.C., Army of the Cumberland (F). After crossing, Butterfield moved to Dogwood Valley at Trickum; Geary, to Dug Gap.

May 8. Logan's 15th A. C., Army of the Tennessee (F), after passing the ridge, joined Dodge's 16th A. C. (F) at Villanow & Snake Creek Gap.

(Located on GA 151, 1.3 miles north of junction with GA 95. GHM 146-6, 1953.)

ROCK SPRINGS

OLD TAVERN ROAD

May 7, 1864, McPherson's Army of the Tennessee (F) (15th & 16th A. C.), having marched by Lee & Gordon's Mill, turned S. E. at this point and via Rock Springs Ch. on the old Tavern Rd. (State Highway 95), marched to its intersection with State Highway 151, & camped there that night.

McPherson's objective was to outflank Johnston's forces (C) at Dalton by seizing Snake Cr. Gap.

As originally planned, this flanking march was to have been made from Guntersville, Ala. via Rome & Kingston, but failing to secure additional forces, Sherman decided on a more restricted approach to Johnston's rear, via Villanow & Snake Creek Gap.

(Located on Old US 27 and GA 95/Rock Spring Drive. GHM 146-4, 1953.)

COURTESY, BUREAU OF AMERICAN ETHNOLOGY

JOHN ROSS (1790–1866)

ROSSVILLE

JOHN ROSS HOME

This comfortable two-story log house was the home of Cherokee Chief John Ross from boyhood until he went west over the "Trail of Tears," losing his Indian wife enroute. Although only one-eighth Indian himself, Ross was the elected "Principal Chief" of the Cherokee Nation for 40 years and their advocate for justice for 57 years. He voluntarily chose exile with his people.

In the War of 1812, Ross served with a regiment of Cherokees under Gen. Andrew Jackson against the Creek allies of the English.

This house was built in 1797 by John McDonald, grandfather of John Ross.

(Located at US 27 and Spring Street. GHM 146-12, 1954.)

OLD FEDERAL ROAD

The first vehicular and postal route of Georgia to Rossville was the Federal Road across the Cherokee Nation. Beginning on the southeast Indian boundary in the direction of Athens, Georgia, the thoroughfare led this way toward Nashville via Tate, Jasper, Talking Rock and Spring Place.

Formal permission by the Cherokees to open the road was granted in the 1805 Treaty of Tellico, Tennessee.

CHIEF JOHN ROSS HOME

Prior to that time the trace served as an Indian trading path to Augusta.

The earliest post office in northwest Georgia was established on this route at Rossville, on April 5, 1817, with John Ross as postmaster.

(Located on US 27 just south of the Georgia–Tennessee line. GHM 146-14, 1992.)

VILLANOW

WEST ARMUCHEE VALLEY

Southward for several miles is the pleasant little valley of W. Armuchee Creek; Dick Ridge on the E.; Taylor's Ridge on the W.

Situated 3 mi. S. are Old Shiloh Ch. & the Wm. Little res. – where Maj. Gen. John B. Hood (C) was taken from the field of Chickamauga to recover from a leg amputation, Sept. – Oct., 1863.

May 8, 1864. Maj. Gen. Grenville Dodge & the 16th A.C. marched E. on this road from Ship's Gap being joined enroute near Villanow by Maj. Gen. John A. Logan's 15th A.C. These were Army of the Tenn. troops (F), commanded by Maj. Gen. J. B. McPherson – enroute to a surprise seizure of Snake Creek Gap near Resaca.

(Located on GA 136 at junction with West Armuchee Road, 4.1 miles west of Villanow, 2.5 miles east of junction of GA 136 and GA 151. GHM 146-8, 1953.)

VILLANOW

Ante-bellum cross-roads settlement; name taken from Jane Porter's novel: "Thaddeus of Warsaw."

May 7, 1864. Kilpatrick's Cav., having crossed Taylor's Ridge at Nickajack Gap, moved to Gordon's Springs where it was joined by Ireland's brigade (Geary's Div., 20th A.C.). May 8, these troops moved to Villanow to meet & support McPherson's forces (F) moving E. from Ship's and Gordon Springs Gaps in Taylor's Ridge.

McPherson's troops reached Villanow at noon & continued E. to Snake Creek Gap – a surprise move to outflank Johnston's forces (C) at Dalton. The seizure of Snake Cr. Gap was effected while Geary's Div. (20th A.C.) (F) attacked Dug Gap.

(Located at GA 136 and GA 201. GHM 146-9, 1953.)

McPHERSON'S ARMY AT SNAKE CREEK GAP

A narrow, 3 mi. passage between two ridges, beginning 1 mi. S. of this marker & ending at the fork of Sugar Valley & Resaca roads.

May 8, 1864. While Geary's Div. (20th A.C.) (F) stormed Rocky Face Ridge at Dug Gap, 5 mi. N.E., McPherson's Army of the Tenn. (15th & 16th A.C.) (F), gained a lodgment in Snake Cr. Gap & held it while the 14th, 20th & 23d Corps (F) left the Dalton front & marched through the gap.

Outflanked in his position at Dalton, Johnston (C) evacuated it, May 12, & withdrew to Resaca, which he defended against Sherman's forces in two days of battle, May 14 &15.

(Located on GA 136, 0.3 mile west of junction with GA 201. GHM 146-10, 1953.)

WALTON COUNTY

Named in honor of George Walton (1749–1804), one of three Georgians who signed the Declaration of Independence. County Seat: Monroe.

GOOD HOPE

THE POPPY LADY

Moina Michael, educator, patriot, and internationally known as "The Poppy Lady," was born near here August 15, 1869. A granite boulder marks her birthplace. She received her early education at Braswell Academy and at Martin Institute, Jefferson, Georgia. Her first teaching was in a log cabin on her father's plantation and in an old store at Good Hope. Miss Michael's inspiration for the Flanders Field Poppy as the memorial emblem came to her November 9, 1918, just before Armistice Day, while she was serving with the YMCA in New York. From the sale of poppies made by disabled war veterans in hospitals, millions of dollars are realized annually for their

MOINA MICHAEL (1869–1944)

aid. Miss Michael died May 10, 1944, and is buried in Monroe, Ga.

(Located at GA 83 and Moina Michael Road, 2 miles south of Good Hope. GHM 147-7, 1958.)

LOGANVILLE

GARRARD'S CAVALRY RAID

On July 20, 1864, Union forces under Maj. Gen. W. T. Sherman, USA, were closing in on Atlanta. Hq. 2nd Cavalry Division (F), Brig. Gen. Kenner Garrard, was in Decatur, 6 miles E of Atlanta, Garrard's three brigades were guarding bridges over the Chattahoochee River and picketing the left flank. That night, Garrard was ordered to assemble his command and march to Covington (18 miles S) to burn the bridges over the Yellow and Ulcofauhachee (Alcovy) rivers and destroy the Georgia Railroad in that area.

He marched late on the 21st. Next morning the destruction was begun. At Covington, he burned the depot, a newly-built hospital center, 2,000 bales of cotton, and large quantities of quarter-master and commissary supplies. After destroying 2 railroad and 4 wagon bridges, 3 trains and 6 miles of track, he turned north toward Loganville, arriving here about noon on July 23rd.

After sending Minty's brigade to Lawrenceville (11 miles NW) on the same mission, Garrard stripped this vicinity of horses and mules, then marched back to Decatur, arriving on the 24th.

Garrard's raid cut off all communication between Atlanta and Augusta and destroyed any hope that the Army of Tennessee (C) the hard-pressed defenders of Atlanta – might receive supplies or reinforcements from the Eastern Confederacy.

(Located at US 78/GA 10 and GA 81. GHM 147-6, 1958.) ♦ ★

MONROE

WALTON COUNTY

This County created by Acts of the Legislature of Dec. 15 & 19, 1818, is named for George Walton, signer of the Declaration of Independence. Walton, born in Va. in 1749 came to Savannah when 20 to study law. Elected Secretary of the first Provincial Congress of Ga. in '75 he was also President of the Council of Safety. He served in the Continental Congress from Jan. '76 til Oct. '81. As a Col. of militia he was wounded and captured at the Battle of Savannah. He was Governor in '79 & '80 and again in '89 & '90, U. S. Senator in '95 & '96. He died Feb. 2, 1804.

(Located at South Broad and Spring Streets on the courthouse lawn. GHM 147-1, 1954.)

JAMES MONROE

This City of Monroe, settled in 1818 and incorporated Nov. 30, 1821, was named for James Monroe, fifth President. Born in Virginia in 1758, he fought in the Continental Army. He served in the Virginia legislature, in Congress and the Senate, and as Governor of Virginia twice. He was Minister to France, helped negotiate the Louisiana Purchase and was Minister to England and Spain. He served as Secretary of State, and later of War for President Madison. He was elected President in 1816 and again in 1820 and is best known as author of the Monroe Doctrine. He died in New York in 1831.

(Located at South Broad and Church Streets in front of city hall. GHM 147-3, 1955.)

SEVEN GOVERNORS HAVE LIVED IN WALTON COUNTY

Walton County has been the home either through birth or short residence of the following Georgia Chief Executives:

WILSON LUMPKIN (1831–1835)
ALFRED HOLT COLQUITT (1877–1882)
JAMES S. BOYNTON (1883)
HENRY D. McDANIEL (1883–1886)
CLIFFORD WALKER (1923–1927)
RICHARD B. RUSSELL, JR. (1931–1933)

Two of these illustrious sons, Colquitt and Russell, became United States Senators. Richard B. Hubbard, born on a plantation in Walton County in 1836, later moved to Texas and became Governor of that State.

(Located at South Broad and Church Streets in front of city hall. GHM 147-4, 1955.)

THE BATTLE OF JACK'S CREEK
SEPT. 21, 1787

The principal battle of white settlers and Creek Indians between the Revolution and the War of 1813–14 left on record was Clark's fight near here at a branch called Jack's Creek, on Sept. 21, 1787. The attacking force of 130 whites, some distinguished veterans of the Revolution, was drawn up in three divisions: General Elijah Clark commanded the center, Major John Clark, his youthful son, later Governor of Georgia (1819–1823), commanded the left wing, and Colonel Holman Freeman commanded the right.

COURTESY, GEORGIA DEPARTMENT OF ARCHIVES AND HISTORY

HENRY D. McDANIEL

The Indians, thought to be some 800 in number were completely routed from their encampment, escaping in small parties. The battle terminated in a brilliant victory for the whites. Dr. Anthony Poulain attended the wounded at Jack's Creek.

(Located on US 78/GA 10 in the northeast edge of Monroe. GHM 147-2, 1954.) ♦ ★

SOCIAL CIRCLE

THE MARCH TO THE SEA

On Nov. 15, 1864, after destroying Atlanta and cutting his communications with the North, Maj. Gen. W. T. Sherman, USA, began his destructive campaign for Savannah – the March to the Sea. He divided his army (F) into two wings. The Right Wing marched south from Atlanta, to feint at Macon but to cross the Ocmulgee

River above the city and concentrate at Gordon.

The Left Wing (14th and 20th Corps), Maj. Gen. H. W. Slocum, USA, marched to Decatur where the 20th Corps, Brig. Gen. A.S. Williams, USA, took the road to Social Circle to strike the Georgia Railroad here and destroy it through Madison.

Late on the 17th, the 20th Corps reached Centerville Box (Jersey), 6 miles NW, and camped between Cornish and Big Flat creeks, with its leading division (Geary's) on the west bank of the Ulcofauhachee (Alcovy) River, 3 miles from Social Circle.

On the 18th, elements of the 2nd and 3rd Divisions destroyed the Georgia Railroad from Social Circle to Madison (16 miles). At Rutledge (7 miles SE), the depot, water tank, warehouses and other RR facilities were burned, those at Social Circle having been destroyed in July by Garrard's cavalry (F). That night, the 20th Corps camped west of Madison on the Covington road.

Between Atlanta and Milledgeville, the movements of the Left Wing were unopposed, the few Confederate troops available being employed against the Right Wing to protect Macon, a principal arsenal center, and the Central of Georgia Railway.

(Located on GA 11 at the Methodist Church. GHM 147-5, 1955.) ♦ ★

HIGHTOWER TRAIL

This road is a portion of Hightower Trail, old Indian path to Etowah River, which ran from High Shoals of the Appalachee westward to Shallow Ford on the Chattahoochee. It formed a boundary between Cherokee lands to the north and Creek lands to the south. In 1817–21, it marked the Georgia frontier, and was used by pioneer families settling this section.

On November 17th and 18th 1864, the left wing of Sherman's Army passed down this trail on its "march to the sea."

(Located at South Cherokee Road and East Hightower Trail. WPA-C8, 1940.)

WHITE COUNTY

Named in honor of David Thomas White (1812–1871), representative from Newton County, who backed the bill to form White County. County Seat: Cleveland.

CLEVELAND

WHITE COUNTY

White County, created by Act of Dec. 22, 1857, was cut off from Habersham and Lumpkin Counties. Wm. H. Shelton, Repr. from Habersham at the session tried twice to have the county formed but failed. Repr. David T.

White of Newton Co. backed the bill and it passed. In gratitude, Repr. Shelton had the county named for Repr. White. First county officers were: Isaac Bowen, Sheriff; Wm. L. Sumpter, Clk. Sup. Ct.; Wm. R. Kimsey, Clk. Inf. Ct.; Willis A. England, Cor.; Wm. Burke, Tax Rec.; Champion Ferguson, Tax Col.; Vincent F. Sears, Surveyor; Wilkes T. Leonard, Ord.; J. Cicero Bell, Treasurer.

(Located in the center of town on the lawn of the old courthouse, now the home of the White County Historical Society. GHM 154-3, 1955.)

CLEVELAND

When White County was formed in 1857, Mt. Yonah was selected as the County-seat. The majority of its residents wished to rename it Sheltonville for William H. Shelton, who sponsored the formation of the new county. Shelton asked that it be named Cleveland for his good friend and mentor, Benjamin Cleveland, who served 6 terms as representative, 8 terms as senator from Habersham County and was Brigadier-General from 1820 to 1826. Built of handmade brick by slave labor, the White County Courthouse is modelled after Independence Hall in Philadelphia.

(Located in the center of town on the lawn of the old courthouse, now the home of White County Historical society. GHM 154-4, 1955.)

DISCOVERY OF GOLD

In 1828 gold was discovered here on Duke's Creek, White County, by two people. John Witheroods of North Carolina found a 3-ounce nugget and a Negro servant of Major Frank Logan of Loudsville, Georgia, also discovered gold on the creek. Early discoveries came almost simultaneously as prospectors drifted into Northeast Georgia from the North Carolina diggings. One merchant in the Nacoochee Valley purchased and shipped 1 to 1.5 million dollars worth of gold in a thirty year period.

The pits visible along the creek are evidence of recent hydraulic mining.

(Located on GA 75, 6.5 miles north of Cleveland, on the south side of Duke's Creek. GHM 154-9, 1962.)

GOLD – DUKES CREEK

In 1828, gold was discovered here on Dukes Creek, then called Nacoochee Creek, by a negro servant of Major Frank Logan of Loudsville, Georgia. Other mines were opened and in the first 30 years one merchant in Nacoochee Valley purchased and shipped between two and three million dollars worth of Gold.

The pits visible along the Creek are evidence of recent hydraulic mining.

(Located on GA 75, 6.5 miles north of Cleveland, at Dukes Creek. WPA 154-B6.) ♦ ★ – not standing.

NACOOCHEE

THE UNICOI TURNPIKE

This road is the Old Unicoi Turnpike, first vehicular route to link East Tennessee, Western North Carolina and North Georgia with the head of navigation on the Savannah River system. Beginning on the Tugalo River, to the east of Toccoa, the road led this way, thence through Unicoi Gap and via Murphy, N. C. to Nine Mile Creek near Maryville, Tenn.

Permission to open the way as a toll road was given by the Cherokees in 1813 to a Company of Indians and white men. Tennessee and Georgia granted charters to the concern.

Prior to its establishment as a road, the trace was part of a trading path from Augusta to the Cherokees in East Tennessee.

(Located at GA 75 and GA 17, south of Helen. GHM 154-1, 1954.)

NACOOCHEE INDIAN MOUND

Nacoochee Indian Mound was the center of the ancient Cherokee town of Gauxule, visited by DeSoto in 1540 in his search for gold, according to legend. On this ceremonial mound, 190 feet long, 150 feet wide and 20 feet high, stood the Town House where a sacred fire burned unceasingly. Ceremonial dances were performed in and around the Town House. Residents of the town lived on the flat land surrounding the mound. The findings of Heye Foundation archaeologists who explored the mound in 1915 indicate the advanced cultural development of the builders.

(Located at the junction of GA 75 and GA 17, south of Helen. GHM 154-2, 1955.)

STARLIGHT

"Starlight" was built 1824–1830 of handhewn sills, handmade brick and hardware. Its builder, Major Edward Williams, wrote of his new home, "In comfort and convenience it would vie with some of the finest homes in Boston . . I can convey as good spring water as ever ran to each or all of the rooms" by gravity in wooden pipes. Major Williams came to Nacoochee Valley from N.C. in 1822, purchased a large tract of land for $1 an acre, part payable in corn and wheat. After building a temporary home and planting he brought his family down in late 1823. He died in 1856, leaving his home to his daughter, Hannah Williams Starr, wife of Dr. E. F. Starr. "Starlight" became the name of the home after that.

(Located on GA 17 just east of the Nacoochee Indian Mound. GHM 154-7, 1956.) ♦ ★ – not standing. **Note:** Starlight was destroyed by fire in 1959.

NACOOCHEE INDIAN MOUND

NACOOCHEE VALLEY
VALLEY OF THE EVENING STAR

This valley has long fascinated travelers, writers and artists. It was farmed for centuries by Indians and white men alike. The valley was devastated by Spanish and American gold hunters and timbermen and has been carefully nurtured by prosperous summer residents and progressive farmers.

The valley is watered by Sautee and Duke's Creeks and the Chattahoochee River. These streams formed the rich alluvial soils, laced the soils with placer gold, and powered small industries. Longtime residents of the valley have been the Dyers, Glens, Hardmans, Lumsdens, Nichols, Richardsons and Williams.

(Located on GA 17, 0.7 mile east of junction with GA 75. GHM 154-10, 1980.)

EARLY TRADING POST

At this point, just north of the safest ford in the Chattahoochee River, the first white settlers in this area built their campfires in 1822. A trading post was soon established on the site and Indians traded gold nuggets and gold-dust to the settlers for merchandise. The first Nacoochee post office was established at the trading post with Charles Williams, son of one of the first settlers, serving as Postmaster for more than 50 years. To this same site in 1838 soldiers gathered the Indians from surrounding valleys and highlands to begin their "Trail of Tears" to the West.

(Located on GA 17, 0.8 mile east of junction with GA 75. GHM 154-6, 1955.)

WHITE METHODIST CHURCH

A Methodist Church has stood on this site since the early 1820's when one was built by the first white settlers in Nacoochee Valley. Six acres of land to be used for the church and cemetery were deeded to the Methodist Episcopal Church in 1836 by Major Edward Williams at the death of his wife. Maj. Williams came to the Valley in 1822, purchased a large tract of land, built the home known as "Starlight" and lived there until his death in 1856. The first permanent building, with its gallery for slaves to worship with their masters, was painted white. Since that day the church has been known as the "White Church."

(Located on GA 17, 1.2 miles east of junction with GA 75. GHM 154-8, 1956.)

JOE BROWN PIKES

On Sautee Creek just north of here are remains of a dam constructed as part of a grist mill owned by Edwin P. Williams. During the War Between the States, to arm the Home Guard, Gov. Joseph E. Brown had made a great number of pikes, daggers on long poles, for close fighting. This mill was converted to the manufacture of "Joe Brown Pikes." Though church bells and used iron were given for making the pikes, iron from a forge near Clarkesville was probably used here.

After the war the mill was reconverted to grinding corn.

(Located on GA 17, 0.5 mile east of junction with GA 155 at Sautee Creek. GHM 154-5, 1955.♦ ★

WHITFIELD COUNTY

Named in honor of George Whitefield (1714–1770) who followed John and Charles Wesley to Georgia and Founded Bethesda Orphanage, the oldest in America, at Savannah in 1740. County Seat: Dalton.

DALTON

GEORGE WHITEFIELD

George Whitefield (1714–70) was a noted evangelist, born in Gloucester, England. He met John and Charles Wesley, at Oxford and with them formed the Holy Club. Ordained deacon in 1736, he followed the Wesleys to Georgia in 1738 and founded Bethesada Orphanage (oldest in America) at Savannah (1740).

After doctrinal differences with the Wesleys he founded the Calvinistic Methodists.

He made seven trips to America, preaching in Georgia, Pennsylvania and New England. He died while holding a meeting in Newburyport, Mass., and is buried there.

Whitfield County (1851), created from Murray, originally Cherokee County, was named for him.

(Located on Selvidge Street between Crawford and King Streets on the courthouse lawn. GHM 155-28, 1953.)

TRISTRAM DALTON

Tristram Dalton (1732–1817) was born in Newburyport, Mass; graduate of Harvard, 1755; admitted to bar but followed mercantile pursuits.

Delegate to Convention of Committees of New England Provinces, Providence, R. I., 1776; member Massachusetts House of Representatives 1782–88; Speaker 1784–85; U S Senator 1789–91; Surveyor, Port of Boston 1814–17.

COURTESY, GEORGIA HISTORICAL SOCIETY

GEORGE WHITEFIELD (1714–1770)

COURTESY, GEORGIA DEPARTMENT OF ARCHIVES AND HISTORY

EDWARD DALTON WHITE (1811–1898)

His grandson, Edward White, laid out the City of Dalton, Ga., donating land for a City Park and church sites. The city was named in honor of Senator Dalton and his daughter, Mary, mother of Capt. White.

(Located at King and Pentz Streets in front of city hall. GHM 155-29, 1953.)

THE BLUNT HOUSE

This house, built in 1848 by Ainsworth Emery Blunt, pioneer settler of Dalton, has been continuously occupied by members of his family. Appointed postmaster of Cross Plains in 1845, Mr. Blunt was elected mayor when that town became Dalton in 1847 and served for many years. He was the moving spirit and founder of the First Presbyterian Church in 1847 and held office as ruling elder in that

church until his death in 1865. While Federal troops were in possession of Dalton during the War Between the States, this house was used by them as a hospital.

(Located on Thorton Avenue/US 41 between Church and Emory Streets. GHM 155-30, 1955.)

CONFEDERATE CEMETERY

421 unknown Confederate, four known Confederate and four unknown Federal soldiers are buried here. Some of these men died of wounds received in the Battles of Stone's River, Perryville, Chickamauga, Lookout Mountain, Chattanooga, Missionary Ridge, and other battles fought north of here.

COURTESY, GEORGIA DEPARTMENT OF ARCHIVES AND HISTORY

THE BLUNT HOUSE ABOUT 1868

THE BLUNT HOUSE TODAY

Others died of disease and sickness. Located here, in 1862–1864, were several important Confederate Hospitals where thousands were treated and nursed back to health. Hospitals were moved south of this point in early May 1864 to get out of the path of invading Federals.

(Located near Emory Street and Greenwood Drive within Westhill Cemetery. GHM 155-31, 1956.)

DUG GAP

Dug Gap was so named because a pioneer road, cut out of the hillside, passed through a cleft in Rocky Face Ridge at this point.

The road led east to Dalton and the Western and Atlantic Railroad, important military objectives. Federals sought in February and again in May, 1864, to pass through the gap, but were repulsed.

May 8, 1864, as the Atlanta Campaign began, Geary's Division of the Federal Twentieth Corps attacked Dug Gap, but was driven back after a brisk action. Direct attacks on Dalton failing, Sherman flanked toward Resaca through the broken, wooded area to the west.

(Located south of Dalton on US 41/GA 3 at Carpenter Creek, 0.1 mile south of Treadmill Road and 0.1 mile north of West Ezzard Avenue. GHM 155-34, 1956.) ★

BATTLES OF TILTON

2.8 miles E. of here, on May 13, 1864, a delaying action was fought as Confederates moved south toward Resaca. On Oct. 13, 1864, part of French's Division of Stewart's Corps, Confederate Army of Tennessee, attacked this place, then garrisoned by 300 men of the 17th Iowa Veteran Volunteer Infantry, under the command of Lt. Col. S. M. Archer, U. S. Army. Many of the garrison took refuge in the blockhouse just north of the town. Selden's Battery brought into action, battered the blockhouse and, after a battle that lasted several hours, the garrison surrendered.

(Located south of Dalton at US 41/GA 3 and Carbondale Road. GHM 155-33, 1988.)

BATTLE OF RESACA

May 14, 1864. The 20th Corps (F) was shifted from Camp Creek Valley, 0.5 mi. W. & aligned across rd. – the 2d & 3d Divs. in reserve; the 1st Div. prolonging Stanley's Div. (4th A.C.) (F) to the State R. R., E.

May 15. Butterfield's (3d) & Geary's (2d) Divs. of 20th A. C. (F), astride rd., moved in assault on Hood's line (C) 0.7 mi. S. in an attempt to break through.

Butterfield, W. of the rd. led off, followed by Geary, E. of the rd., brigades in all. They failed to break Hood's line (C), but seized & removed the 4 guns of Corput's Cherokee Battery (C).

(Located on US 41/GA 3 and East Nance Springs Road, south of Dalton, near Whitfield/Gordon County line. GHM 155-1, 1953.) ♦ ★

BATTLE OF RESACA

May 15, 1864. The 23d A.C. (F) was shifted from Camp Cr., 1.5 mi. W., to this vicinity where it extended the left of Sherman's line (F) to the Conasauga River.

Hovey's (1st) div., supported Williams' (1st) div., 20th A.C. (F) between the Scales house and R.R. during Stewart's (C) 2d attack.

May 16. Johnston's forces (C) evacuated his position and withdrew S. followed by 4th and 14th A.C. (F). The 20th and 1st and 2d divs., 23d A.C. (F) moved SE to the Coosawattee River; Cox's (3d) div., (F) moved N. to Hogan's Ford, Conasauga R. near Tilton and via Holley to Field's Mill, Coosawattee R.

(Located off US 41/GA 3, south of Dalton, near the Whitfield/Gordon County line. On East Nance Spring Road, 0.4 mile east of junction with US 41/GA 3. GHM 155-4, 1986.)

R. R. WOOD STATION

Approx. site of John H. Green's wood station during the 1860's – which was a fuel supply depot of the State R.R.

April 12, 1862: Andrews' Raiders, (F) with the locomotive GENERAL, paused to wood up while closely pursued by the locomotive TEXAS (C).

WILBUR G. KURTZ

THE GENERAL

COURTESY, GEORGIA DEPARTMENT OF ARCHIVES AND HISTORY

THE TEXAS

May 9, 1864: 18 men of the 9th Illinois mounted infantry, (F) burned station and cut telegraph wires – an episode of McPherson's (F) first move on Resaca. The severed wires were spliced by two intrepid women of the vicinity: Mrs. Bachman and her sister, Miss Carrie Sims.

(Located off US 41/GA 3, south of Dalton, near the Whitfield/Gordon County line at East Nance and Gracie Roads, 0.6 mile east of junction with US 41/GA 3. GHM 155-5, 1953.)

BATTLE OF RESACA

At this point the intrenched line of Stanley's (1st) Div., 4th A. C. (F) crossed the highway, facing Hood's line (C) 0.5 mi. South.

May 14, 1864; 0.4 mi. E. (near Nance's Spring) Hood's rt. (C) made a spirited attack on Stanley's left, (F) which was foiled by timely arrival of 20th Corps troops (F).

May 15: Hood's rt. (C) attacked 1st Div., 20th A. C. (F) near State R R., E., & the 2d & 3d Divs., failing to break Hood's line (C) in their front, captured Corput's 4-gun battery.

(Located on US 41/GA 3, south of Dalton, at the Whitfield/Gordon County line. GHM 155-2, 1953.)

BATTLE OF RESACA

May 14. Stewart's Div., Hood's Corps (C) moved from intrenchments near the John Green house and attacked left of Federals then extending toward the State R. R.

This attack fell upon the left of Stanley's (1st) div., 4th A.C., and 5th Ind. Battery (F) (on ridge NW). The timely arrival of Williams' (1st) div., 20th A.C. (F) checked Stewart's (C) advance and stabilized the left flank of the Federal forces.

May 15. Stewart (C) repeated attack of 14th – the assault falling on Williams' div. (F) astride road here – and with like result.

(Located off US 41/GA 3, south of Dalton. Follow US 41/GA 3 into Gordon County. Take Chitwood Road east 0.7 mile to marker. GHM 155-3, 1986.)

HAMILTON HOUSE

This brick house & the stone spring house in the low ground back of it, were built by John Hamilton about 1840.

During the Winter, 1863–1864, when the Confederate Army of Tennessee, under Gen. Joseph E. Johnston, occupied Dalton, Brig. Gen. J. H. Lewis of the celebrated "Orphan Brigade," of Kentucky, had h'dq'rs here – his tent near the spring house.

The Army of Tennessee, under Gen. Bragg, withdrew from Missionary Ridge, Nov. 25, 1863, to Dalton, where Gen. Johnston succeeded to the command, Dec. 27. Outnumbered & outflanked, by Sherman's forces, Johnston evacuated Dalton May 12–13, 1864.

(Located at Chattanooga Avenue and Matilda Street. GHM 155-17, 1954.)

HAMILTON HOUSE

SITE: AULT'S MILL

In this vicinity stood Ault's Mill & residence cited in Official Records as Lt. Gen. Wm. J. Hardee's h'dq'rs, May 8–13, 1864.

Hardee was in temporary command of units of Hood's A. C. (Hindman's div.) together with those of his own corps at various places. This sector was the rt. of the Confederate line across Crow Valley, from Rocky Face Ridge on the W. to Potato Hill (Picket Top) and Ault's Gap on the E.

This N. line of Dalton's defenses was 2 mi. further N. than the one used in repelling Federal attacks in February.

(Location undetermined. GHM 155-18, 1953.) ♦ ★

STEVENSON'S LINE

During demonstrations on Rocky Face and in Crow Valley, by 4th & 23d A.C. troops (F), the N. line of Dalton's defense works crossed the road here.

Stevenson's div. (Hood's A.C.) (C) held this sector, his left at Cheatham's line, at Signal Station on Rocky Face; his right, at Ault's Creek, E.

May 9, 1864. Stevenson's men repulsed the 23d A.C. in Crow Valley, and the desperate attempt by Harker's and Wagner's brigades, Newton's div., 4th A.C., to break the left of Stevenson's at and near the top of Rocky Face, where Pettus' and Brown's brigades were posted behind stone breastworks.

ROCKY FACE AS SEEN FROM STEVENSON'S LINE

(Located on Crow Valley Road, 1.9 miles north of junction with Willowdale Road. GHM 155-20, 1985.)

NORTH LINE
DALTON'S DEFENSES

April, 1864. Pending Federal moves on Dalton a strong line of defense works was built across Crow Valley. Beginning at the Signal Station on Rocky Face,W., it crossed the road at this point & ascended the wooded hill E., where artillery was placed. Beyond a creek to a high ridge it turned S. across Ault's Gap.

N. of ridge & prolongation of it, is Potato Hill (Picket Top), which was also fortified.

May 8–13. Stevenson's div. (Hood's A.C.) occupied the line W. On the E. were portions of Hindman's div., under temporary command of Hardee – his h'dq'rs at Ault's Mill.

(From Willowdale Road, follow Crow Valley Road north 2.7 miles, turn right on Poplar Springs Road and continue 0.1 mile. Marker is 100 yards off to the right on a gravel road. GHM 155-19, 1954.)

CROW VALLEY

Feb. 25, 1864. Federal forces moved S. on this rd. in an attempt to outflank the Confederate defenders at Mill Creek Gap, which was being threatened by 2 Fed. divs. from the W. These movements were to test the strength of Johnston's army at Dalton, said to have been depleted by a shift of Hardee's A. C. to Mississippi. All Federal attacks failed.

Troops in this area were Cruft's div. 4th A. C., Baird's div., 14th A. C., & Long's cavalry.

5 Landmarks of the Feb. operations in Crow Valley, still survive: The Crow House, opp. this marker; the Davis House 500 ft. N., the Burke house, spring & log barn, 2 mi. N.E.

(From Willowdale Road, follow Crow Valley Road north 2.7 miles, turn left and follow 1.2 miles to marker at junction with Reed Pond Road. GHM 155-21, 1954.)

SCHOFIELD'S 23D CORPS IN CROW VALLEY

May 9, 1864. Two divs. 23d A.C., having deployed abreast between the Burke and Harris houses moved S. astride this wooded ridge in the fork of Crow Creek.

This move was made in conjunction with 4th A.C. troops on the summit & eastern slope of Rocky Face Ridge,

together with pressure by the 14th A. C. at Mill Creek Gap from the W.

Schofield's troops pressed S. of this point until halted by Stevenson's & Hindman's divs. (aligned across the valley), & the artillery fire from Potato Hill (Picket Top), the high point to the S.E.

(From Willowdale Road, follow Crow Valley Road north 2.7 miles, turn left and follow 1.2 miles to Reed Pond Road. Turn right and follow 1 mile to Reed Road. GHM 155-22, 1954.)

MILITARY OPERATIONS IN CROW VALLEY

There were 2 demonstrations by Federal forces on Dalton, in 1864; Feb. 24–26; May 7–12. On these over-lapping fields of operations, the Burke house & spring were noted landmarks.

Feb. 25, Cruft's & Baird's divs. (4th & 14th A. C.), via the low ridge W., moved to outflank the Confederates at Mill Creek Gap, but were forced back. May 9, 2 divs., Schofield's 23d A. C., were halted at S. end of ridge, by Stevenson's div., Hood's A. C., & the artillery at Potato Hill.

The log barn at the Burke house was used as a hospital by Surg. S. C. Menzies, Med. Director, Cruft's div., 4th A. C., Feb. 25.

(From Willowdale Road, follow Crow Valley Road north 2.7 miles, turn left and follow 1.2 miles to Reed Pond. Turn right and follow 1 mile to Reed Road, turn left on Reed Road and follow 1.6 miles to marker. GHM 155-23, 1954.)

HARRIS' GAP

In 1864 the direct road from Tunnel Hill to Varnell's, passed through Harris Gap at this point, which is just N. of where Rocky Face drops off into continuous foot-hills.

Federal operations in Crow Valley by the 23d A.C., began with its march S. from the Dr. Lee house to this road. Schofield had h'dq'rs at the Harris house (which stood opp. this marker until 1952), May 8–10, 1864.

May 9. Judah's 2d & Cox's 3d divs. moved S. from this road, astride the low ridge (E. of Rocky Face), toward Stevenson's sector of the Dalton defenses. Hovey's 1st div., in reserve, guarded the gap and supported Judah & Cox.

(From Willowdale road, follow Crow Valley Road north 2.7 miles, turn left and follow 2.6 miles to New Hope Road, turn right and travel 100 yards, turn right and follow 100 yards to marker. GHM 155-26, 1954.)

GEORGE DISNEY'S GRAVE

High up on Rocky Face, S. of gap, is the lone grave of English-born George Disney, Co. K., 4th Ky. Inft., Lewis' "Orphan Brigade," Bate's div., Hindman's Corps (C).

The 4th Ky. was deployed to form a living telegraph line from base to summit of the ridge at the point where the view commanded Federal movements in open valley N.W. Disney, atop the ridge, was killed by a random bullet, Feb. 25, 1864; he was buried where he fell.

Dalton Boy Scouts, on a hike, found the grave, & directed by Scout Master, Wm. M. Sapp, Sr., replaced the inscribed heart-pine board with a marble marker, May 13, 1912.

(Located on US 41/GA 3, 0.4 mile north of Tibbs Road. GHM 155-16, 1954.)

ATLANTA CAMPAIGN
ROCKY FACE RIDGE
MAY 7–12, 1864

Federal frontal attacks failing completely here Sherman ably outflanked the Confederate Army, strongly entrenched across Rocky Face Ridge and this Gap whereupon Johnston with great skill reestablished a position by withdrawing to Resaca.

(Located on US 41/GA 3, 0.6 mile north of Tibbs Road at the Georgia State Patrol Station. NPS 155-99.)

THE FLOODED GAP

May, 1864. The Confederate defenders of Dalton impounded the waters of Mill Creek by a dam in the gap, as a measure of defense when Federal forces under Sherman assailed this opening in Rocky Face Ridge. This temporary lake, together with fortifications in and bordering the gap, prevented its seizure by the 14th A.C.

May 8: Three abortive attempts to cut the dam were made by detachments from the 34th Ill.

14th A.C. operations against Mill Creek Gap (May 8–12), served to engage the attention of Dalton's defenders (as did the attacks in Crow Valley), while McPherson's Army of the Tenn. seized Snake Creek Gap 14 miles southward.

(From Tibbs Road, follow US 41/GA 3 1.2 miles north to junction with Old US 41 next to Mill Creek. GHM 155-15, 1953.) ♦ ★

MILL CREEK GAP

Otherwise known as Buzzard Roost. This natural gateway through Rocky Face Ridge, was heavily fortified by Confederate forces at Dalton, after their retreat from Missionary Ridge.

February 25, 1864, the Federal 14th A.C., Dept. of the Cumberland, moving by Tunnel Hill, attempted to seize the gap, but were driven back by Stewart's & Breckinridge's divs. At the same time, the gap was assailed from Crow Valley, E. of Rocky Face, by Cruft's & Baird's divs., which were repulsed by Hindman's A.C.

These Federal moves were prompted by rumors that Johnston's command had reinforced Polk, facing Sherman's forces at Meridian, Miss.

(From Tibbs Road, follow US 41/GA 3 1.2 miles north. Turn east on Old US 41, a dirt road beside Mill Creek, and travel 0.2 mile to marker. GHM 155-13, 1987.)

CONFEDERATE DEFENSE OF MILL CREEK GAP

Feb. 25, 1864. Stewart's & Breckinridge's divs. in the gap, repulsed the attacks of the Federal 14th A.C., from the N.W., while Hindman's A.C. drove back Cruft's & Baird's divs. in Crow Valley E. of Rocky Face Ridge & N. of the R.R.

May 8–9. Attempts by 14th A.C. troops from the W. were resisted by Stewart's and Bate's divs. posted in and on both slopes of the gap – a further protection, the impounded waters of Mill Creek.

Cheatham's div. on summit of Rocky Face N. of the Creek, together with Hood's A.C. aligned on the slope and across Crow Valley E. of it, repelled attacks by the 4th and 23d Corps.

(From Tibbs Road, follow US 41/GA 3 1.2 miles north. Turn east on Old US 41, a dirt road beside Mill Creek, and travel 0.4 mile to Rocky Face Railroad Street. Turn right, follow 0.1 mile and park at dirt path on the right next to railroad tracks. Cross the railroad tracks by foot to the marker. GHM 155-14, 1989.)

TWENTIETH CORPS IN DOGWOOD VALLEY

May 7,1864. Gen. Hooker's 20th A.C. crossed Taylor's Ridge at Nickajack & Gordon Springs Gaps, moving E. toward Rocky Face Ridge.

Geary's 2d & Butterfield's 3d divs., via Gordon's Springs, reached this point that afternoon. Butterfield's troops moved N. toward Trickum; Buschbeck's & Candy's brigades of Geary's div. camped at the Thornton farm 1.5 mi. N. E.; Ireland's brigade was detached to support Kilpatrick's cavalry.

May 8. Buschbeck's & Candy's brigades moved 2 mi. S. on this road to the County Line, where they turned E. to Dug Gap.

(Located north of Dalton on GA 201 at Gordon Springs Road, 6.1 miles west of US 41/GA 3. GHM 155-7, 1954.)

"CALLAWAY PLACE" – 1814

Jesse Callaway, soldier of 1812, son of Joseph Callaway, soldier of '76, lived in this house from 1852 to 1867. The house, built with bricks made on the place, remained in the family until after 1900. It is said to have been built about 1814. Callaway, born in Wilkes County in 1796, was a Sergeant in Capt. Jones' Co., Col. Booth's Regiment, Ga. Militia, 1814–15. He was married 4 times and had 18 children, most of them having living descendants in Ga. Deeding this house to his son John in 1867 he moved to another house on his land 2 miles north, where he died in 1875 and is buried in a family cemetery.

(Located north of Dalton on GA 201 at Gordon Springs Road, 6.1 miles west of US 41/GA 3. GHM 155-29C, 1954.) **Note:** The house is no longer standing.

GEARY'S DIVISION TO DUG GAP

May 8, 1864. Gen. J.W. Geary, with Buschbeck's & Candy's brigades, 2d div., 20th A.C., marched S. on this road from near Gordon's Springs.

Turning E. here (near Whitfield–Walker County line), Geary's troops moved to Dug Gap in Rocky Face Ridge, 5 miles from this point.

This move was made to outflank Johnston's army at Dalton by seizing Dug Gap & also to give support to McPherson's Army of the Tennessee which moved via Ship's Gap & Villanow to Snake Creek Gap. Geary failed to take Dug Gap; McPherson's occupation of Snake Cr. Gap led to the evacuation of Dalton by Johnston's forces.

(Located north of Dalton on GA 201 at the Whitfield/Walker County line, 8.2 miles west of US 41/GA 3. GHM 155-8, 1954.)

DR. ANDERSON'S HOUSE

Hd'q'rs., Maj. Gen. Joseph Hooker, commanding Federal 20th A.C., May 7–9, 1864.

These troops, having crossed Taylor's Ridge, May 7, moved E. to this vicinity. Williams' 1st & Butterfield's 3d divs. camped in Dogwood Valley near Trickum; Geary's 2d div., at the Thornton farm, one mi. S.

The 20th A.C. occupied the Federal Sector between Mill Creek Gap & Villanow, during Sherman's move toward Rocky Face. Demonstrations were made at both Mill Creek Gap & Dug Gap, May 8 – the latter, 5 mi. S.E., being the scene of Geary's vain attempt to dislodge the Arkansas & Kentucky defenders, while McPherson's troops occupied Snake Creek Gap.

(Located north of Dalton. From US 41/GA 3, follow GA 201 south 3.7 miles, turn right onto Dunnagan Road and proceed to marker. GHM 155-6, 1953.) ♦ ★

BATTLE OF DUG GAP

May 8, 1864. Maj. Gen. J. W. Geary, with Buschbeck's & Candy's brigades of the 2d div., 20th A.C., moving from near Gordon's Springs, reached this, the Babb Settlement, at 3p.m.

Planting McGill's Penna. Battery (3 inch Rodman guns) near Joel Babb's house, the Confederate position at Dug Gap in Rocky Face Ridge was shelled. This was followed by a concerted assault up the steep scarp by Buschbeck's brigade on the right, Candy's on the left.

Repeated attempts by the Federals to seize the gap ended in failure, but under cover of this engagement, McPherson's troops occupied Snake Creek Gap, 6 mi. S.W.

(Located north of Dalton. From GA 201 take Old Lafayette Road 0.1 mile, turn right on Mill Creek Road and follow 4.9 miles to junction with Babb Road. GHM 155-10, 1954.)

BABB'S SETTLEMENT

Antebellum domain of Joel Babb (1809–1882) – on Mill Cr., foot of Rocky Face at Dug Gap.

May 8, 1864. 1 A.M.; Col. W. C. P. Breckinridge's 9th Ky., Grigsby's brigade, Wheeler's cav., descended from Dug Gap & patrolled the roads N. & W. to ascertain if any Federals were there.

By 1:30 P.M., Breckinridge found Dogwood Valley swarming with Federals, a brigade of which, in support of Kilpatrick's cav., was enroute S. to Villanow. Later, the 9th Ky., confronted by 2 brigades, Geary's div., 20th A.C., moving E., was forced to retreat to Dug Gap. Geary, reaching this vicinity at 3 p.m., deployed his 2 brigades for the storming of Dug Gap.

(Located north of Dalton. From GA 201 take Old Lafayette Road 0.1 mile, turn right on Mill Creek Road and follow 5.1 miles to junction with Masters Drive. GHM 155-9, 1954.)

ASCENT TO DUG GAP

1.5 mi. W. this road ascends to and crosses the summit of Rocky Face Ridge – a direct route between Dalton and LaFayette.

May 7, 1864. Grigsby's brigade (Wheeler's Cav.), after retreating from Tunnel Hill to Mill Creek Gap, camped on this road at foot of the ridge – all except Dortch's battalion, which ascended to the gap, joining the infantry post of Williamson's Arkansans.

Dortch's arrival there, being reported to h'dq'rs. at Dalton, prompted a peremptory order to Grigsby to send cavalry scouts across the ridge. The 9th Ky., on reaching Dogwood Valley, early the 8th, found the Federals advancing.

(Located at Dug Gap and Dug Gap Mountain Roads. GHM 155-12, 1989.)

DUG GAP

An excavation at the summit of Rocky Face Ridge on the direct route between Dalton and LaFayette.

This gap was guarded by Confederate forces when Dalton was occupied after the retreat from Missionary Ridge in Nov. 1863.

Federal forces made 2 efforts to seize the gap: Feb. 25 & May 8, 1864. The latter attempt was made by Buschbeck's and Candy's brigades of Geary's (2d) div., 20th A.C. These troops scaled the W. scarp of the ridge, but failed to dislodge the defenders: 1st & 2d Arkansas reg'ts., under Col. J. A. Williamson, and Grigsby's brigade of Wheeler's cav., supported by Cleburne's div. of Hardee's Corps.

(Follow Walnut Avenue/GA 52 west, crossing I–75 at Exit 136 where road name changes to Dug Gap Battle Road. Follow 1.8 miles to marker. GHM 155-11, 1986.)

TUNNEL HILL

TUNNEL HILL

May 7, 1864. The Federal forces, under Maj. Gen. W. T. Sherman, began the campaign for Atlanta by seizing Tunnel Hill. Howard's 4th A.C., having marched from Catoosa Springs, drove Wheeler's Cav. from the R.R. tunnel S. to Mill Creek Gap.

Palmer's 14th A.C., moving from Ringgold (U.S. Highway 41), supported Howard on his right and extended the Federal front to Mill Cr. Gap, where its rt. joined left of 20th A.C. in Dogwood Valley.

These operations were designed to engage the Confederate forces at Dalton, while McPherson's army moved from the W. to Snake Creek Gap, 18 miles S. of Tunnel Hill.

(Located at US 41/GA 3 and Oak Street. GHM 155-24, 1985.)

CLISBY AUSTIN HOUSE

400 yds. S.E., at the big spring, is the brick residence known as the Austin house.

May 7, 1864. The Federal forces, having seized Tunnel Hill – their first movement in the campaign for Atlanta – Maj. Gen. W. T. Sherman had headquarters at the Austin house, until May 12.

While here, Sherman learned that McPherson's forces had failed to cut the R. R. at Resaca, after seizing Snake Creek Gap – May 9, whereupon the attempts at Rocky Face, Crow Valley & Mill Creek Gap, were dropped and all Federal units but the 4th A.C., Stoneman's, & McCook's cav. were shifted May 12, to the Resaca front via Villanow and Snake Creek Gap.

(Located on Oak Street at the railroad crossing. GHM 155-25, 1954.)

VARNELL

HISTORIC VARNELL HOME

This historic home was built in 1847 by "Dry Dan Dold" for M. P. Varnell, a pioneer settler of this community. In the War Between the States, this home was used as a temporary hospital by Federals and Confederates. Several skirmishes and engagements were fought around this place in May, 1864. Gen. Joe Wheeler and his Confederate Cavalry attacked here on May 12, 1864, and drove Federals from this town, killing and wounding more than 150. Federals immediately returned, and this home was used as Headquarters by several Federal commanders. Many "minnie balls" struck this house in the battles fought here.

(Located on GA 2 near the junction with GA 201. GHM 155-32, 1956.)

OLD FEDERAL ROAD

The highway crossing east and west at this point is the Old Federal Road, northwest Georgia's earliest vehicular route. It led across the Indian Country from the southeast boundary of the Cherokees, in the direction of Athens,

toward Nashville via Rossville. Another branch ran from a fork at Ramhurst, Ga., toward Knoxville, Tenn. Formal permission to use the trace was granted by the Cherokees in the 1805 Treaty of Tellico.

This way was the first postal route of this section of Georgia and was the earliest emigrant trace from the lower Southeast to Tennessee and north Alabama.

(Located at GA 71 and GA 2. GHM 155-29B, 1953.) ♦ ★

HISTORIC RED CLAY

Red Clay, one mile W, was once an important Council Ground for the Cherokee Indians who called it "Red Earth Place." During the War Between the States, on May 2, 1864, the 2nd Brigade, First Cavalry Division, Dept. of the Cumberland, in. S. Army, after a hard fight drove the Confederates from this town. It then became an important depot of supplies for Federal forces. A heavy force of Federals guarded this town to prevent Confederate raids from capturing valuable stores here. The Federal Army of Ohio, moving South toward Dalton passed through this town.

(Located on GA 71 and Stancil Road, 1.6 miles north of Cuhutta. GHM 155-34, 1956.) ♦ ★

WILKES COUNTY

Named in honor of John Wilkes (1727–1797), a member of the British Parliament, who opposed the actions against the colonies. County Seat: Washington.

RAYLE

ROCK METHODIST CHURCH
WILKES COUNTY

Rock Methodist Church was instituted about 3 miles from here in 1839. The present building was erected in 1870. Charter members were: Tom and Lizzie Willis; John and Mary E. Mattox; John P., Martha, and Mrs. T. C. Latimer; Luke Turner, Sr., Wm. and Mary Turner; Ivey Barrett; B. W. Tuck; Richmond and Olive Bryant; Miles G. and Rebecca Dorough; Terry P., Wm. and Caroline Sherrer; W. R., Martha, and John C. Perteet; Mary Gresham; Jane Staple; Sara F. Wynne; Simeon C. and Sara F. Arnold; Betty Strozier. Descendants of the Latimer, Turner, Bryant, Wynne, and Mattox families are present members.

(Located on US 78/GA 10, 3 miles from the Wilkes/Oglethorpe County line or 2.1 miles west of Rayle. GHM 157-14, 1958.)

SANDTOWN

HEARD'S FORT
(EARLY GEORGIA CAPITAL)

Heard's Fort was designated the Seat of Government for Georgia on February 3, 1780. The Executive Council met and transacted the affairs of the State in this temporary Capital until early in 1781. This designation was made by the Governor and Council in session at Augusta, and was necessary because of the danger that City might at any time be captured by British forces who were practically in control of the State. The fort was a stockade built by Stephen Heard about 1774, when he settled in the area. Stephen Heard served as President of the Executive Council of Georgia, February 18, 1780–1781.

(Located on GA 44, 1 mile south of junction with Sandtown Road. GHM 157-16, 1958.)

FIRST COURT NORTH
OF AUGUSTA

Near here, in the home of Jacob McLendon, the first Court held north of Augusta convened August 25, 1779, by order of the Executive Council of Georgia. Absalom Bedell, Benjamin Catchings, William Downs were Justices; Henry Monadue, Clerk; Joseph Scott-Riden, Sheriff. John Dooly was Attorney for the State. Grand Jurors were: Stephen Heard, Barnard Heard, George Walton, Daniel Burnett, Thomas Carter, Richard Aycock, Robert Day, John Gorham, Dionysius Oliver, Holman Freeman, Sen. Daniel Coleman, Thomas Stroud, Micajah

Williamson, James McLean, Jacob Herington, William Bailey, John Glass, Charles Bedingfield.

(Located on GA 44 at Sandtown Road. GHM 157-17, 1958.)

FISHING CREEK
BAPTIST CHURCH

Fishing Creek Baptist Church, the second of this denomination to be constituted in the upcountry of Georgia, was organized in 1782, under the leadership of the Rev. Sanders Walker, who became its first pastor. It was one of five churches represented at a meeting held at Kiokee in October, 1784, to organize the Georgia Baptist Association. In May, 1786, the Association met at Fishing Creek. The original church building stood a short distance from this site.

(Located on Sandtown Road, 0.4 mile west of junction with GA 44. GHM 157-26, 1958.)

TIGNALL

INDEPENDENCE
UNITED METHODIST CHURCH

Old Independence Church, built for all denominations, was situated near the campground across the road from its present site. The Methodists organized a membership and claimed the church. The matter was carried to the courts. A young lawyer, Robert Toombs, defended the Methodists and won the case. The beginning of Old Independence was around 1783, and it

became a Methodist Church in the 1830's. In 1840, Thomas L. Wootten deeded the lot on which the Old Church building stood to the trustees. In 1870, the church building was sold to the black people who moved it to land given them in Tignall. A new church building was erected, and in 1871 Bishop George F. Pierce preached the dedication sermon. A Sunday School celebration was held in 1879 with almost 1,000 attending. Dr. A. G. Haygood, President of Emory College delivered the address. The church has been remodeled many times. In 1950 the Church School Annex was added and a Fellowship Hall was built in 1974. Many prominent families in the county have been identified as members of this church. Several have been licensed to preach at her altars, the more prominent being, Reverend J. W. Hinton, D. D. a preacher and writer of national fame.

(Located on Church Street, 0.2 mile west of junction with GA 17. TUMC 157-99, 1978.)

POPE'S CHAPEL
UNITED METHODIST CHURCH

The Methodist Society, which was later organized into Pope's Chapel Church, was first organized in August 1786 by Thomas Humphries at the home of James Marks located in what is now Elbert County about 1½ miles Northeast of Old Baker's Ferry on Broad River. When Elbert County was formed in 1790 from Wilkes County, it left most of the church members in Wilkes County., so the church was moved south into Wilkes and located about 2 miles from Broad River on property owned by John Landrum adjoining his homeplace on the east side of Baker's Ferry Road. It was in this location that it received its name, in honor of Rev. Henry Pope who supplied much of the timber for the building. Bishop Asbury preached the Dedication Sermon there in 1805. In 1852 the church was again moved about 2 miles southeast to its present location. In 1871 Trustees of the church were Benjamin W. Fortson, M. T. Cash, Augustus A. Neal and James W. Boyd. A second building was constructed here in 1897 in which two stained glass windows were installed as a memorial to Benjamin Winn Fortson and his wife Hannah Rebecca Ogilvie by their children. The Dedication Sermon was preached by Lundye Harris in 1898. This building, severely damaged by a windstorm, was replaced in 1957 by the present building.

(From Tignall, travel 3.2 miles north on GA 17, turn right and follow road 3.8 miles, turn right at stone marker and follow road 0.2 mile to marker and church. TUMC 157-98, 1978.)

WASHINGTON

WILKES COUNTY

Wilkes County, an original county, was created by the Constitution of Feb. 5, 1777, from Creek and Cherokee Cessions of June 1, 1773. At first, it contained all of Oglethorpe, Elbert, Lincoln and parts of Taliaferro, Hart, Warren and Madison Counties. It was named for John Wilkes (1727–1797), English politician and publicist, who

strenuously opposed measures leading to war with the colonies. First County Officers were: John Dooly, Sheriff, comm. Feb. 9, 1778; Samuel Creswell, Surveyor, comm. Feb. 18, 1783; Benjamin Catching, Clk. of Sup. and Inf. Cts, comm. Jan. 2, 1785; Howell Jarrett, Coroner, comm. 1790.

(Located on Court Street at the Public Square on the courthouse lawn. GHM 157-11, 1956.)

JEFFERSON DAVIS

On May 4, 1865, Jefferson Davis arrived in Washington where he performed what proved to be his last duties as President of the Confederate States of America. Shortly thereafter, with a small staff and escort, he departed enroute to the trans-Mississippi Department where, undaunted by the tragic surrenders at Appomattox and Durham Station, he intended to unite the forces of Generals E. Kirby Smith, Taylor, Forrest, Maury and Magruder "to form an army, which in the portion of that country abounding in supplies, and deficient in rivers and railroads, could have continued the war until our enemy, foiled in the purpose of subjugation, should, in accordance with his repeated declaration, have agreed, on the basis of a return to the Union, to acknowledge the Constitutional rights of the States, and by a convention, or quasi-treaty, to guarantee the security of person and property."

After a hard journey via Sandersville, Dublin and Abbeville, his party camped a mile north of Irwinville (178 miles SW), in the present Jefferson

JEFFERSON DAVIS (1808–1889)

Davis Memorial State Park. At dawn on May 10th, his camp was surrounded by men of the 1st Wisconsin and 4th Michigan cavalry regiments (F), and the President of the Southern Confederacy became a "state prisoner," his hopes for a new nation, in which each state would exercise without interference its cherished "Constitutional rights," forever dead.

(Located on Court Street at the Public Square on the courthouse lawn. GHM 157-12, 1957.)

OLD INN SITE

This building stands on the site of one of the most popular inns of the early stagecoach days. Under it are the ancient handhewn timbers, hand

made brick and massive beams of the inn basement. In the basement is the rock vault with heavy iron door and tremendous lock where the gold shipments and mail pouches were kept in safety for the stagecoaches.

Washington people were proud of their stagecoaches. They did not give them up until 1870 – 20 years after the coming of the railroad.

(Located on Robert Toombs Avenue and the Public Square. GHM 157-4, 1953.)

THE TUPPER HOUSE

This was the home of Dr. Henry Allen Tupper, grandfather of the wife of General George Marshall, former U S Army Chief of Staff, U. S. Secretary of State and originator of the Marshall Plan. Dr. Tupper was pastor of the Baptist church here for 20 years, but never accepted one penny of salary, as he was already wealthy. The 18 white columns on all four sides and the graceful, divided stairway make the house outstanding architecturally.

In ante-bellum days the daylight basement was used as a kitchen and office.

THE TUPPER HOUSE

(Located on West Robert Toombs Avenue/US 78B and Allison Street. GHM 157-1, 1953.)

FIRST METHODIST CHURCH

Organized in 1819, this Church is an outgrowth of Grant's Meeting House, the first Methodist Church building in Georgia, erected 5 miles E. in 1787. In 1820, the Methodists built the first church building in Washington. It was shared by other denominations. In 1823, Rev. Alexander Webster, first pastor of the Washington Presbyterian Church, was ordained there. A Methodist Sunday School was organized in 1871. A Woman's Missionary Society, started in 1878, was the first in the Conference. On the site of the first structure, a second, now the Masonic Temple, was erected in 1882. In this building, erected in 1907, the first Methodist Men's Club in Methodism was chartered in 1919, during the pastorate of Rev. G. S. Frazer.

Bishop Francis Asbury visited Washington many times during his 17 trips to Georgia. He held the second Methodist Conference in Georgia in the log Courthouse, near the site of the present Wilkes County Courthouse. Rev. Hope Hull and Rev. Lorenzo Dow were among the famous pioneer Circuit Riders to hold revival meetings in Washington. Rev. Lovick Pierce, leader in early Methodism, was the first recorded pastor of this church.

(Located on Spring and West Liberty Streets. GHM 157-20, 1958.)

THE CAMPBELL HOME

CAMPBELL HOME

This was once the home of two distinguished Georgians – father and son. Duncan G. Campbell was noted for drafting the treaty that removed the Cherokee Indians from Georgia and also for introducing in the Georgia legislature the first bill providing for higher education for women. John Archibald Campbell, born here in 1811, was an Associate Justice of the United States Supreme Court from 1853 until 1861, when he resigned to become Assistant Secretary of War for the Southern Confederacy. After the war he practiced law in New Orleans.

This house is really two houses in one. It had two identical front doors and the wainscoted panels under the front windows open.

(Located on Liberty Street between South Alexander Avenue and Jefferson Street. GHM 157-5, 1953.)

HOLLY COURT

This lot, originally sold by the Town Commissioners in 1804 to John Griffin, was later owned by Henry Anthony.

This structure combines two separate houses. The back part probably dates from 1817; the front was moved by oxcart from 7 miles out in the County by Dr. Fielding Ficklen in the 1840's. In this house, Mrs. Jefferson Davis and her two children spent a few days awaiting President Davis' arrival after the fall of Richmond.

Dr. James Pettigrew Boyce; Co-founder and first President of the Southern Baptist Theological Seminary, Louisville, Ky., married Elizabeth L. Ficklen here, Dec. 20, 1848.

(Located at South Alexander Avenue and Water Street. GHM 157-13, 1957.)

WASHINGTON PRESBYTERIAN CHURCH

The Presbyterian Church at Washington was organized in 1790, under the Presbytery of South Carolina, with the Rev. John Springer as first pastor. Services were held in private homes, in the Court House, the Academy, and in the Methodist Church, until 1825, when the first church edifice was erected. On July 29, of that year, the lot upon which the present church building stands was conveyed by Dr. Joel Abbott to Thomas Terrell, Samuel Barnett, Andrew G. Semmes, Constantine Church and James Wingfield, Trustees of Washington Presbyterian Church.

The Georgia Presbytery was organized at a meeting of the South Carolina and Georgia Synod in Washington in 1821, and in 1826 the Synod met in the new church building. Many famous ministers have been pastors of

the Washington Presbyterian Church, among them: the Rev. Alexander H. Webster, the Rev. S. J. Cassels, the Rev. Francis R. Goulding, the Rev. John Brown, the Rev. H. W. Petrie, the Rev. Nathan Hoyt, the Rev. J. K. S. Axson, and the Rev. Thomas Dunwoody. Alexander H. Stephens and Duncan G. Campbell were lifelong members of this church, as were many other distinguished men and women.

(Located on East Robert Toombs Avenue at East Liberty Street. GHM 157-21, 1958.)

HOME OF ROBERT TOOMBS

This was the home of Robert Toombs – planter, lawyer and distinguished Southern statesman. Born July 2, 1810, Robert Toombs was educated at Franklin College, Georgia, at Union College, New York, and the University of Virginia. He was a member of the Georgia House of Representatives, 1837–1840, 1842–1845; of the United States House of Representatives, 1845–1853; of the United States Senate from 1853 until his resignation in 1861. He served as Secretary of State, C.S.A., resigning to become a Brigadier General in the Confederate Army. He was a member of the Constitutional Convention in 1877.

Robert Toombs died in this house on December 15, 1885, an "Unreconstructed Rebel." After his death this became the home of his devoted niece, Mrs. Frank Colley. This marker replaces one erected by the Children of the Confederacy of Georgia in June, 1941.

ROBERT AUGUSTUS TOOMBS (1810–1885)

(Located at 216 East Robert Toombs Avenue between Poplar and Liberty Streets. GHM 157-30, 1959.)

HOME OF ROBERT TOOMBS

Here stands the home of Robert Toombs, distinguished Southern States-man. Born July 2, 1810, he was a member of the Georgia House of Representatives, 1837–1840, 1842–1845; United States Congressman 1845–1853; United States Senate 1853–1861, resigned. Member Secession Convention and Provisional Congress, 1861. Secretary of State, C.S.A., resigned to become Brigadier General in the Confederate Army. Member Constitutional Convention, 1877. Toombs died here on Dec. 15, 1885, "an Unreconstructed Rebel."

Sponsor: Ga. Division Children of the Confederacy Mrs. Joseph Mason, Madison, GA.

(Located at 216 East Robert Toombs Avenue between Poplar and Liberty Streets. WPA 157D-12, 1941.) ♦ ★ – not standing.

HISTORIC DUGAS HOME

This home was built by Mr. and Mrs. Louis Dugas, French refugees from Santo Domingo, in the early 1790's. Here, until 1810, Mrs. Dugas conducted the Boarding School for Select Young Ladies which was attended by the daughters of many of Georgia's outstanding early settlers. In this home was born Louis Alexander Dugas (1806–98) who became one of the State's most distinguished physicians

COURTESY, GEORGIA DEPARTMENT OF NATURAL RESOURCES

HOME OF ROBERT TOOMBS IN 1903

THE TOOMBS HOME TODAY

and surgeons. Educated at home, he studied medicine under Dr. John Dent, later was graduated from the University of Maryland, and after spending some time in Europe as a student returned to settle in Augusta, Georgia. A founder of the Medical College of Georgia, Dr. Dugas was for many years Professor of Surgery there. He was President of the Medical Society of Augusta and of the Medical Association of Georgia, and from 1851 to 1858 edited the Southern Medical and Surgical Journal. During the War Between the States he served as Volunteer and Consulting Surgeon of Military Hospitals.

In later years this home was occupied by Dr. Thomas Dunwoody, distinguished Presbyterian minister, pastor of the Washington Presbyterian Church.

(Located on East Robert Toombs Avenue across from Grove Street. GHM 157-2, 1961.)

WASHINGTON–WILKES HISTORICAL MUSEUM

This museum shows the splendors of plantation life in Georgia before the War Between the States, displays relics, mementoes and keepsakes of the era that tried men's souls, and adds a fine collection of Indian relics for variety.

Washington had many ties with the Confederacy. The Confederate Cabinet held its last meeting just down the street. President Jefferson Davis met his wife and daughter in this city at the end of the war. Mr. Davis' field desk and camp chest are on display. The well-named, Last Cabinet Chapter of the U.D.C., has on display many precious keepsakes and mementoes of the war, together with Joe Brown Pikes, guns, swords, pistols, documents, and pictures.

The big house dates back to about 1800. It was occupied after 1857 by Samuel Barnett, first Georgia Railroad Commissioner, and W. A. Slaton, forty-year occupant. Washington's benefactor, Dr. Francis T. Willis, half-brother of Mr. Barnett, lived with him here. Francis T. Willis moved to Richmond, Va. in his later years but told his sons that he wanted his ante-bellum furniture returned to Washington when there was a place for it. Edward

WASHINGTION–WILKES HISTORICAL MUSEUM

Fauntleroy Willis, brought the furniture from Richmond. It makes a beautiful display.

(Located on East Robert Toombs Avenue at Grove Street. GHM 157-31, 1960.)

First Presbyterian Ordination in Georgia

In the shade of a giant poplar tree which stood 200 feet East of this spot, on the 22nd of July, 1790, the Rev. John Springer was ordained to the Presbyterian ministry and installed Pastor of Smyrna, Providence and Washington churches. This was the first Presbyterian ordination held in Georgia. A Commission from the Presbytery of South Carolina conducted the service, with the Rev. Robert Hall preaching the ordination sermon and the Rev. Francis Cummins presiding and giving the charge.

The tree, always afterward known as The Presbyterian Poplar, stood for more than 150 years after the ordination.

(Located on Poplar Drive/GA 17B, 0.4 mile south of junction with US

78/GA 10/44 **or** 0.2 mile north of junction with East Robert Toombs Avenue/US 78B/GA 10B. GHM 157-18, 1958.)

GILBERT–ALEXANDER HOUSE

In the 1780's Felix and William Gilbert, Virginians, camped in a beautiful grove here and were so pleased with the scenery that they returned later to take land grants. In 1808 they erected the brick portion of this house, one of the oldest brick structures north of Augusta. Their descendants are the only families who have occupied it. The burial grounds on the property attest the continuity of the family for more than 150 years.

The Alexanders, descendants of the Gilberts, served with distinction in the War Between the States. Porter Alexander, who lived here, was a Brigadier General of Artillery in the Confederate Army.

(Located on Alexander Drive between North Alexander Avenue and Poplar Drive. GHM 157-3, 1953.)

THE CEDARS

The high hill on which The Cedars stands was a home-site for the Indians before the arrival of white men. Not long after the Revolutionary War, Anthony Poulain, a Frenchman of noble birth who came to the aid of Georgians against the British, built The Cedars. His son, Dr. T. N. Poulain, accompanied LaFayette on his visit to Georgia in 1825 as personal physician.

There are 20 rooms in the present house, two kitchens and parlors stretching to 90 feet. In the spacious dining room are many panes of hand-blown glass. A cabinet contains a pair of Gen. Cornwallis' knee buckles.

(Located on Sims Street at North Jefferson Street. GHM 157-6, 1953.)

GRANT'S MEETING HOUSE

On this site the first Methodist church building in Georgia was erected in 1787. Daniel Grant and his son, Thomas, prosperous merchants of this area, were its builders.

Bishop Asbury often visited the Grants at their home nearby, on his trips through Georgia, and in the church here he held the second and third Methodist conferences in the State, in 1789 and 1790.

Thomas Grant was for many years a prominent Methodist layman in Georgia.

(From US 78 and US 378 east of Washington, follow US 78 2.2 miles, turn right on GA 80 and travel 1.4 miles to marker. GHM 157-25, 1958.)

THE CEDARS

SMYRNA CHURCHYARD

This burying ground was laid out in 1788 when Sir John Talbot gave two acres of his vast estate for use as a Presbyterian Church and churchyard. Sir John was descended from the Earl of Shrewsbury. His own son, Matthew Talbot, served as a Superior Court judge, President of the Georgia Senate in 1811, 1817–22, and as Governor of Georgia from Oct. 24 to Nov. 5, 1819. Both are buried here.

W. H. T. Walker, Confederate General killed in the Battle of Atlanta, was a descendent of Sir John Talbot.

The Presbyterians moved to a new building in Washington in 1825.

(From US 78 and US 378/GA 47 east of Washington, follow US 378/GA 47 3.5 miles to marker and church. GHM 157-7, 1953.)

SMYRNA CHURCH

Smyrna Church was organized about 1786, by the Rev. John Newton and the Rev. John Simpson, Presbyterian ministers under the jurisdiction of the South Carolina Presbytery. Services were at first held in the homes of the members. The first Smyrna church edifice, built on this site in 1793, was of logs, with a steeple. The first regular pastor was the Rev. John Springer, who preached here until 1801. About 1820, the church membership declined to fifteen, and these removed to Washington, to affiliate with the Washington Presbyterian Church.

At this time, the Smyrna Presbyterians, through their elders, tendered the use of the church edifice to the Methodists, who accepted and soon established a flourishing Methodist Society here. The old church was in use until 1860, when it was torn down and a new building erected. On October 6, 1886, the title to Smyrna Church was passed from the Trustees of the Washington Presbyterian Church to the Trustees of the Smyrna Methodist Church. In 1911, a new building was constructed, the third Smyrna on this site.

In the 1840's, an encampment was prepared near the church, and was used as a camp ground by both Presbyterians and Methodists.

(From US 78 and US 378/GA 47 east of Washington, follow US 378/GA 47 3.5 miles to marker and church. GHM 157-19, 1958.)

WALNUT HILL ACADEMY

Walnut Hill Academy, one of the famous schools of its time, was established in 1788 by the Rev. John Springer, in a building erected close to his house on this plantation. Among the students taught by Mr. Springer at the Academy were John Forsyth, afterward Governor of Georgia, Member of Congress, and U.S. Minister to Spain; Nicholas Ware, Senator from Georgia; Jesse Mercer, founder of Mercer University and one of the State's leading Baptist ministers. The Rev. Hope Hull, noted Methodist minister, was for some time assistant to the Rev. Mr. Springer at Walnut Hill Academy.

(Located on GA 17, 3.7 miles north of junction with US 78/GA 10/44. GHM 157-28, 1958.)

THE REV. JOHN SPRINGER

The Rev. John Springer, 1744–1798, distinguished minister and educator, is buried in the garden on this plantation, Walnut Hill. A graduate of Princeton, he taught there and at Hampden–Sydney, and was first Rector of Cambridge College in South Carolina. He was a soldier of the American Revolution. Following his ordination to the ministry in 1790, his activities centered in Wilkes and adjoining counties, but he traveled widely, preaching the Gospel, often serving churches in South Carolina. He was several times Moderator of Presbytery, was President of Wilkes Academy, and held other offices of distinction.

(Located on GA 17, 3.7 miles north of junction with US 78/GA 10/44. GHM 157-29, 1958.)

JESSE MERCER'S HOME

This was the home of Jesse Mercer, pioneer Baptist preacher and largest contributor to the founding of Mercer Institute at Penfield, now Mercer University of Macon.

Jesse Mercer, born in North Carolina Dec. 16, 1769, was the son of Rev. Silas Mercer, a Baptist preacher who moved to Wilkes County in the early 1770's and founded several pioneer churches. He baptized Jesse Mercer at the age of 18, and the youth at once

started holding prayer meetings in the log home of his grandmother. He married Miss Sabrina Chivers of the Phillips' Mill community when 19, and was ordained for the ministry at 20. Sardis Church, originally called Hutton's Fork, was Mr. Mercer's first charge. In 1796 he succeeded his father as pastor of the Phillips' Mill Church, which he served for 39 years, baptizing 230 persons. He also served as pastor of Bethesda Church (1796–1827); Powell's Creek Church, in Hancock County (1797–1825); and the Baptist Church at Eatonton (1820–26).

Mr. Mercer's first wife died Sept. 23, 1826 and in his loneliness he moved to Washington. In December, 1827, he married Mrs. Nancy Simons, a wealthy widow, who joined him in large gifts to Mercer Institute.

Early in life Mr. Mercer had published a popular song book under the title "Mercer's Cluster." In later years he published the Christian Index and a Temperance paper in Washington. In 1828 he became the first pastor of the Washington Baptist Church, which he served until his death in 1841.

(Located on US 78B/GA 10B near the junction with GA 44. GHM 157-10, 1954.)

SITE OF
WILKES COUNTY ACADEMY

This is the site of the Wilkes County Academy, built in 1797. The Academy was authorized by the Legislature in 1783, one of the first public schools chartered by the State of Georgia.

Commissioners were: Stephen Heard, Micajah Williamson, Robert Harper, Daniel Coleman and Zachariah Lamar. Samuel Blackburn was the first teacher. Classes were held in rented houses until 1797, when, with funds raised by public subscription, a commodious two story brick building was erected for an Academy and Church. The Academy was in active use until 1824, when it was torn down and the school removed to a location nearer the business section of Washington.

(Located on US 78B/GA 10B near the junction with GA 44. GHM 157-27, 1958.)

KETTLE CREEK
BATTLEGROUND

One and one-half miles North and one-half mile West is War Hill, site of the Battle of Kettle Creek, one of the decisive battles of the Revolutionary War.

It was at Kettle Creek, on February 14, 1779, that Col. John Dooly, Col. Elijah Clark and Col. Andrew Pickens defeated overwhelmingly a superior number of Tory forces, turning back forever the British troops in Upper Georgia.

(Located on GA 44, 8.3 miles west of junction with US 78B/GA 10B. GHM 157-24, 1958.)

BATTLE OF KETTLE CREEK

The Battle of Kettle Creek, fought here on February 14, 1779, was one of the most important battles of the Revolutionary War in Georgia. At that time,

the State was almost completely under British control. Col. Boyd, with 600 British sympathizers (Loyalists or Tories) crossed the Savannah River into present-day Elbert County enroute to the British army then at Augusta. Patriots Col. Andrew Pickens with 200 S. C. militia and Col. John Dooly and Lt. Colonel Elijah Clark with 140 Georgia militia marched to overtake the Loyalists. On the morning of the 14th, Boyd and his men were camped here at a bend in the then flooded Kettle Creek. Their horses were grazing, sentries were posted, and most of the men were slaughtering cattle or searching for food. The Patriots attempted to attack the Loyalist camp by surprise but failed and a desperate battle raged on both sides of the creek for three hours before the Loyalists finally broke and fled. Col. Boyd and 20 of his men were killed and 22 captured. Pickens and Dooly lost seven men killed and 14 or 15 wounded. Pickens later wrote that Kettle Creek, "was the severest check and chastisement, the tories ever received in South Carolina of Georgia."

(From GA 44 and US 78B/GA 10B, follow GA 44 west 8.3 miles, turn right and follow road for 1.2 miles, turn left and travel 1.3 miles, turn left on dirt road and follow for 1.2 miles to marker and site. GHM 157-15, 1978.)

THE BATTLE OF KETTLE CREEK

BATTLE OF KETTLE CREEK

Nine miles Southwest, the Revolutionary Battle of Kettle Creek was fought on the morning of Feb. 14, 1779. Col. Boyd leading a large Tory force, had crossed the Savannah River northeast of here and was seeking by a circuitous march to join Col. Campbell, stationed at Augusta. A smaller band of Americans under Col.'s Pickens, Dooly, and Clarke overtook the Tory forces while encamp upon Kettle Creek, and defeated it after a severe battle ending upon nearby War Hill, now crowned by a U. S. Marker. This decisive victory ended Tory supremacy in North Georgia.

(Located on US 78/GA 10, west of Washington. WPA 157-D10.) ♦ ★ – not standing.

PHILLIPS MILLS BAPTIST CHURCH

On June 10, 1785, 16 members met in a mill on this site owned by Joel Phillips, a Revolutionary soldier, and organized Phillips Mills Baptist Church. The Rev. Silas Mercer, leader of the group, became the first pastor of the church, and served in this capacity for 11 years. His son, Jesse Mercer, was received into the church on July 7, 1787, at the age of eighteen. Later he was ordained to the ministry in the old church, and followed his father as its pastor, serving this church for thirty-seven years.

The present edifice is the second to be built on the site, which was donated to the church by Joel Phillips. Since its organization, many impor-

PHILLIPS MILL BAPTIST CHURCH

tant conferences have been held in Phillips Mills Church, and young men whose names are now famous in the ministry have preached their first sermons here.

(Located on GA 44, 9.9 miles west of junction with US 78B/GA 10B. GHM 157-23, 1958.)

CLARKE'S CREEK ENCAMPMENT

At Clarke's Creek, near here, on the night of February 13, 1779, American troops commanded by Col. Elijah Clark, Col. John Dooly and Col. Andrew Pickens, encamped. Very early the next morning, they launched a surprise attack on the British forces under Colonel Boyd, encamped at Kettle Creek, four miles away. The victory prevented the British troops from joining the notorious McGirth, and broke their devastating march through Georgia.

(From US 78B/GA 10B and GA 44, travel west on US 78B/GA 10B, joining US 78, 5.6 miles. Turn right on the road at the end of the airport runway, travel 1 mile and bear left at the fork. Follow road 7.3 miles to marker. GHM 157-22, 1958.)

These markers were erected just before publication of this book.

CHEROKEE COUNTY

CANTON

FORT BUFFINGTON

One-half mile north is the site of Fort Buffington, built in the 1830's by local militia. It was one of about 25 stockades in the Cherokee Indian Nation used by Federal and State troops during the Cherokee Removal in 1838. In May and June, 1838, 7,000 soldiers forced over 15,000 Cherokee Indians from their homes and held them in the stockades until removal west could take place. Many Indians from the local area were held at Fort Buffington. As many as 4,000 Cherokees may have died while held in the stockades and on the 800 mile journey west. Their ordeal has become known as the "The Trail of Tears."

(Located on Ga 20, east of Canton in front of Buffington Elementary School. GHM 028-6, 1992.)

CLARKE COUNTY

ATHENS

HERTY FIELD

This marker overlooks the site of the first intercollegiate football game played in the state of Georgia and one of the first to be played in the deep south. On January 30, 1892, Georgia defeated Mercer College 50 to 0 on the stubbly grounds that served as an athletic field. Several hundred spectators watched from the sidelines, some of them spilling out on the playing ground. Students living in New College close by the field had a splendid view of the action from their dormitory windows.

Georgia played all its home games on this field until 1911 when a new field was constructed off Lumpkin Street. The old grounds were thereafter used for informal intramural games and as a drill field for the R.O.T.C. trainees.

The original field, later converted into a parking lot, was named in honor of Dr. Charles H. Herty, professor of chemistry at the University and sports enthusiast. He introduced football to the college boys and was unofficial coach and trainer of the early teams. Herty later earned fame as a scientist in the development of the turpentine and pine pulpwood industry.

(Located in a parking lot behind the University Chapel on the campus of the University of Georgia. GHM 029-17, 1991.)

OCONEE COUNTY

WATKINSVILLE

JEANNETTE RANKIN'S GEORGIA HOME

Jeannette Rankin (1880-1973) was the first woman to serve in Congress; being elected from Montana in 1916 before women had the right to vote in other states. She was active in women's suffrage and was a peace advocate who opposed all war. She was one of only fifty persons in Congress who voted against entry into WWI. Her position was unpopular and she did not return to Congress. She purchased land near the Oconee-Clarke County line in the twenties and lived there on a seasonal basis. She purchased 44 acres on this site in 1933. She renovated an old farm house and used it as a seasonal residence that became her beloved "Shady Grove."

In the 1920s she helped found the Georgia Peace Society that worked for over ten years to support the Kellogg-Briand Pact which would have outlawed war as a way of settling disputes. She was re-elected to Congress in 1940 from Montana.

She cast the only vote against entry into WWII after President Roosevelt's "Day of Infamy Speech." Steadfastly she remained active in peace movements during the Vietnam Era, participating in the "Jeannette Rankin Brigade" march in Washington on January 15, 1968.

(Located off GA 53 on Mars Hill Road across from the Oconee Middle School, west of Watkinsville. GHM 108-6, 1992.)

WHITFIELD COUNTY

TUNNEL HILL

WESTERN & ATLANTIC RAILROAD TUNNEL

The 1447 foot long Chetoogeta Mountain railroad tunnel is one-half mile east of this marker. The tunnel was completed in 1850 and this opened the W&A RR from Atlanta to Chattanooga. This was the first railroad tunnel completed south of the Mason-Dixon Line and linked railroads from the Atlantic to the Mississippi River. The railroad was operating during the late 1840s and goods and passengers were portaged over Chetoogeta Mountain while the tunnel was under construction. A community grew up near the construction activity and Clisby Austin built a three story hotel in

1848. Tunnel Hill was incorporated on March 4, 1848. The W&A was approved by the Georgia Legislature in 1836 and surveyed by Stephen Harriman Long. Construction of the 137 mile line took 13 years and cost more than four million dollars. William L. Mitchell was Chief Engineer and William Gray was Chief Mason. Gray was given the honor of being the first to pass through the tunnel when the two headings were driven through on October 31, 1849. The tunnel was in use until larger locomotives and loads necessitated a larger tunnel in 1928.

The tunnel played a role in one of the most colorful exploits of the Civil War, The Great Locomotive Chase. James J. Andrews and his band of Union "engine thieves" raced the stolen GENERAL through the tunnel closely pursued by the TEXAS, under Wm. Fuller, and Confederate forces.

(Located on Oak Street near the railroad crossing in Tunnel Hill. GHM 155-36, 1992.)